Victoriana – Histories, Fictions, Criticism

For Dave

Victoriana – Histories, Fictions, Criticism

Cora Kaplan

Edinburgh University Press

Edinburgh University Press Ltd
22 George Square, Edinburgh

Typeset in 10.5/13 Adobe Sabon
by Servis Filmsetting Ltd, Manchester, and
printed and bound in Great Britain by
Cromwell Press, Trowbridge, Wilts

A CIP record for this book is available from the British Library

ISBN 978 0 7486 1147 8 (hardback)
ISBN 978 0 7486 1146 1 (paperback)

Contents

List of Figures

Acknowledgements

My warmest thanks to artist Paula Rego, who has, with great generosity, allowed me to use 'Come to Me' from her astonishing series on *Jane Eyre* for the cover, and 'Loving Bewick', a further image from the same series, to illustrate my discussion of her work. My thanks also to filmmaker Jane Campion and to Jan Chapman for kind permission to use a still from *The Piano* in 'Retuning *The Piano*'.

One of the unexpected pleasures of writing about contemporary fiction, film and television is how much informal, enthusiastic exchanges with friends help to shape and reshape one's arguments. I am especially indebted in this regard to Michèle Barrett, Norma Clarke, Nell Druce, Catherine Hall, Stuart Hall, Annie Janowitz, Alison Light, Mandy Merck, Peter Middleton, Patrick Parrinder, Alyson Pendlebury, Adam Phillips, Martin Ryle, Jacqueline Rose, Sally Shuttleworth, Jenny Taylor, Judith Walkowitz and Ann Whitehead. My colleagues and students at Southampton University, and more recently at Queen Mary, University of London, have provided exemplary critical support. So too – and much more – has my writing group: Sally Alexander, Catherine Hall, Lynne Segal and Barbara Taylor. Special thanks to the members of the PhD Reading Group at Queen Mary for their thoughts on Hegel and aesthetics. I have lectured on aspects of the book's various topics to academic audiences in Britain, the United States and Australia – the questions they have raised have always helped me to clarify my arguments. Michèle Barrett, Alison Light and Barbara Taylor have read drafts of part of the book at different stages and offered extremely helpful criticism and suggestions. Sabine Clemm and the late Chris Willis, two passionate Victorianists, have been ideal research assistants.

Many thanks too, to Fiona Wade whose careful, courteous copy-editing has given order to my anarchic notions of punctuation, and to Ann Vinnicombe in production for piloting *Victoriana* through to publication.

My superb Edinburgh editor, Jackie Jones, has given me astute advice about structure, content and style from the beginning – all of which I have taken gratefully. Her unstinting encouragement and her enthusiasm for the book have been matched only by her angelic patience with my tortoise-like crawl towards the finish line. As informed interlocutor and ideal reader she has made writing *Victoriana* a pleasure.

David Glover, my partner, has read all of the book in draft, some sections several times over. We have discussed its interpretations, its form and its component texts at great length over the years; some of the best ideas in the book are undoubtedly his. He will know which they are. We met almost two decades ago through common interests in contemporary popular fiction, cultural theory, gender and nineteenth-century writing, and the conversations begun then have continued uninterrupted ever since. *Victoriana*, perhaps especially, is indebted to lines of enquiry and ways of seeing that I had never considered and which he has opened up for me. This book is dedicated to him.

Introduction

In Brian Moore's comic novel *The Great Victorian Collection* (1975), a young Canadian, Anthony Maloney, an assistant professor of British history whose subject is Victorian things, falls asleep in the Sea Winds motel in Carmel-by-the-Sea, California, and dreams that he is walking through an exhibit of Victorian objects, rivalling and sometimes reproducing those on display in Britain's Great Exhibition of 1851.[1] In a typical aberration of dream life, the collection, which takes up a modern city block, is located not in some virtual London, but, to Anthony's amazement, in the Sea Winds parking lot. He wakes to find himself the custodian of just such an exhibition outside his motel room, whose contents not only perfectly replicate actually existing historical objects – from a glass fountain to a toy engine, to erotic playthings he has only read about – but has created others, many of which were not known to have survived the inevitable triage of history, or even to have ever existed in more than descriptive or imaginary form. Media attention to the collection brings Anthony, as its realiser and reluctant curator, a brief celebrity, but its mysterious origin in his psyche, and its curious dependence for its integrity on his presence at the site of its appearance, ultimately prove fatal to the dreamer and his dream; the story ends with Anthony's macabre death, while the collection – subtly degraded, no longer newsworthy, but not destroyed – survives him.

A meditation on the modern obsession with things Victorian, *The Great Victorian Collection* explores the late twentieth-century desire to know and to 'own' the Victorian past through its remains: the physical and written forms that are its material history. Maloney's academic interest in Victorian 'collectibles' – Victoriana in its earliest definition as material culture – provides the occasion for a surrealist exposure of the grotesque and even dangerous side of the historical imagination – the incommensurability of the Victorian past and its late capitalist legacy. California, in Moore's evocation of the 1970s, represents the horizon of

Britain's influence as America's Pacific rim: postmodernity's monstrous elaboration of a consumer society derived in part from Victorian ingenuity, invention, high ideals and greed, the effect of the nineteenth century's insatiable desire for commodities, as well as its perverse sexual imagination. Carmel, at first glance, is the antithesis of Victorian Britain. A second look tells us that it is the logical evolution of the 1851 Exhibition's utopian and imperial impulses. Reworked fantastically in his unconscious, Maloney's projected archive, the cultural capital drawn from his historical research, materialises in the land of the dream factory, and is no more or less surreal than Hollywood or Disneyland.

The tone and texture of Moore's California novel are variously indebted to the state's dystopic chroniclers, F. Scott Fitzgerald, Nathaniel West and Raymond Chandler. Asocial, unstable, *The Great Victorian Collection*'s characters are radically unsecured in their own history, and they move helplessly towards disaster in a landscape whose distinctive character is its anomie. It is in this California-like space, in which the past itself is a waning concept, that Moore implies we must now know it. *How* we know the Victorian past, Moore seems to suggest, is irrevocably altered not just by a leap in time and in context, but by the elaborate theorisation of the self and the work of art in the twentieth century. Nowhere credited, the novel's conceits about material culture and the mind adapt elements of Walter Benjamin's argument about 'The Work of Art in the Age of Mechanical Reproduction' and is indebted to Freud's *The Interpretation of Dreams*. There are parallels too to Jean Baudrillard's 'Simulacra and Simulations', published in English in the same year as Moore's novel.[2] A *jeu d'ésprit* that probes and satirises the late twentieth-century interest in Victoriana, *The Great Victorian Collection* is also a wonderfully complex example of it.

Brian Moore, like his doomed protagonist Anthony Maloney, was Canadian, and Moore's take on Maloney's lethal curatorial passion for the objects gathered for or made in the metropolitan centre of the British Empire at its triumphal moment, is suffused with postcolonial irony. But Britain's own revived appetite for its past has far outstripped that of its former possessions. Sanderson's William Morris range of fabric and wallpaper, Peter Ackroyd's monumental *Dickens* (1990), the historical pastiche of A. S. Byatt's *Possession* (1991), Sarah Waters's *Tipping the Velvet*, *Affinity* and *Fingersmith* (1999–2003), a spate of successful television and film adaptations, including Dickens's *Bleak House* (2005) and Elizabeth Gaskell's *North and South* (2004) – the fascination with things Victorian has been a British postwar vogue which shows no signs of exhaustion.[3] At the beginning of the fad in the 1960s, 'Victoriana' might have narrowly meant the collectible remnants of material culture in the corner antique shop, but by the late 1970s its reference had widened to embrace a complementary miscellany of evocations and recyclings of the nineteenth century, a constellation of images which became markers for particular moments of contemporary style and culture. I can see my younger self – just – watching television costume dramas like the longrunning Victorian series, *Upstairs, Downstairs* (1971–75): an American expatriate living in an English seaside town, curled up on a re-upholstered Victorian chesterfield in a Laura Ashley dress. Today 'Victoriana' might usefully embrace the whole phenomenon, the astonishing range of representations and reproductions for which the Victorian – whether as the origin of late twentieth century modernity, its antithesis, or both at once – is the common referent.

Describing the making and circulation of such objects, histories, stories, adaptations, pastiches and parodies is easier than pinpointing their collective significance. But we might start by asking whether the proliferation of Victoriana is more than nostalgia – a longing for a past that never was – and more too than a symptom of the now familiar, if much debated, view that the passage from modernity to postmodernity has been marked by the profound loss of a sense of history. This loss, some theorists of the postmodern argue, has meant that what was once a depth model of historical time has been compressed into a single surface, so that the past has become a one-dimensional figure in the carpet, a thematic element in the syncretic pattern of a perpetual present.[4] Individual instances of Victoriana – a film, a pastiche fiction, a retro style, even a biography – may superficially fit this latter description. Yet in the wider definition that I am proposing, one that includes the self-conscious rewriting of historical narratives to highlight the suppressed histories of gender and sexuality, race and empire, as well as challenges to the conventional understandings of the historical itself, the transformation of the Victorian past cannot be so neatly characterised. The variety and appeal of Victoriana over the years might better be seen as one sign of a sense of the historical imagination on the move, an indication that what we thought we knew as 'history' has become, a hundred years and more after the death of Britain's longest-reigning monarch, a kind of conceptual nomad, not so much lost as permanently restless and unsettled.[5]

I would like to offer the five essays and the Afterword that follow – on Victorian literature and culture as read through its modern interpreters, on biographical treatments of Victorian writers and on late twentieth-century Victoriana in fiction and film – as at once an example of Victoriana in its most inclusive definition, and as an extended commentary on the phenomenon as a whole. For while the essays are freestanding and come

at their subjects from different angles, together they extend and elaborate
the analysis of Victoriana in some of the many genres it has colonised or
invented from the late 1960s forward, considering it as a discourse
through which both the conservative and progressive elements of
Anglophone cultures reshaped their ideas of the past, present and future.

My own interest in writing about the Victorian period, in particular the
stormy middle decades of the nineteenth century, began in the mid 1970s,
overtly as an offshoot of research on feminism and women's poetry, but
subliminally inspired, I now think, by the many ways in which the rein-
vented Victorian was incorporated in my everyday life. My modest 1870s
terraced house in Brighton, like those of my professional neighbours, was
full of Sanderson and Laura Ashley reproduction wallpaper and fabrics,
a confusion of the plebeian and the bourgeois in its furnishings of stripped
pine and reupholstered button-backed chairs, but my politics and my
other cultural tastes were not in any sense retro; both left-wing and
feminist, they were emphatically of the moment. The productive incon-
gruity of these influences found its form in my initial project to republish
Elizabeth Barrett Browning's narrative poem, *Aurora Leigh* (1855), an
almost forgotten proto-feminist Victorian text, and to reinterpret its
moment of writing in the light of late twentieth-century political
concerns. In the process of working on the edition, published by
The Women's Press in 1978, I began to think of myself for the first time
as a 'Victorianist', albeit one working from a Marxist and feminist
perspective, and open to the kinds of contemporary theoretical influences – German critical theory, psychoanalysis, semiotics, poststructuralism, deconstruction – which seemed (and still seem) to have an odd
affinity with an interest in the Victorian period and its literature. I knew
that the theory-friendly feminist Victorianist was not an invention of my
own but an identity shared with other Anglophone academics, ubiquitous
enough to be affectionately parodied at a later moment in David Lodge's
Nice Work (1988) with its red-haired protagonist Robyn Penrose, a spe-
cialist in the Industrial Novel, and in A. S. Byatt's *Possession* (1991),
whose cool, blonde, English lecturer Maud Bailey writes about the life
and work of her fictional forebear, the composite Victorian woman poet
Christabel LaMotte.

Over time my interest in women's writing, and in social hierarchy, led
me to read and teach Victorian women's prose and poetry, setting Barrett
Browning's *Aurora Leigh*, Christina Rossetti's *Goblin Market*, Charlotte
Brontë's *Villette*, *Jane Eyre* and *Shirley* alongside *The Diaries of Hannah
Cullwick*, a Victorian maid-of-all-work.[6] For many left-wing Victorianists
in the 1960s and 1970s it was class hierarchies, class injustice and class
antagonism that were the worst of the nineteenth century's legacy to

modern Britain, a judgement made stronger, the remnants of the system more despised, just because those structures of deference that class imposed were definitively weakening in the postwar years, and Labour policies were promising, if not delivering, a more equitable, supposedly 'classless' society. In the fourteen years that I lived among Brighton's Regency and Victorian streets and waterfront I grew deeper into that scholarly identity. Increasingly I began to think of myself as British as much as American. My relationship to things Victorian – from the built environment, to fashion, to books and domestic furniture – redefined my sense of national identity, influenced my politics and changed my academic signature. As a writer, teacher, scholar, reader – as a woman and a British resident – I am myself written through, like a stick of Brighton Rock, with the contradictions inscribed in that complicated encounter with Victorian culture. My pleasure in the period's literary language, which went back to my adolescence in Massachusetts when I first read Brontë and Dickens, became crossed with my outraged fascination, translated into respectable critical analysis, at Victorian social conventions and prejudices which surface unexpectedly in much-loved texts – for example in the vicious and grotesque representations of the poor in Barrett Browning's *Aurora Leigh*, a poem I still teach and read, and, as I came to see by the mid-1980s, in the imperial and racial discourse that is a leading trope in my favourite *Jane Eyre*.

These abiding concerns about class, gender, empire and race run through these essays and are joined by another preoccupation: the high degree of affect involved in reading and writing about the Victorian past, an indication that more is at stake in the ongoing popularity of Victoriana than can be registered in the categories of historical investigation, aesthetic appreciation or entertainment. As I have suggested, I am as implicated in the contradictory sets of feelings that the Victorian provokes as any other writer and reader, and my intention in analysing such emotions is not to rationalise or depoliticise them, or to suggest that I or anyone else can finally stand outside them. The Victorian as at once ghostly and tangible, an origin and an anachronism, had a strong affective presence in modern Britain in the supposedly libertarian 1960s and 1970s, when the nation was thought to be on its way to becoming a classless and multicultural society. Its idiomatic function was enhanced in the 1980s and 1990s when Victorian Values – thrift, family, enterprise – were brought back as the positive ethic of Conservative government. It was then that I began seriously to consider the curious appropriation of the Victorian for disparate political and cultural agendas in the present, to see Victoriana's peculiar role, not simply as that always selective and unreliable thing, historical memory, so easily cloyed with nostalgia or soured into persecution of the dead, but as what we might call history out of place, something atemporal and almost spooky in its effects, yet busily at work constituting this time – yours and mine – of late Capitalist modernity.

In exploring some of the cultural and political ramifications of Victoriana, these essays try to account for the pleasures and dangers evoked by imitation or reference to the narrative forms, individual histories and systems of belief of nineteenth-century Britain. For while the high literary modernism and the popular culture in the first half of the twentieth century defined itself through an explicit or tacit rejection of the cultural preferences and social mores of the Victorian world, distance from the period has not only produced detailed – and controversial – historical analyses of its customs, practices and influence, but has gradually lent it over time the charm of antiquity and the exotic, so that increasingly, in the new millennium, even its worst abuses seem to fascinate rather than appal. Genealogically speaking, the Victorian is no longer seen as a disapproving parent of the louche modernity of the opening of the last century – indeed, the modernist period may have increasingly replaced the Victorian as a still coercive but more wayward antecedent. Certainly the postwar left's characterisation of the Victorian as the bullying bourgeois patriarch responsible for the twin cruelties of capitalism and empire, has less purchase on the general historical imagination today than it did some twenty years ago, and has become the subject of vigorous debate in the humanities.

An aggressive and politically focused putsch by academic and popular historians has set itself the task of demolishing the critique of the Victorian. The present moment has gone much further than Margaret Thatcher ever did in extolling the virtues of the Victorian – it was in her interests to keep that association positive but vague. Now TV programmes such as the BBC's 'What the Victorians Did for Us' endlessly praise its invention and enterprise.[7] Matthew Sweet, in an acute and engaging study, *Inventing the Victorians*, suggests that most of our assumptions about them are wrong – the Victorians are neither our skeleton in the closet nor our moral saviours, but are more like us in their differences than is commonly supposed. Sweet rejects the 'sentimentality' and opportunism which made Margaret Thatcher praise Samuel Smiles, and Tony Blair in 1996 describe himself as a 'Christian Socialist, in order to create a continuity between New Labour and a progressive political tradition that predated the formation of his own party' – and, we might add, to explicitly distinguish his 'socialism' from the socialism of 'Old Labour' and the Bennite left.[8] The tradition of Christian Socialism itself is a little more of an ethical minefield than Blair knows or at least implies: one of its founders and most prominent members was the Reverend Charles Kingsley, author of the Victorian classic *The Water Babies* and an outspoken racist.[9] British Chancellor of the Exchequer, Gordon Brown, follows the line of recent revisionist historiography – David Cannadine's *Ornamentalism* (2001) and Niall Ferguson's *Empire* (2002) have been particularly influential – when he told Anglophone Africa on a 2005 visit that the Empire had been on balance a progressive and modernising force, and Britain has 'nothing to apologize for'.[10] This anti-apologetic stance is, even so, couched in defensive terms, and can take a range of contradictory positions, so that we might now see the Victorian in the Blair years as a key term in the struggle to define the 'conservative modernity' of New Labour, as well as a period once again wide open not only to the endless revision of historical interpretation, as it should be, but also especially porous to highly politicised forms of representation.[11]

The first essay, 'Heroines, Hysteria and History: *Jane Eyre* and her Critics', discusses the revision of women's writing of the 1840s by twentieth-century criticism. It traces the critical fortunes of Charlotte Brontë's *Jane Eyre*, a novel whose enduring popularity, rewriting and translation to small and large screen make it a leading example of narrative Victoriana. *Jane Eyre* remains a classic, I suggest, because its themes and rhetoric have summoned up for generations of readers the powerful politics of affect at the heart of gender and modernity. Working forward from Virginia Woolf's condescending treatment of Charlotte Brontë as a writer, to more recent feminist rethinking of her best-known fiction by Elaine Showalter, Gayatri Chakravorty Spivak, Nancy Armstrong, Sally Shuttleworth and Heather Glen, it ends with a consideration of artist Paula Rego's stunning series of drawings on *Jane Eyre*, which comprise a strikingly original commentary on accompanying passages from Brontë's text. I explore *Jane Eyre* as a popular icon which acts as what Freud called a 'mnemic symbol', a memorial or narrative that embodies and elicits a buried psychic conflict which cannot be resolved in the present. The essay asks what *Jane Eyre* is to her twentieth-century readers that they should still weep for her, but it also questions whether the disentangling of the novel's critical genealogy and political history dispels, or only renews in new ways, the strong affective responses it has evoked over time.

'Biographilia' considers the high – and still rising – profile of Victorian literary biography in the last two decades. Less a craving on the part of readers for a full-frontal exposure of the private lives of Victorian writers, the ongoing enthusiasm for biography satisfies a more bookish desire, perhaps equally subversive in its way, to revisit the nineteenth century's realist forms through a modern genre that borrows from them.

Conservatively viewed, this urge can be seen as a wish to recapture the cultural and social optimism of the period, that time of high humanism in which the 'man of letters' could be a hero, and individuals could be seen as having both cultural and ethical agency. Yet I argue that the vogue for nineteenth-century literary biography today is more culturally complicated than this perspective has allowed. Ideas about authorship, and about agency more generally have been deeply affected by the theoretical moment of the late 1960s and 1970s in which Roland Barthes and Michel Foucault jubilantly, but prematurely, announced 'the death of the author'.[12] The author whose comeback from the culture wars of the 1970s and 1980s is being celebrated is not quite the confident figure who left. Survivors of an uncertain philosophical and political détente, authors past and present emerge as a new sort of hero for these less than heroic times. 'Biographilia' explores our undiminished *fin de siècle* appetite for life histories, commenting on the invention, ambition and appeal of Victorian literary biography through three celebrated examples: Peter Ackroyd's potboiling, late-romantic *Dickens* and two biofictional treatments of Henry James, Colm Tóibín's melancholy *The Master* and David Lodge's briskly comic *Author, Author*. Throughout, the essay raises some broader questions about Victorian literary biography as an occasion for elegy in its capacity both to retrieve and to bury the past, and as an ambivalent site of identification for biographers and readers.

'Historical Fictions: Pastiche, Politics and Pleasure' looks at a constellation of historical novels which thematise the Victorian and whose styles and narrative procedures are influenced by postmodern fiction and theory. The original of this sub-genre was John Fowles's *The French Lieutenant's Woman* (1969), but by the early 1990s a flood of such narratives had appeared, flowing across the different categories of the novel. Detective fiction, for example, has developed a lucrative little line of mass-market Victorian pastiche, much of it written by Americans whose acquaintance with England, much less the Victorian period, seems both slight and second-hand. Successful novels with more literary aspirations include David Lodge's *Nice Work* (1988), A. S. Byatt's *Possession* (1991) and Michael Faber's *The Crimson Petal and the White* (2002). Sarah Waters's trio of novels, thematising lesbianism in the Victorian, have been so successful that they have nicknamed a new subgenre: the slyly metrosexual 'Vic Lit'. All these novels engage the Victorian through a mix of narrative strategies. *Possession* cross cuts between the nineteenth century and the present, tracking a lost manuscript by an imaginary woman poet who is a synthesis of Elizabeth Barrett Browning, Christina Rossetti and Emily Dickinson, comparing sexuality and literary cultures then and now; *Nice Work* cleverly updates Mrs Gaskell's *North and South* for post-industrial Britain under Thatcher. The historical side of their ambition has less to do with the faithful reproduction of Victorian language, landscapes and mores – *Possession* is full of these, but in *Nice Work* they are a lightly referenced backstory – than with constructing a virtual relationship between past and present, one which experiments with the kaleidoscopic configurations of two key moments of modernity. Intimately dependent on, and in critical dialogue with, the last quarter century of radical revisions of Victorian social and political history, the pedagogic dimension of these novels is matched, from Fowles forward, by their experiments with form and their speculative aesthetics. At once philosophical, political and generic, the new historical fiction positions itself as both a complement and rival to academic writing on the period.

The last long essay in the collection, 'Retuning *The Piano*', traces the network of Victorian sources and intertexts at play in Jane Campion's 'dark' postcolonial romance which opened in 1993. Set in nineteenth-century New Zealand, Campion's film about the mute but musical Ada McGrath and her illegitimate daughter Flora contains a web of references to Anglophone fictions from the nineteenth century, many of them American texts. Fragments – both figure and story borrowed from Hawthorne's *The Scarlet Letter*, James Fenimore Cooper's *Leatherstocking Tales*, Herman Melville's *White-Jacket*, Charlotte Brontë's *Villette*, Henry James's *The Turn of the Screw* – are recomposed to emphasise both the film's origins in nineteenth-century narrative, and its emphatically 'modern' take on colonialism and sexuality. In the same way *The Piano* keeps before us the competing terms of nineteenth-and twentieth-century science and philosophy. The film invites us to interpret Ada's supposedly self-willed disability through romantic psychologies of the self and/or psychoanalysis; its tongue-in-cheek evocation of Claude Lévi-Strauss's structural anthropology in its central narrative conceit about the exchange of women and pianos, runs alongside its emphasis on the common-sense racial assumptions of nineteenth-century settler societies. These various ingredients blend almost magically at the level of the film's narrative diegesis, but separate out as discrete, even radically incompatible, elements if one tries to follow their social and political logic. The feminist, or some might say post-feminist, motifs in *The Piano* undermine its somewhat truncated critique of British colonial and imperial practices. 'Retuning *The Piano*' explores the peculiar dissonances between the film's twin political imperatives.

Campion's film nevertheless maps out fresh and interesting terrain. While narrative Victoriana in books, film and television has always sold well on the international market, trading on a sentimental attachment to

English or British cultural heritage, *The Piano* daringly abandons this limited focus, representing the Victorian more comprehensively as the *modus vivendi* of empire, as travelling cultural capital that included the methods of conquest as well as the social, psychic and material baggage that British colonisers carried with them. This ideological dissemination is examined and criticised within the film text, but it is ironically reproduced in the mode in which the film functions as a commodity. A successful example of postcolonial cultural enterprise, *The Piano*'s crafting of a new kind of 'global' Victoriana with its exotic antipodean setting, its English-speaking cast drawn both from the metropolitan homeland and its now fully-detached empire, its erotically charged, sexually explicit romance coupled with 'artistic' cinematography, is cleverly fashioned to appeal to multiple audiences worldwide. Although the film can itself be seen as a period piece which has taken on classic status, Jane Campion's compelling staging of the Victorian has not been surpassed in its disturbing complexity. In a short Afterword to the book I reflect further on some of the questions raised throughout the book about the thematising of Empire in Victoriana from Jean Rhys through Julian Barnes.

Once a month for the past eight years, on my way to my London hairdresser, tucked away in a converted warehouse off the Gray's Inn Road, I walk past the Charles Dickens Museum at 48 Doughty Street, where one may presumably (I have never looked in) see the writing environment in which Dickens lived and worked from 1837–39, together with paintings, rare editions, manuscripts, original furniture and personal items. While I have dutifully, and with some profit and pleasure, visited Hardy country and Kipling's house, and am a regular at V & A exhibits, I have been resistant to this particular tourist attraction, which in any case never seems mobbed by visitors. Perhaps Dickens's twenty-first century fans, finding him alive and kicking in his novels, their adaptations, popular biography and in his vivid evocation in Peter Ackroyd and Simon Callow's camp, tragicomic one-man show, *The Mystery of Charles Dickens*, are put off, as I am, by four floors of material culture offering Dickens as fixed and frozen in cultural memory through a reconstruction of one of the houses in which he briefly lived, however historically meticulous that reconstruction may be. The Museum is there, however, if you like that sort of thing. You can even preview your visit by taking a 'virtual tour' of the house on the web, as if it were a hotel you might book in some far-flung resort. Dickens certainly exists today 'out there' in his texts, adaptations and in his always-changing reception by academic and common readers, as well as in his appropriation by the heritage industry (of which this museum is a part). Personally too he exists 'inside' for me as a sort of palimpsest of all my encounters with his work from the age of fourteen, when his fiction was a way out of 1950s provincial America and the loneliness of adolescence, to my latest rereading of *Bleak House* this year – to remind myself of what Andrew Davies's consummate TV adaptation had added or subtracted – but I would want to resist making too much of this idiosyncratic association also.

A few days after the 7 July 2005 London bus and tube bombing I was interested to see that another blue-plaqued residential site, in Tavistock Square, which reads '1851–1860 Charles Dickens, Novelist/Lived in Tavistock House near this site' was chosen as the front cover of *The Guardian*'s G2 magazine section, ostensibly to illustrate its cover story, a piece by novelist John Lanchester, 'Why the bombers want to obliterate our history'. Oddly, Lanchester's thoughtful, complex essay never mentions Dickens once. For him it is W. B. Yeats, not Dickens, who was the significant literary figure who lived near the site of the bus bombing, and what was memorable about Yeats's residence in Woburn Walk was that he lost his virginity there.[13] One could add, although Lanchester doesn't choose to, that Tavistock Square and its environs have been associated rather more with the Bloomsbury set than with either Dickens or Yeats. Yet it seems that even for that cosmopolitan liberal daily *The Guardian*, neither the Irish Yeats, nor the feminist and pacifist Woolf (not to mention her scandalous friends and relations), can properly represent 'our history' at a moment of trauma; it must be Charles Dickens who memorialises London and British historical identity. The irony is that Dickens's response to July's terrorist outrage might well have echoed his infamous genocidal wish to 'exterminate' the whole 'Race' of those responsible for the death of British subjects at the time of the Indian Mutiny of 1857.[14] Perhaps *The Guardian*'s choice of Dickens as the long-dead cultural figure who the bombers, themselves British subjects, were out to get, was an unconscious expression of an atavistic revenge motif, one that could not legitimately surface in its editorial pages. Victoriana has a constantly shifting politics. It is usually complicated, not always obvious and not always nice.

Such disturbing stories, however, do not account for the aesthetic pleasure we continue to take in invoking the Victorian, a pleasure tinged with another sort of unease, associated with the mix of familiarity and strangeness which Freud theorised as the uncanny, and which surfaces when we do that tempting and transgressive thing and try to imagine ourselves in the past or the past in our present. For the last fifteen years of his life Henry James tried and failed to complete an historical novel, *The Sense of the Past*, which, like Moore's *The Great Victorian Collection*, was, at its heart, a commentary on the gothic effects of the historical imagination; its ability to make us doubt the stability of chronology and subjects. In it, a young man of James's time, Ralph Pendrel, goes back to the 1820s, taking the place of another young man in a family portrait. He is desperate to get back to his own late nineteenth-century modernity, and James, in his notes for the unfinished novel, suggests that as frightened as he feels among them, the historical characters begin to 'fear' him also, experiencing him 'as abnormal, as uncanny, as not *like* those they know of their own kind etc., etc.'[15] Ralph, who according to James's plan for the novel was to be allowed to return to 1910, is luckier than Moore's Anthony Maloney, who, failing to destroy the past that he has dreamed into the present, commits suicide. A correlative to the everyday estrangement of being a subject in time, the fantasised threats to subjects who play fast and loose with dreams of history provide, I would suggest, that necessary frisson of imperilment that makes narrative Victoriana so pleasurable.[16]

The historical imagination may have shifted its philosophical ground – may have seemed to abandon ground altogether as a base-line figure for thinking about the past – but this shift, whether self-conscious or more simply the effect of the altered cultural climate of postwar societies, has acted to reignite rather than suppress interest in particular past times, especially those traditionally thought to constitute an origin, however resisted, disavowed or superseded, of our present. What happened or was believed in Victoria's long reign has been read as one of those origins, and if our ambivalent attachment to it is less literally oedipal than that of, say, Virginia Woolf's generation, who were born into it and parented by its central figures, it is nevertheless a cultural and political genealogy that, rather surprisingly, still presses on us in a personal as well as a public form. *Victoriana: Histories, Fictions, Criticism* will, I hope, provide some clues to its continuing cultural hold on twenty-first century subjects.

Notes

1. Brian Moore, *The Great Victorian Collection* (London: HarperCollins, 1994). First published by Jonathan Cape in 1975, *The Great Victorian Collection* won the James Tait Black Memorial Prize.
2. Walter Benjamin, 'The Work of Art in the Age of Mechanical Reproduction', *Illuminations* (London: Fontana, 1973) pp. 219–54; Sigmund Freud, *The Interpretation of Dreams* (Harmondsworth: Penguin Books, 1976); Jean Baudrillard, 'Simulacra and Simulations', in Mark Poster (ed.), *Jean Baudrillard, Selected Writings* (Stanford: Stanford University Press, 1988) pp. 166–84. Benjamin suggests that today the work of art 'by the absolute emphasis on its exhibition value . . . becomes a creation with entirely new functions', p. 227. Baudrillard invents the term

'hyperreal' for simulation which dissolves the 'distinction between the real and the imaginary'. Benjamin sees the invention of film as changing both visual perception and attitudes towards art; Baudrillard argues that 'Disneyland is a perfect model of all the entangled orders of simulation'. Moore's location of his surreal fiction in California suggestively aligns his story with both these analyses.

3. Andrew Davies has been responsible for some of the most successful adaptations for television of Victorian fiction and Victoriana. See for example his versions of George Eliot's *Daniel Deronda* and Sarah Waters's self-styled 'lesbian romp', *Tipping the Velvet*, both from 2002. His 2005 version of Charles Dickens's *Bleak House* with actor Gillian Anderson was especially memorable.

4. See Fredric Jameson, 'Postmodernism, or The Cultural Logic of Late Capitalism', *New Left Review*, I: 146, July-August 1984, pp. 53–92.

5. John Kucich and Dianne F. Sadoff (eds), *Victorian Afterlife: postmodern culture rewrites the nineteenth century* (Minneapolis: University of Minnesota Press, 2000) highlights the Jamesonian position in its introduction and some of its essays, but the volume as a whole, as the editors say, 'stages a debate' rather than takes a position about the loss of historicity in what they call the 'post-Victorian' , p. xxv.

6. *The Diaries of Hannah Cullwick, Victorian Maidservant*, Liz Stanley (ed.) (London: Virago Press, 1984).

7. See also the accompanying book by the presenter. Adam Hart-Davis, *What the Victorians Did for Us* (London: Headline Book Publishing Ltd, 2002).

8. Matthew Sweet, *Inventing the Victorians* (London: Faber and Faber, 2001) p. 227.

9. For a discussion of Kingsley's views, see Catherine Hall, *Civilising Subjects: metropole and colony in the English imagination 1830–1867* (Cambridge: Polity Press, 2002) pp. 438–40.

10. See David Cannadine, *Ornamentalism: how the British saw their Empire* (London: Allen Lane, 2001). Cannadine argues that questions of race were less important than the class dynamics of Empire, while Niall Ferguson, in *Empire: the rise and demise of the British world order and the lessons for global power* (London: Allen Lane, 2003) p. 358, makes a much fuller defence of Empire, arguing that 'liberal capitalism' exists around the world because of 'the spread of British rule', which 'pioneered free trade, free capital movements, and, with the abolition of slavery, free labour'. Gordon Brown, *The Daily Mail*, 15 January, 2005. For an illuminating response to these views see Geoff Eley, 'Beneath the Skin. Or: How to Forget About the Empire Without Really Trying', *Journal of Colonialism and Colonial History*, 3: 1, Spring 2002, and for an alternative view of the effects of Empire, Catherine Hall, *Civilising Subjects*.

11. See the special issue on 'Conservative Modernity', David Glover and Cora Kaplan (eds) *New Formations*, 28, Spring 1996.

12. See Andrew Bennett, *The Author* (New York: Routledge, 2005) for a short, clear account of the debates on authorship.

13. John Lanchester, *The Guardian*, G2, 12 July 2005, pp. 1–3.

14. Dickens told his friend Miss Burdett-Coutts that if he were Commander-in-Chief in India he 'should do his utmost to exterminate the Race upon whom

the stain of the late cruelties rested . . . to blot it out of mankind and raze it off the face of the Earth . . .', cited in Peter Ackroyd, *Dickens* (London: Minerva, 1991) p. 844. Ackroyd, typically, reads Dicken's genocidal 'rage' as more to do with his personal frustrations at the time than his political beliefs.

15. Henry James, *The Sense of the Past* (New York: Charles Scribner's Sons, 1945) p. 295. James is seemingly using 'uncanny' in its more traditional sense as simply the fear of strangeness, but the situation he describes comes nearer to Freud's emphasis on fear caused by the mix of familiarity and strangeness.

16. See the treatment of a similar theme in Mark Twain, *A Connecticut Yankee in King Arthur's Court* (1889), a book James is very likely to have read.

Chapter 1

Heroines, Hysteria and History: *Jane Eyre* and her Critics

An arresting, surreal urban vignette from the first of Freud's *Five Lectures on Psychoanalysis* (1910) illustrates and extends one of his best known formulations: 'Hysterical patients suffer from reminiscences.' 'Their symptoms,' he suggests, are 'residues and mnemic symbols of particular (traumatic) experiences', symbols which function in the patient's psyche like public 'monuments and memorials', such as the column at London's Charing Cross erected in memory of Richard Plantagenet's beloved Queen Eleanor, or the 'towering column' near London Bridge that was 'designed as a memorial of the Great Fire' of 1666. Hardly registered by the urban dweller 'going about his business in the hurry that modern working conditions demand', 'unpractical Londoners', Freud's figure for the hysteric, would 'pause in deep melancholy' before Charing Cross, or 'shed tears' beside the monument to the Great Fire. 'Hysterics and neurotics' 'remember' and 'still cling to' 'painful experiences of the remote past', for they 'cannot get free of the past and for its sake they neglect what is real and immediate'.[1]

The history of feeling that narrative or visual Victoriana seeks at once to memorialise and renew for the modern reader – the melodramatic excess of nineteenth-century fiction, the unembarrassed sentiment in its poetry – has something in common with the overemotional response to historical trauma that Freud described in his 'impractical Londoners'. It might be an association too far to align the writer or reader of modern Victoriana with Freud's hysteric, yet his urban analogy catches something about the affective dynamics both of modern subjects and national history that speaks to Victoriana's affective relationship to the past, and to its compulsive recycling of Victorian material and discursive culture. Without stretching Freud's comparison too far, we might see Charlotte Brontë's most-read novel, *Jane Eyre*, as yet another type of mnemic symbol, a Western cultural monument which has moved generations of its mainly women readers to tears of desire and rage, as well as of loss.

In this chapter I want to annex Freud's evocative analogy as a tool for exploring the highly charged emotions that, over time, have frequently accompanied critical responses to Charlotte Brontë's most enduring novel, and which surface especially in those assessments which consider *Jane Eyre* in direct or oblique relationship to its proto-feminist themes.

A classic and now firmly canonical fiction, *Jane Eyre*, as its multiple paperback editions attest, has a life beyond its place on school and university syllabi. Imitations and variations on its plot and character began to appear within a few years of its publication, but Brontë's original remains a steady seller and a popular read. While popular cultural artefacts, as opposed to the sort of sober civic emblems in Freud's example, might suggest things too ephemeral to serve as mnemic symbols, over an extended period they may, like Brontë's book, attain a similar cultural status, condensing in their images or stories traumatic tropes and narratives which surprisingly continue to trigger strong affective responses, responses which seem strangely excessive in relation to their catalyst.

Cultural theorist and filmmaker Laura Mulvey has made this argument persuasively in relation to a wide range of 'artefacts of popular culture', including 'stories, scenarios, jokes, myths, images' – even whole genres like film. They 'supply', she suggests, 'a collective pool of imagery, like a bank or resource', that provides a release for the individual psyche, unable to express itself 'in so many words'. However the performance of this cultural work, she warns us, 'would depend, not on any essential or ahistorical shared human psyche, but on shared social formations that install ideals and taboos in the individual and then mark and mould the consequent desires and anxieties that characterize a shared culture'. '[L]egendary figures and stories' that 'persist through history' 'come to form part of the psychic vocabulary both of the individual and the collective culture', and these 'collective mnemic symbols . . . allow ordinary people to stop and wonder or weep, desire or shudder . . .'.[2]

Mulvey's nuanced discussion of the heavy psychic traffic between the 'individual' and 'collective' points towards the difficulty of drawing firm lines between those discrete elements of culture deemed to be distinct or even opposed – social or psychic, public or private, collective or individual, political or personal. The critical literature which has homed in on *Jane Eyre*'s agency in introducing a new, highly personalised 'voice' into nineteenth-century fiction, a voice which critics often argue confers a particular cultural value on subjective experience, has been typically concerned with trying to develop new ways of understanding these perceived oppositions. Indeed in feminist thinking in recent years both women's subjective voice and the experience to which it testifies have become hotly debated issues which have put into question the antecedents, present character and future of Western feminism. *Jane Eyre*, its heroine and its author (the distinctions between book, character and writer are frequently blurred) have acted as a kind of cultural magnet in these debates, drawing widely dispersed issues into the novel's field of meaning. While a graph of its rising and falling reputation in the last quarter century gives too historically limited and too linear an impression of the controversy it continues to stir, we should remember that in the 1970s *Jane Eyre* briefly attained a unique status as a positively valued 'cult text' for second-wave Anglophone feminism. Since Gayatri Chakravorty Spivak coined that description in her influential 1985 essay on the novel, *Jane Eyre* has become a much more tarnished and controversial cultural emblem of Western feminism's ambiguous political legacy. As mnemic symbol therefore, *Jane Eyre*'s narrative and its mode of telling memorialise no single event but a shifting constellation of stories, images and interpretations. An iconic cultural artefact for feminism, it amplifies the dissonances within and among contemporary feminisms.

Rather than joining the heated conversation about the ethical status of *Jane Eyre* for feminism, I want, in this essay, to challenge some of the terms of that debate both historically and in the present. It may be fruitful to read the often violent responses to Brontë's novel as Freud does the melancholy and tears of his 'unpractical Londoners', as a sign not only of the text's catalytic power, but, more painfully, as a symptom of a condition in which the relation between affect and object, as well as between the feeling subject and a history that may be both personal and collective, has become dangerously skewed.

From the first months of its publication in 1847, at a time when the identity and the gender of its author was still a matter for intense speculation, it was clear that *Jane Eyre* was capable of provoking ferocious critical commentary. Elizabeth Rigby's notorious review of the novel in *The Quarterly Review* of December 1848, attacking it as 'unchristian', 'coarse' and politically incendiary, was by far the most extended negative notice that the book received, but a highly critical one in *The Christian Remembrancer* of April 1848, which suggested that the 'love-scenes glow with a fire as fierce as that of Sappho' and that 'every page burns with moral Jacobinism' was not much kinder, declaring that 'there never was a better hater' than its author. These levels of outrage indicates how disturbing Brontë's work could appear to contemporary sensibilities, the anger certain readers found in her writing provoking an answering fury on the part of the hostile critic, male or female. Brontë recognised this circulation of anger from text to reader, writing to her publisher, W. S. Williams that she hoped 'that their anger will not make *me* angry'.[3] But the differences in the way in which that anger is read and reinscribed as criticism in different historical conjunctures, and from different national, social and cultural positions, concerns me as much as its remarkable power over time to unsettle its readers.

The 'hard to articulate', 'long lost psychic structures' that Mulvey believes are resurrected by the emotions generated by popular artefacts, when put into words by the critic, may both express and conceal not a single psychic narrative or fantasy, but multiple versions of them. Just such striking continuities and differences mark the highly charged treatment of *Jane Eyre* by the first two of my twentieth-century examples, British critics Virginia Woolf and Raymond Williams, whose pivotal use of Brontë's novel set the stage, in some sense, for the controversies of the last twenty-five years. Neither of these brilliant and idiosyncratic critics are exactly exemplary figures, although they explore, respectively, themes at the heart of first-wave feminist and post-World War II socialist cultural analysis. The question of feminism and women's writing is always central to Woolf's discussion, and it haunts Williams's work as well, emerging most explicitly in the essay on *Jane Eyre* and *Wuthering Heights* in *The English Novel* (1970). For each of these critics the personal voice of Brontë's narrators is of great importance, yet only in part as an innovation in the history of fiction in English. Both Woolf and Williams are concerned in very complicated ways with the relationship of that personal voice to questions of gender and class, not exclusively as these are given expression in *Jane Eyre*, but as they resonated in the 1840s and are embodied in the figure of the author.

For Virginia Woolf, *Jane Eyre* and Charlotte Brontë are the avatars both of the type of nineteenth-century women's fiction she wished her modernist aesthetic to transcend, and of a pre-twentieth-century feminism too freighted with female anger and too concerned with the personal and domestic. Her essay '*Jane Eyre* and *Wuthering Heights*' emphasises the spatial, temporal, cultural and economic differences between Brontë and the twentieth-century reader, and highlights the effects of provincialism and poverty in her writing, whose only redeeming virtue is its passionate poetic power. Brontë's heroine is similarly located at the margins of bourgeois culture and normalcy, her social and psychic condition made to seem both voluntary and deeply eccentric. 'The drawbacks of being Jane Eyre are not far to seek. Always to be a governess and always to be in love is a serious limitation in a world which is full, after all, of people who are neither one nor the other.'[4] Woolf's parodic echo of Keats's 'Ode to a Grecian Urn' freezes Jane in an attitude almost as grotesque as the poses of Charcot's hysterical patients at Salpêtrière. She is poised on the anomic social border between gentility and service, imprisoned in an intensity of feeling that is only bearable or

sane, Woolf implies, when transient. In a parallel move, Charlotte Brontë
is freeze-framed in a lost time and place; an anachronism, she is someone
with 'no lot in our modern world' who 'remains forever' in the 1850s,
'in a remote parsonage upon the wild Yorkshire moors'.[5] With an adroit
and deadly sleight of hand, the substantial Yorkshire parsonage is transformed into a much humbler rural address, and the writer's imagination
mirrors the cramped solipsism of the isolated artisan, rather than the
sublime freedom of the lonely artist. 'For the self-centred and self-limited
writers have a power denied the more catholic and broad-minded. Their
impressions are close packed and strongly stamped between their narrow
walls.'[6] The figure evokes a worker's cottage, in which 'impressions'
crowd like too many children, and of cottage industry – of weaving or
spinning in particular – is extended in Woolf's comment on Charlotte's
style: likened to that of 'any leader-writer in a provincial journal', it is
'stiff and decorous' founded on a 'staple' prose that, like the raw material of cheap cloth, 'is awkward and unyielding' to work upon. Without
'speculative curiosity', philosophy, comedy, learning or the ability to
create characters that are more than 'vigorous and elementary', it is not
surprising that even Woolf's praise of 'the country parson's daughter' and
her 'authentic voice' locates her writing in the most modest domestic
space imaginable, besides the 'red and fitful glow of the heart's fire which
illumines her page'.[7] It is in the disdainful voice of a metropolitan intellectual that Woolf carefully crafts the degradation of Brontë's class status
and education – one that wilfully distorts the breadth of her reading as
well as her experience of other places.[8] Woolf's distaste for the first personal singular in Charlotte Brontë, in spite of what she calls 'the eloquence and splendour and passion' of Charlotte's 'I love', 'I hate',
'I suffer', reveals her very different aesthetic stance to be sure, but her
critical strategy goes further to devalue that voice, pre-emptively eroding
its ability to speak either universally, for 'most people' or for women.[9] In
the novel, of course, Jane is neither 'always a governess' or 'always in
love', but Woolf's compelling image of a plot in stasis, of an author stuck
in a temporal, social and intellectual backwater, inevitably suggests that
the reader who identifies with either governess or love addict is suffering
from a peculiarly unglamorous form of reminiscence.

In her 1929 essay 'Women and Fiction', and in *A Room of One's Own*
of the same year, Woolf extends this argument through her focus on
female anger, arguing in the first piece that the consciousness of a
'woman's presence' in *Jane Eyre*, 'of someone resenting the treatment of
her sex and pleading for its rights', 'creates a distortion and is frequently
the cause of weakness' in the writing, a flaw that is shared by the male
writer only if 'he happens to be a working-man, a Negro, or one who for

some other reason is conscious of a disability'.[10] Feminist politics, as I have argued elsewhere, is thus reduced to the status of 'personal cause' and 'personal discontent'.[11] In *A Room of One's Own*, the most general proto-feminist statement in *Jane Eyre*, Jane's soliloquy from the top of Thornfield in Chapter 12 is perversely interpreted by Woolf in a unparalleled example of punitive excess as the 'flawed passage' in which the personal voice of the author dominates, a passage which proves that Brontë's

> books will be deformed and twisted. She will write in a rage where she should write calmly. She will write foolishly when she should write wisely. She will write of herself when she should write of her characters. She is at war with her lot. How could she help but die young, cramped and thwarted?[12]

For Woolf then, *Jane Eyre* as mnemic symbol evokes a cluster of overt anxieties about gender, feminism and anger which threaten to weaken or disable the novelist's (though not the critic's) craft as Woolf wished to define it for herself. When Woolf's separate critiques of Charlotte Brontë and *Jane Eyre* are brought together, the imperious condescension touched with malice that links them acquires a logic which is missing when they are read separately. Jane/Brontë's subjective voice – a voice that once given permission to speak cannot be contained or regulated but will interrupt a story to complain about women's lot – marks not the origin of the modern novel, as it will do for Raymond Williams, but constitutes the most profound danger to its possibilities when undertaken by women. Each attack on *Jane Eyre* and its author is in reality a defensive screen against Woolf's own potential, and potentially lethal, identification with her, a reassurance that no psychic, social, intellectual or aesthetic similarity can be established between the 'country parson's daughter' and the 'catholic and broad-minded' daughter of the metropolitan intellectual, Sir Leslie Stephen. *Jane Eyre* structures the critical and political genealogy that Woolf attempts to set up in these several pieces – one in which feminist modernism and modern feminism transcend their flawed precursors and survive in a safe space where, she insists, the 'woman writer is no longer bitter. She is no longer angry', an assertion that is put into question by Woolf's treatment of Brontë's first novel.[13]

There is more than thirty years between Woolf's lethal assault on *Jane Eyre* and Raymond Williams's oblique celebration of it in *The Long Revolution*, a distance marked too by Williams's very different social location as the working-class son of a railwayman from the Welsh border country who eventually joined the faculty of the Cambridge from which Woolf felt herself, for all her advantages, so profoundly excluded. *The Long Revolution* takes the 1840s as the exemplary decade for his second chapter, 'The Analysis of Culture'. In this remarkable essay

Williams theorises the relationship of the traumatic social and political events of the 1840s to the whole field of narrative fiction from the now forgotten best sellers sold on railway bookstalls – a radical innovation in mass marketing in those years – to those novels more highly acclaimed for their literary merit. The 'connection between the popular structure of feeling and that used in the literature of the time,' Williams writes, is where 'at a level even more important than that of institutions that the real relations within the whole culture are made clear'.[14] Williams points out that the novels which have since become classics shared many of their narrative features with the most poorly crafted periodical fiction of the day, and he goes on to speculate that the elusive difference between the 'good novel' and the rest may be simply that in some 'good novels the ordinary situations and feelings are worked through to their maximum intensity', in others 'one element of the experience floods through the work, in such a way as to make it relevant in its own right, outside the conventional terms'. Here 'Charlotte Brontë, taking lonely personal desire to an intensity that really questions the conventions by which it is opposed', and the stories that figure the 'orphan, the exposed child, the lonely governess, the girl from a poor family', are made to express 'a *general* judgement of the human quality of the whole way of life'.[15] These novels, less obviously concerned with social and political upheaval, most profoundly address the fears they evoke. Moreover the 'intensity of the central experience' could, Williams thought, transcend the ordinary structure of feeling of a period and even teach 'a new feeling'.[16] *Jane Eyre* is not mentioned by name in this passage, so familiar a part of his readers' everyday cultural baggage does Williams assume it to be; the juxtaposition of 'orphan' and 'governess' in his summary of 'the lonely exposed figure' is enough to evoke it as the classic of the archetype.

A different kind of obliqueness in this essay governs the absence of any reflective account of why middle-class women writers and their female protagonists in particular can stand as the symbolic representatives of the generic state of 'Man alone, afraid, a victim'.[17] It is as if the critic assumes that readers will silently agree that terror, loneliness and poverty will be felt as states of feminised abjection whether men or women suffer them. Williams's unqualified praise of these novels for challenging convention and representing 'radical human dissent' is related to his emphasis on their protagonists as victims. When, in his 1970 essay on 'Charlotte and Emily Brontë', Williams highlights the social and psychological agency of Charlotte Brontë's subjective voice as a woman's voice, both his analysis and his emotional response to Charlotte Brontë and *Jane Eyre* – as cultural artefact, as mnemic symbol – undergoes a profound change. This shift makes sense if we read this later essay as in an uneasy, implicit dialogue with the early arguments of second-wave feminism which began to appear in Britain in the late 1960s. It is, for example, much more self-conscious about the gender of the character and the reader, as when it acknowledges that the 'depressing image' of the governess may be a problem for the 'male middle-class' reader who is likely to find her 'repressive, unfeminine, dowdy'.[18] Yet it is when we tune in to the new intensities that have crept into Williams's restated view that Charlotte and Emily Brontë's 'emphasis on intense feeling, on a commitment to what we must directly call passion' in the English novel that we can hear the way in which the 'intensity of desire' disturbs him when it takes the form of what he calls 'secret sharing' in Charlotte Brontë's writing.

> The connecting power of Charlotte Brontë's fiction is in just this first-person capacity to compose an intimate relationship with the reader [and this] private confidence, this mode of confession: the account given as if in a private letter, in private talk; a private talk; the account given to a private journal includes – as it were involuntarily, yet it is very deliberate and conscious art – the awareness of the friend, the close one, the unknown but in this way intimate reader: the reader as writer, while the urgent voice lasts.[19]

This passage with its urgent, somewhat hostile repetition of 'private' speaks of a forced, uncomfortable intimacy with an alien, even feared intensity of feeling; at the same time it seems to register an almost equal fear of exclusion from the 'secret sharing'. Against this voice in *Jane Eyre* (and in *Villette*) Williams sees the 'multipersonal' *Wuthering Heights* as 'fresh and open air'. Yet it is Charlotte, not Emily, *Jane Eyre* and *Villette*, not *Wuthering Heights*, that stand very obviously at the head of a tradition of the 'fiction of special pleading'.[20]

No longer representative of the general structure of feeling of the mid-century, the

> particular weakness of this form has become very obvious. Its persons outside this shaping longing demanding consciousness have reality only as they contribute to the landscape, the emotional landscape, of the special, the pleading, the recommending character. That is all we know of them, all we really know of her, and some extraordinary things have been done in its name: use of others, abuse of others; a breakdown of discourse – and with discourse so much else, so many other needs and realities – as the all including voice, the voice pleading for this experience, for the understanding of it, for the exclusion of alternatives – alternative voices, alternative viewpoints – comes through and creates its own world.[21]

Here it is clearly the critic's voice that seems close to breakdown, as it resists, with passionate accusation, the voice initiated by and associated with Charlotte's 'her', which, in Britain in the late 1960s, was aiming to change broad definitions of politics; to make the political more personal and to place the uneven and unequal conditions of men and women at the top of its agenda. Williams, interestingly, does not call this voice 'individualism', as many socialist cultural critics after him will do, for 'individualism' cannot capture what fascinates and appals him about its gendered intensity of feeling. However unlike Virginia Woolf, who wants to relegate it to the Victorian past, Williams is not afraid – indeed he is rather driven – to call it the voice of modernity.

Both Woolf's and Williams's response to *Jane Eyre* imagined a primary audience of readers domiciled in the British Isles, readers for whom, whatever their class, gender or geographical location within Britain, would be reminded in so many ways – through the built environment, natural landscape, family history, the legacy of economic and political institutions – of their present and historic connections to the regional and class cultures in which Brontë lived and wrote. Their criticism acknowledged, if only through strong denial (Woolf) or a kind of angry despair (Williams), the continuities between the tradition she headed and their own. It is a very different matter with the American-born feminist critics for whom *Jane Eyre* and Charlotte Brontë are at least in one sense a composite evocation of an alien 'Englishness' towards which they may well have a sort of desiring identification, but from which they inevitably have a national, cultural difference, and a psychic distance. And this means that they have a radically different relationship to the anger which they heard in the novel, a difference which helped them to begin to address and negotiate that anger.

Forging a specifically feminist, Anglophone, international cultural genealogy was the task that critics like Elaine Showalter in *A Room of Their Own: British women novelists from Brontë to Lessing* (1977) and Sandra Gilbert and Susan Gubar in *The Madwoman in the Attic: the woman writer and the nineteenth-century literary imagination* (1979) set themselves. These two groundbreaking and influential studies gave *Jane Eyre* a central place in the history of women's writing, Showalter interpreting it as a 'feminine' novel, Gilbert and Gubar as the quintessential novel of 'rebellious feminism'. Each of these books confidently place *Jane Eyre* in the cultural context of its production and reception, yet in illuminating aspects of gender in that culture, other aspects of the 1840s seem to fall into shadow; for example neither binds it closely, as Williams does, to the social upheavals of the decade. In slightly different ways each book pursues the psychological and sexual themes and symbols in the novel. However both single out Brontë's proto-feminist anger as *Jane Eyre*'s most salient feature. As a mnemic symbol for American-based feminist critics in the 1970s, that anger is no longer the book's 'flaw', its 'special pleading' or even its anti-Christian dissent. Instead anger becomes the ground of a radical new aesthetic. In retrospect we can see feminist criticism in this period developing a feminist aesthetics of anger, for which the Victorian period serves as a literary and social origin. Showalter and Gilbert and Gubar argue that the 'gothic' and 'surreal' narrative devices, part of Brontë's innovative experimentation, create scenarios that Jane successfully negotiates 'to achieve 'a full and healthy . . . Womanhood' (Showalter), rewarded in 'the marriage of true minds at Ferndean' (Gilbert and Gubar).[22] In these American feminist readings, angry female selfhood, one that repudiates 'a crucifying denial of the self', is not punishable by the kind of certain death that Woolf retroactively confirmed for Charlotte Brontë, but is instead rewarded, valued as a sign both of aesthetic excellence and emotional health.[23]

Although critical studies of fiction inevitably select different parts of narratives for special attention, it is remarkable that in these two watershed critiques of *Jane Eyre*, elements of the story that are hardly mentioned by Woolf and Williams become the most important sections. Showalter highlights to good effect the childhood passages. In the 1970s 'second-wave' feminism was experiencing the rapid development, internal upheavals and struggles with authority that had a certain resonance with the rebellious childhood and difficult adolescence represented in *Jane Eyre*. The early sections of the book certainly struck an especially strong chord with feminist readers and fledgling feminist critics. Yet these correspondences do not explain every shift in emphasis. Gilbert and Gubar, interestingly, consider Rochester's place in the story – and the story he tells – in great detail. All three critics consider the role of Bertha Mason, but none find in the representation of Rochester's mad white Creole wife the disturbing discourse of race and empire that would concern critics only a few years later. Neither *A Literature of Their Own* or *The Madwoman in the Attic* represented the radical arm of feminist thought. These liberal feminist studies occupy a middle ground and are, if anything, somewhat less critical of men and masculinity than Brontë was for her time. Both books, for example, see the novel's happy heterosexual resolution as a harbinger of the new equality between the sexes that the women's movement would bring about in the late twentieth century. The popular structure of feeling of certain strands of feminism in the 1970s, especially perhaps in the United States, made room both for anger and euphoria, for an honourable past for Anglophone feminism, in which, for some feminist thinkers, the feminine and the feminist could happily coexist.

So far in this essay I have been exploring discrete moments in the history of *Jane Eyre*'s reception in order to suggest how a popular and canonical fiction that takes gendered feeling as its overt topic has elicited in its turn a powerful affective response from some of its most influential critics. I have been arguing that criticism, like the imaginative literature it analyses, has an emotive history that we can best understand by specifying the cultural sites – of class, gender, nationality, political persuasion – from which the critic speaks. Situating such criticism in its cultural grid, I would argue, involves thinking about aspects of the critic's biography as both public and exemplary rather than private and idiosyncratic, and it leads to a more illuminating analysis than approaches which reduce a critic's strong reaction to a novel to their personal psychological history. If popular literary icons like *Jane Eyre* act like the mnemic symbols in Freud's discussion of hysteria, triggering responses that, as Mulvey, says are 'hard to articulate' and evade 'the precision of language' (although here they erupt within critical arguments), they signal the presence of clusters of 'anxieties and desires' which are not so much beyond analysis or structurally inexpressible, as not yet worked through. The fact that *Jane Eyre* continues to incite a highly charged contentious response within feminist criticism, a response so full of present feeling that it seems out of sync with the novel's historical status, suggests that its narrative condenses unresolved questions in and for feminism today. One of these is clearly the status of female feelings in feminism, of anger and of desire, the latter both in its specifically sexual and more generally utopian definition. Another is the status of female individualism, of independent agency when advocated by and on behalf of white middle-class subjects.

Revisionist feminist critiques of *Jane Eyre* since 1985 have challenged the novel's positive and radical profile in the previous two decades by reading it as deeply conservative about class, race and empire. These approaches tie both Brontë's feminist individualism and her emphasis on the feeling self to a particularly problematic strand of feminist history, one whose pretensions to speak on behalf of 'women' as a group masks its own considerable cultural biases, and its implication in the development of imperialism. They ask, in specifically historical terms, what social meanings *Jane Eyre*'s rhetoric of desire might conceal and which groups are the targets of its anger. Instead of simply celebrating the derepressed discourse of feeling in the novel, they are more suspicious about the way in which the rhetoric of feeling enables less liberatory cultural narratives. At the same time these new, highly critical readings, aimed at dislodging the novel from its too honorific position within feminism by offering a wider social and political context in which to read it, are marked by some of the same rhetorical excesses that I have noted in earlier critiques. Again it seems as if *Jane Eyre* performs its function of mnemic symbol by allowing present anxieties about the late twentieth-century politics of feminist cultural analysis to become displaced onto the historical text.

This is certainly true of the way *Jane Eyre* and the Brontës are treated in Nancy Armstrong's *Desire and Domestic Fiction: a political history of the novel* (1987), an important and influential study which responds to attacks on and self-criticism within feminism for its Eurocentrism and its blindness to race and class issues. Armstrong's book is also part of a paradigm shift in feminist literary scholarship in which Marxist, psychoanalytic, poststructuralist and postcolonial theory challenge and displace the liberal humanism of Showalter and Gilbert and Gubar. Armstrong's remarkable long view of domestic fiction as a crucial subgenre of the novel is most obviously indebted to the theoretical framework of Michel Foucault, especially *The History of Sexuality* (1978). Paraphrasing Foucault she argues that 'sexuality is a cultural construct and . . . has a history . . . that written representations of the self allowed the modern individual to become an economic and psychological reality', adding her key point, 'that the modern individual was first and foremost a woman'.[24] Instead of celebrating women's vanguard role, as Showalter or Gilbert and Gubar might have done, Armstrong regards this development as deeply problematic. And this means that her specific account of the importance of the work of Charlotte and Emily Brontë, together with her close reading of *Jane Eyre*, echo the highly coloured critical views of both Woolf and Williams. Like Woolf in 'Women and Fiction', and *A Room of One's Own*, Armstrong sees the domestic, private life, the world of personal feelings, as in opposition to, and less important than, the public and political world. Like Woolf, and like Williams in his 1970 essay, she hears something terrifying and transforming in the narrative of desire. While the Brontës do not quite stand for Armstrong, as they do for Williams, 'at the head of a tradition', they are seen as the most expert practitioners of that aggrandising category of the novel, domestic fiction, which, she argues, 'actively sought to disentangle the language of sexual relations from the language of politics'.[25] This fiction not only formulated 'universal forms of subjectivity' for men and women, but translated 'all kinds of political information into psychological terms. As they displaced the facts and figures of social history, the Brontës began producing new figures of desire that detached the desiring self from place, time and material cause.'[26] While Raymond Williams, in *The Long Revolution*, saw the political point of such a universalising imperative, which could make female orphans stand for 'man alone', Armstrong views the creation of 'universal forms of subjectivity' as wholly politically retrograde.

Armstrong's description of the Brontës's universalising practice is, interestingly, very close to what Mulvey suggests is the labile effect of mnemic symbols, which trigger weeping that cannot be located in a history either public or private, tears which both speak and suppress that history. Yet the charge that the Brontës's writing does in fact work to evade history and materiality, rests, in my view, on a shaky and very idiosyncratic definition of 'history', which seems to exclude anything at all to do with gender. One of Armstrong's textual examples from *Jane Eyre* suggests the weakness of her case. Choosing the scene in Chapter 4 in which the bullying Mr Brocklehurst, the governor of Lowood School, 'chatechises' Jane, who refuses to be cowed by him, Armstrong argues that this scene of rebellion is a 'displacement of class conflict onto sexual relations', contrasting it to a real political intervention which appeared 'during the coal miners' strike of 1844, the "Miner's Catechism"', in which 'Peter Poverty' is mockingly interrogated by an anonymous ruling class authority.[27] The comparison implies that women and gender are somehow not implicated in class relations but stand outside them, unconnected and in opposition to them, an argument that implicitly rejects feminism's claim that gender hierarchy is articulated with, and of the same order as, all other hierarchical relations such as race and class. It also, perversely, takes the most historically rooted episode in the novel, Brontë's thinly veiled attack on the governor of the charity school that she and her sisters actually attended, and places it outside the public, classbound history of such institutions. Armstrong argues that *Jane Eyre* belongs to a key moment in an anti-historical tradition of the novel. One of the most powerful texts of domestic fiction, it inhabits a 'private' space reserved for women and their doings, a space whose temporality seems oddly commensurate with the skewed, stopped time of the hysteric. In *Desire and Domestic Fiction* the domain of the private – which may just be the home and domesticity – and the psychic – the domain of individual feeling – are both conflated and pathologised. The reader and the modern critic, living in what Armstrong takes to be the real time of 'history', are encouraged to break their identification with that hysterical, ahistorical fictional world – told to stop crying, as it were, for and about *Jane Eyre*.

The anger directed at *Jane Eyre* by Brontë's contemporaries was aroused by the novel's unfeminine discontent and its supposed 'anti-Christian' Jacobinical sentiments: Elizabeth Rigby did not 'hesitate to say that the tone of mind and thought which has overthrown authority and violated every code human and divine abroad, and fostered Chartism and rebellion at home, is the same which has also written *Jane Eyre*'.[28] For the late 1840s the novel was read as explicitly radical, affectively if not overtly aligned with just the sort of political rebellions, the European revolutions of 1848 and chartism in Britain, that Nancy Armstrong would accept as 'political'. Neither Woolf nor Williams read it quite that way; – for each of them Brontë's novel represents something both innovative and disquietingly anti-political if not quite conservative, something embedded in the affect it describes and produces, a response that Armstrong builds on and expands. Gayatri Chakravorty Spivak also endorses the view that *Jane Eyre* is an innovative but politically right-wing text; however, her critical reading locates *Jane Eyre* neither in the home nor in the wounded female psyche, but firmly in history. For Spivak the novel is one of the exemplary fictions of its time about the Empire at home, a text in which Jane and St John Rivers represent the complementary elements of the nineteenth-century ideology of empire, 'childbearing and soul making'. 'The first,' Spivak explains, 'is domestic-society-through-sexual reproduction cathected as "companionate love"; the second is the imperialist project cathected as civil-society-through-social-mission'.[29] Spivak accuses 'the emergent perspectives of feminist criticism' of reproducing 'the axioms of imperialism'. She challenges her readers to distance themselves from the version of *Jane Eyre* which has become a 'cult text' of eurocentric liberal humanist feminism, so that they may focus instead on the novel's construction of the subjects and dynamics of empire. Rather than producing a close historical reading of the novel, Spivak's essay opened up the possibility, indeed the necessity, of such a reading. In this sense we might see the effect of Spivak's piece in relationship to the operation of hysteria, where the patient's symptoms are the effects of traumatic memories which have become blocked. By highlighting the forgotten or suppressed racial and imperial figures in *Jane Eyre*, the reader is released from her fantasmatic fixation on the heroine's narrative.

Although the essay provoked, and I believe continues to provoke, a fair amount of hostility among Brontë fans and scholars, it did have the effect of repositioning *Jane Eyre* within the nineteenth-century history of empire in which it is so imaginatively rooted. A number of critics – Susan Meyer, Jenny Sharpe and myself among them – took up Spivak's challenge, producing historicist readings in which the novel's thematisation and figuration of race and empire are seen to emerge from the twin contexts of the British empire at home and abroad.[30] Yet there is, in retrospect, a small difficulty with this postcolonial critique; as in the commentary of Williams, Gilbert and Gubar, Showalter and Armstrong, it tends to reify *Jane Eyre*'s position as an ur-text – not just an origin for modern fiction and modern subjectivity, or of progressive and aspirant feminism, but a uniquely powerful articulation of the project of empire. Paradoxically, the more the novel is critiqued and its canonical and popular status queried, the more trauma it seems to embody for critics, even if that violence – circling around the negative rather than the positive site of female individualism – is read as differently as it is in Armstrong and Spivak. The very iconic status of the novel, its 'cult' properties that Armstrong and Spivak wish to debunk, is reaffirmed.

Spivak carefully situates her intervention as a critique of the unconscious imperialism of Western feminism, and her essay traces *Jane Eyre*'s influence through its revision and rewriting in Jean Rhys's *Wide Sargasso Sea*. Her essay remains a watershed in *Jane Eyre*'s critical genealogy, in that it puts the novel's politics for a modern reader in the context of divisions within feminism worldwide and nationally. Rereading *Jane Eyre* in this way is a sign of the cultural effects of postwar decolonisation: it marks the growth of postcolonial studies, and is an example of what Spivak and others call the 'worlding' of Western literature. From this perspective, *Jane Eyre* is rightly seen as a cultural artefact read all over the English-speaking world and beyond, and it would follow that the identifications and affect it has generated ought to be more widely assessed from the point of view of readers from former British colonies as well as from a more heterogeneous 'global' readership. Even the mere consciousness that these 'other' readers exist, changes the book's resonance for a white Western reader.

Bringing a high degree of political awareness to the reading of the novel – understanding that *Jane Eyre* is enmeshed in the history and politics of its time and ours – makes it harder for the scholar and student to identify so wholeheartedly with Jane's trajectory, and this is true whether one takes the view that Brontë's fiction has a highly problematic, complicit relationship with the construction of racial thinking and the empire, or agrees with critics who emphasise her partial but emphatic resistance to it. Making readers conscious and critical about their identificatory relations to texts is, of course, part of the aim of teaching a novel, and like any other analytic or deconstructive process it interferes – at least temporarily – with the simpler pleasures of reading, so that a more reflective process of analysis can take place. Spivak makes that disengagement an urgent political necessity. For Spivak, an 'innocent' Western reading that idealises *Jane Eyre*'s heroine spells complicity with the novel's imperialist agenda. As the comment on its second page that '[s]ympathetic U.S. feminists have remarked that I do not do justice to Jane Eyre's subjectivity' indicates, this was a high-stakes, highly charged argument that aimed to upset the complacent *Jane Eyre* reader as much as possible, even to the point of making her guilty through her readerly association with its heroine.[31]

Critics, like common readers, are reluctant to jettison their literary affiliations and enthusiasms. Questioning the politics and ethics of loved, canonical authors tends to produce an emotional reaction and resistance from ordinary readers, fans and critics.[32] One is almost tempted to personify this resistance as 'belonging' to the text itself, to see it as mounting its own formidable rhetorical defence against criticism – but to take that analysis too far is to ascribe a spurious magical agency to narrative that further mystifies rather than explains its effects. When a once popular text or author falls definitively out of favour with its public for historical reasons to do with shifts in taste and sensibility, readers are not particularly troubled by critical revisions, however politically charged. The fate of texts subjected to powerful critiques vary – a non-literary example would be the way in which Freud's case study of 'Dora' remains fascinating for readers and a key to the interpretation of his oeuvre, although its significance has been hotly debated.[33] Or, with a rich and complex text like *Jane Eyre*, readers can bypass the rationalist function of critique, refuse and reject its political readings, and continue to find other different affective moments to fix on – keeping the novel's ability to evoke tears intact, but shifting the critical emphasis by focusing on scenes and themes that can still make us weep.

Much of the postcolonial criticism of *Jane Eyre* has come from critics based in the United States, while British-based Victorianists have in recent years been pursuing other issues. Sally Shuttleworth's erudite, fascinating *Charlotte Brontë and Victorian Psychology* (1996) uses a Foucauldian approach to rehistoricise Brontë, arguing that her work 'formed an integral part' of the 'wider textual economy' of 'contemporary psychological discourse'.[34] In a very different use of Foucault from Armstrong's, Shuttleworth positions Brontë as an active participant in this discourse, and she looks at the ways she 'both assimilated and challenged Victorian constructs, interrogating received notions, exploring their contradictions, and breaking the bounds of contemporary discourse in the complex structures of her fictions'.[35] Her reading of *Jane Eyre* engages with the racial and class analyses of *Jane Eyre* in the footnotes rather than the main text, and her conclusion accepts that *Jane Eyre* 'can be read as a quintessential expression of Victorian individualism', but argues that Jane's gender makes that expression not the more conservative 'spirit of the age', but something more 'radical, if not revolutionary'.[36] In effect, Shuttleworth attempts to defuse the heat around the more politically charged and divisive debates about *Jane Eyre*, by emphasising the ineluctable historical specificity of the novel's use of the contemporary 'language of psychology', breaking the link between what might be counted politically rebellious in Brontë's time and ours. In this sense she resists the move to locate *Jane Eyre* as part of an almost organically imagined Western feminist psyche – she aims to acknowledge but also to distance its passion and tears, to reduce its function as a mnemic symbol, which she implies is related to its 'traditional' dehistoricisation. In a similar vein, Heather

Glen's *Charlotte Brontë: the imagination in history* (2002) has developed a wonderfully 'thick description' of Brontë's English contexts, while emphasising the aesthetic complexity of the novels. There is a sense, in both Shuttleworth and Glen, that they are bringing Brontë 'back home' from a kind of world tour that has not particularly benefited her reputation, although it may have enhanced her celebrity. In Glen's introduction she acknowledges, but chooses not to engage with, the work on class and race, and it remains largely outside the overt argument of her book.[37] However Glen does focus very productively on the unsettling way in which work so 'passionately loved, so intimately appropriated' continues to stir audiences, an effect that she thinks is related to the way in which the novels continue to 'stir and disconcert' modern readers by seeming to be both deeply familiar and absolutely strange.[38] The reasons for this discomfort, for Glen, lie in the differences between Brontë's social and cultural world and our contemporary one. Glen's emphasis on the uncanny effect of Brontë's work (and I would say *Jane Eyre* especially) takes us back to the question first posed by Freud in his 1910 lecture, as to why mnemic symbols, the repositories of the condensed and unresolved histories of nations and of selves, continue to evoke such passionate and 'unpractical' responses.

This essay has explored the heightened emotions that *Jane Eyre* has provoked in twentieth-century literary criticism in order to give a history to one strand of the affective response to the novel. As I have indicated however, the response itself, including its historicising impulse in recent years, has not, as some critics have hoped, disengaged modern readers from angry or sympathetic identification with the text and its heroine, but rather produced a second order set of feelings about the critical debates, for which, nevertheless, *Jane Eyre* remains a referent. Alongside the critical history of the novel runs an astonishing compendium of *Jane Eyre* spin-offs: imitation, prequel, sequel, adaptation and pastiche. A part of this bulging archive – much of which certainly deserves to be labelled Victoriana – has been documented and well analysed by Patsy Stoneman and Lucasta Miller, among others.[39]

Of this cultural legacy, creative 'reminiscences' we might call them, one strikingly original and non-literary example stands out: artist Paula Rego's recent remarkable series of drawings inspired by the novel, now produced in book form with an introduction by Marina Warner. Set out like illustrations with citations from the text at one side, these images are in fact anti-illustrations; they construct a kind of grotesque dreamscape for which the novel is the occasion. As Warner notes, Rego's portraits of Jane do not 'prettify her'; ugly and stunted, she is visually aligned, Warner suggests, with Bertha, eliding the distinction between heroine

Figure 1.1 *Loving Bewick* by Paula Rego.

and villain, imperial agent and racialised victim.[40] Certain drawings –
'Jane', 'Loving Bewick', 'Crumpled', 'Crying', 'Bertha', 'Come to me' –
depict a female figure in a dramatic attitude – reminding one of the
pictures of the hysterics in Charcot's asylum, Salpêtriére.

In 'Loving Bewick' for example, a giant pelican perches on an adult Jane's fully clothed body and with her full complicity, perhaps invitation, places its phallic, pelican-like beak in her open mouth – a perverse interpretation with, as Warner says, its deliberate reference to Leda and the swan, of a seemingly innocent passage from the opening pages of the novel in which the ten-year-old Jane reads, or rather looks at, the illustrations from Bewick's *Book of British Birds*.[41] In Rego's rendering of 'with Bewick on my knee I was then happy: happy at least in my way', the scene of reading that for Gayatri Spivak establishes Jane's cultural authority as a 'first-world reader' emphasises instead the transgressive reaches of the psyche that art can trigger. From the same passage Rego foregrounds the creative potential of art: 'Each picture told a story; mysterious often to my undeveloped understanding and imperfect feelings, yet ever profoundly interesting . . .' – perhaps the pelican rendered substantial in the child's fantasy, is, as Warner suggests, feeding, not assaulting Jane. Yet the drawn Jane is not a half-formed child, a fact which should remind us that the voice and consciousness of the child Jane is always narrated and negotiated by her adult self.[42] Other images in the series, of grouped and combined figures, of disordered schoolrooms and the preparation for a ball, for example, are equally disturbing but more socially freighted.

Rego's drawings, which in their dark imagination take something from Goya, something else from Käthe Kollwitz, highlight *Jane Eyre*'s thematisation of the pleasures and dangers of the imagination. Her images both depend on and break free of the novel. Like the uses that jazz makes of classical and popular tunes, these works are free improvisation, but while they stand the conventions of nineteenth-century narrative on their end, developing a more syncopated anti-realist story, they selectively memorialise the original, altering it as they do so. Rego's *Jane Eyre* reminds the viewer of the novel's strongly evoked sense of time and place, and of its powerful use of psychology, fairy tale and melodrama, yet its take on them is not mimetic but emphatically twenty-first century. The figures are carefully costumed in nineteenth-century dress, but the exaggerated features and poses are modern: the end product is a wholly new work of art, whose relation to Brontë's novel is never straightforward. Most interesting in terms of the question of affect explored in this essay, the assonance between Rego's drawings and the passages from *Jane Eyre* that go with them poses a question about where the violence and pain, so explicitly visually rendered, comes from. This open-ended question is the work's great strength. Rego highlights the novel's constant evocation of the extreme states of feeling selves, states which depend, as Freud's parallel between monuments and individual trauma implies, on a complex negotiation between two registers of history, social and psychic. In spite of their different temporalities and conventions, these historical registers are always imbricated with each other, never distinct, so that locating the traumatic moment in one place or another – in the mnemic symbol, or the weeping Londoner, angry critic, identifying reader or interpreting artist – is always problematic. Rego emphasises the peripatetic relation between a text like *Jane Eyre*, its audience and its interpreters, among whom the emotion that we try and fail to tie down to one or another, ceaselessly circulates.

Notes

1. Sigmund Freud, *Five Lectures on Psycho-Analysis* (1910), in James Strachey *et al.* (eds), *The Standard Edition of the Collected Works of Sigmund Freud*, vol. 11 (London: The Hogarth Press and the Institute of Psychoanalysis, 1957) pp. 16–17.
2. Laura Mulvey, ' "It Will Be a Magnificent Obsession": The Melodrama's Role in the Development of Contemporary Film Theory', in Jacky Bratton, Jim Cook, Christine Gledhill (eds), *Melodrama: Stage, Picture, Screen* (London: British Film Institute, 1994) pp. 126–7.
3. Charlotte Brontë to W. S. Williams, 3 April 1848, in Margaret Smith (ed.), *The Letters of Charlotte Brontë, Volume Two, 1848–1851* (Oxford: Oxford University Press, 2000) p. 50.
4. Virginia Woolf, '*Jane Eyre* and *Wuthering Heights*', in *The Common Reader*, First Series (London: Hogarth Press, 1925) p. 198. This essay incorporates material from an article on Charlotte Brontë in *The Times Literary Supplement*, 13 April 1916.
5. Virginia Woolf, '*Jane Eyre* and *Wuthering Heights*', p. 196.
6. Virginia Woolf, '*Jane Eyre* and *Wuthering Heights*', p. 199.
7. Virginia Woolf, '*Jane Eyre* and *Wuthering Heights*', pp. 199–200.
8. For a better sense of Charlotte Brontë's breadth of reading and cosmopolitan sensibility one must turn to her letters: Margaret Smith (ed.), *The Letters of Charlotte Brontë*, vols 1–3 (Oxford: Oxford University Press, 1995–2004).
9. Virginia Woolf, '*Jane Eyre* and *Wuthering Heights*', p. 201.
10. Virginia Woolf, 'Women and Fiction' (1929) reprinted in Virginia Woolf, Michèle Barrett (ed. and intr.) *Women and Writing* (London: The Women's Press, 1979) p. 47. This essay first appeared in *The Forum*, March 1929.
11. See my earlier discussion of Woolf's treatment of *Jane Eyre* in 'Pandora's Box: Subjectivity, Class and Sexuality in Socialist Feminist Criticism', *Sea Changes: essays on culture and feminism* (London: Verso, 1986) pp. 170–6.
12. Virginia Woolf, *A Room of One's Own* (New York: Harcourt Brace Jovanovitch, 1957) pp. 72–3.
13. Virginia Woolf, 'Women and Writing', p. 48. Lest it seem that I am arguing that *Jane Eyre*'s ability to provoke the displacement and projection of female anger is particular to Woolf, I would point out that my own heated response to Woolf's treatment of Charlotte Brontë/*Jane Eyre* is equally symptomatic

of the defensive and accusatory feelings that circulate around Brontë's text. In my case, my encounter, as an American expatriate in the 1960s, with the remnants of the British class system surely informs my account of Woolf's mandarin attitude to Charlotte Brontë.

14. Raymond Williams, *The Long Revolution* (Harmondsworth: Penguin, 1965) pp. 84–5.
15. Raymond Williams, *The Long Revolution*, p. 85.
16. Raymond Williams, *The Long Revolution*, pp. 85–6.
17. Raymond Williams, *The Long Revolution*, p. 85.
18. Raymond Williams, 'Charlotte and Emily Brontë', *The English Novel from Dickens to Lawrence* (London: Chatto & Windus, 1970) p. 52. For a longer discussion of Williams's treatment of Victorian women's writing, see my essay ' "What We Have Again to Say": Williams, Feminism, and the 1840s' in Christopher Prendergast (ed.), *Cultural Materialism: on Raymond Williams* (Minneapolis: University of Minnesota Press, 1995). I have drawn some of my argument from this earlier essay.
19. Raymond Williams, 'Charlotte and Emily Brontë', *The English Novel*, p. 70.
20. Raymond Williams, 'Charlotte and Emily Brontë, p. 73.
21. Raymond Williams, 'Charlotte and Emily Brontë, p. 61.
22. Elaine Showalter, *A Literature of Their Own: British women novelists from Brontë to Lessing* (London: Virago Press, 1977) p. 112; Sandra Gilbert and Susan Gubar, *The Madwoman in the Attic: the woman writer and the nineteenth century literary imagination* (New Haven: Yale University Press, 1979) p. 370.
23. Sandra Gilbert and Susan Gubar, *The Madwoman in the Attic*, p. 370.
24. Nancy Armstrong, *Desire and Domestic Fiction: a political history of the novel* (Oxford: Oxford University Press, 1987) p. 8.
25. Nancy Armstrong, *Desire and Domestic Fiction*, p. 3.
26. Nancy Armstrong, *Desire and Domestic Fiction*, p. 187.
27. Nancy Armstrong, *Desire and Domestic Fiction*, pp. 200–1.
28. Elizabeth Rigby, *The Quartely Review*, December 1848.
29. Gayatri Chakravorty Spivak, 'Three Women's Texts and a Critique of Imperialism' in Henry Louis Gates, Jr (ed.), *'Race', Writing and Difference* (Chicago: University of Chicago Press, 1986) p. 263.
30. See for example, Susan Meyer, *Imperialism at Home: race and Victorian women's fiction* (Ithaca: Cornell University Press, 1996); Elsie Michie, 'From Simianized Irish to Oriental Despots: Heathcliff, Rochester, and Racial Difference', *Novel*, 25, 1992, pp. 125–40; Jenny Sharpe, *Allegories of Empire: the figure of woman in the colonial text* (Minneapolis: University of Minnesota Press, 1993); Cora Kaplan, ' "A Heterogeneous Thing": Female Childhood and the Rise of Racial Thinking in Victorian Britain', in Diana Fuss (ed.), *Human, All Too Human* (New York: Routledge, 1995) pp. 169–202.
31. Gayatri Chakravorty Spivak, 'Three Women's Texts and a Critique of Imperialism', p. 263.
32. A related response has been the debate around Edward Said's essay on Jane Austen's *Mansfield Park*, which, like Spivak's interrogation of Brontë, focuses on the way the text negotiates slavery and empire.
33. See Charles Bernheimer and Claire Kahane (eds), *In Dora's Case: Freud, hysteria, feminism* (London: Virago, 1985). The 'rewriting' of Freud's Dora

by late twentieth-century commentators might be seen as another example of Victoriana, as I have defined it.

34. Armstrong uses Foucault also, but to make exactly the opposite case about Brontë's work.

35. Sally Shuttleworth, *Charlotte Brontë and Victorian Psychology* (Cambridge: Cambridge University Press, 1996) p. 5.

36. Sally Shuttleworth, *Charlotte Brontë and Victorian Psychology*, p. 182.

37. Glen has also edited *The Cambridge Companion to the Brontës* (Cambridge: Cambridge University Press, 2002), which, except in the bibliography, does not highlight the imperial and racial themes in their work. The relatively stronger and longlasting influence of postcolonial criticism of Brontë's work in the United States is reflected in Elsie B. Michie (ed.), *Charlotte Brontë's* Jane Eyre: *a case book* (Oxford and New York: Oxford University Press, 2006), which foregrounds this critical perspectives, and excerpts Sharpe's *Allegories of Empire*. Its editor is US based.

38. Heather Glen, *Charlotte Brontë: the imagination in history* (Oxford: Oxford University Press, 2002) p. 2.

39. Lucasta Miller, *The Brontë Myth* (London: Jonathan Cape, 2001), and Patsy Stoneman, *Brontë Transformations: the cultural dissemination of 'Jane Eyre' and 'Wuthering Heights'* (London: Prentice Hall/Harvester Wheatsheaf, 1996).

40. Marina Warner, 'Introduction' in Paula Rego, *Jane Eyre* (London: Enitharmon Editions, 2003) p. 13.

41. Marina Warner, 'Introduction', *Jane Eyre*, pp. 9–10.

42. Paula Rego, *Jane Eyre*, pp. 20–1.

Chapter 2

Biographilia

I have often thought that there has rarely passed a life of which a judicious and faithful narrative would not be useful. *Samuel Johnson* [1]

. . . with regard to the people of past times we are in the same position as with dreams to which we have been given no associations – and only a layman could expect us to interpret such dreams as those. *Sigmund Freud* [2]

In the opening years of this century, the new flagship branch of Waterstone's bookstore in London's Piccadilly, luxuriously housed in the impressive shell recently vacated by the venerable Simpsons Department Store, had the entire left wall of its ground floor running the width of the building to Jermyn Street at the rear devoted to life writing – biography, autobiography, memoir. In front of the shelves holding the massed stories of the dead and living, loaded tables promoted the best-sellers. Even fiction, which once dominated the walk-in trade, was largely relegated to the first floor, along with cookery and travel. As the genre of choice for the common reader, life writing in all its forms is having its day.[3] So much has it encroached on fiction that it has become a commonplace to say that biography has become the new novel. If so, it is the new – superficially at least – as retro, its blockbuster proportions reminiscent of the Victorian three-decker, as are the more traditional examples of its narrative form. Biography's triumphal moment in the twenty-first century might seem, then, like the crude revenge of nineteenth-century realism on the cool ironies, unfixed identities and skewed temporalities of the post-modern.

Certainly the noughts have been comeback years for a humanism which gives priority to individual lives, making biography and autobiography privileged genres. But this return is inevitably a return with a difference, and the elevation of life writing in general cannot be ascribed to a single set of oppositions. If biography now has a prophylactic role as an antidote to theory's provocative death sentence on both subjects and authors, poststructuralism's much decried relativism and postmodernity's love affair with surfaces, its new prominence may also be as a symptom and effect of an argument *within* rather than simply *with* contemporary theory or post-modernity – more broadly, an argument about both the nature and position of the subject. Roland Barthes, whose 1967 essay 'The Death of the Author' kick-started a vigorous debate on authorship that is still going strong, mused that as soon as the author has been relieved – philosophically speaking – of his paternal authority over his work, the reader begins to miss him and look for him in his writing: 'in the text, in a way, *I desire* the author: I need his figure (which is neither his representation nor his projection) . . .'[4] Jacqueline Rose makes a related point regarding the distinctly dissimilar ways in which the subject is understood by deconstruction and by psychoanalysis, emphasising the political nature of that desire, but leaving open the form in which the subject might return. She suggests that

> it is only the dispatching of the subject and its dissolution into a writing strategy which leads to the political demand for its return. For the political necessity of the subject is met in part by the psychic necessity of the subject, but in a way which finds itself suspended between each of these demands, neither pure assertion nor play.'[5]

That paradoxical suspension, especially its tension and its delicate balance, seems to me at work in general in the present currency of life writing, and, as this essay will argue, in Victorian literary biography in particular ways.

Never really out of favour with historians or with the reading public, but often an object of condescension with the new breed of literary critics in the 1970s and 80s, literary biography's surprise revival, from the early 1990s, as one of *the* hot genres of trade publishing and literary studies alike, gave eminent Victorians a new look. No longer were they the repressed and repressive superegos that their intellectual offspring the modernists thought them, or the appalled witnesses glaring down from the schoolroom walls at the entropic end of deference, morals and manners in post-1950s Britain. Writers who had embodied the stuffy middle age of nineteenth-century literature, its radical ambitions and youthful excesses now in the grave with Byron, Shelley and Keats, or left behind, as with Wordsworth or Coleridge, were coming back into style. In a U-turn in taste and cultural politics, those very figures whose busts and portraits, bearded and buttoned up, graced every British institution from hospital to prison, were now being represented in a kinder, gentler and sometimes sexier light.

Feminism's ambitious and ongoing project of recovery and restitution and its interest in life writing and writing lives inspired fat new studies of Victorian women writers. Jenny Uglow's *Elizabeth Gaskell* (1993), Jan Marsh's *Christina Rossetti* (1994), Juliet Barker's family portrait, *The Brontës*, Lyndall Gordon's *Charlotte Brontë* (1994), a new biography of Elizabeth Barrett Browning and at least four of George Eliot, all appeared in the 1990s, testimony to the successful marriage of popular feminism's niche market and biography's bright new image.[6] Feminist interest in Victorian women writers gave the period itself a whole new feel, and may have helped rather than hindered a revived interest in the traditional canon of male authors. Both louche and respectable Victorian men were in line for reincarnation. Among literary biographies since 1990, there have been two of Robert Browning, two of Thackeray, and two new treatments of Trollope as well as reprints of earlier key biographies by C. P. Snow and John Pope Hennessy.[7] Some of the fraught issues to do with the representation of masculinity that dog the renarration of their lives in the last two decades will be explored in the last two-thirds of this essay. Autobiography and memoir are well known for their experimentation with form, and biography, for a long time the most traditional genre of life writing, has developed a more receptive attitude to stylistic innovation, as long as this is not seen to narrow its readership. Fictional devices which loosen up chronologies and allow for more speculative thinking on causes and events that lie beyond the strict evidence provided; authorial reflections, on the genre itself and on the biographer's own relationship to the project and his subject, have found their way into recent biography. The runaway success in this vein has been Peter Ackroyd's much-praised *Dickens* (1990), translated in the late 1990s into a hit one-man stage show with Simon Callow as narrator, eponymous hero, and characters. *Dickens* is a biography with fictional elements and aspirations, but remains, nevertheless, within the traditional conventions of literary biographical writing. The third section of this essay will explore the strange, strained relationship between Ackroyd and his most popular biographical subject, highlighting those problems common to literary biography as a genre as well as those more particularly attached to Victoriana. The transmutation of biography into fiction has been strikingly illustrated by the metamorphosis of that eminent late Victorian, the American-born Henry James, into a fictional character. James is the protagonist of two biographical novels, *The Master* by Colm Tóibín, and David Lodge's *Author, Author*, both of which appeared in 2004, as well as figuring prominently in Emma Tennant's 2002 *Felony*, a novel in conversation with biographer Lyndall Gordon's *A Private Life of Henry James: two women and his art* (1998). Henry James is an explicit referent too, in Alan Hollinghurst's *The Line of Beauty* which won the Man Booker Prize in 2004, beating Tóibín's

The Master. I end by exploring this *fin de siècle* flowering of Jamesiana in Tóibín, Lodge and Hollinghurst.[8]

History, Theory, Masculinity: *The Biographer's Tale*

Life writing's renaissance has a special relevance to literary biography. For if, in theory's gaze, subjects were now no more than the intersection of the discourses that constructed them, then authors were threatened with a double disempowerment. Only a text himself, the writer's dematerialised 'self' was shorn of his romantic right to be the final referent or even a key witness to the sense and significance of his work, and the work itself was denied an idealised aesthetic transcendence. The loss of authorial privilege has been represented in both affective and intellectual terms as a massive cultural insult, one especially damaging to the self-image of writers from the late eighteenth century forward, for whom the right to independent, individual authority was the creed through which 'liberty' and 'identity' were understood. For Victorian subjects it could be seen to constitute a blow to the ideological heart of liberals and conservatives alike. A revaluation of narrated literary lives would appear, in this paradigm, as the return of the repressed subject/author. Biography with its inexorable chronology, its twin foundation in embodiment and achievement, could, in the light of recent debates over the nature of historical truth, become a generic type of 'real' history, certifying the materiality, depth, and moral authority of authors. Indeed biographies – of the wise or the wicked, the genius or the criminal, the canonical and the forgotten – have, in some accounts, been seen as a key element in the rightful restoration of a temporarily mislaid humanism and a wronged, dethroned historicism.

In an alternative narrative, life writing can be seen to respond to new ways of thinking about subjectivity, agency and history. Tempting as it is to represent the return and reinstatement of this prodigal genre as ideological melodrama, a less highly coloured and more textured account makes better sense of the different trajectories around lifewriting in related fields of the humanities, but also within the many subdivisions of literary and cultural studies. It is true that for historians and for traditional literary scholars the humanist subject, unified, self-conscious and in charge of its own destiny in an ideal world if not always in the real one, remained a philosophical and methodological touchstone, and became ever more defended the more it was felt to be under attack by a range of theoretical arguments intent on destabilising its existence and querying its legitimacy. But in certain developing areas of literary and interdisciplinary scholarship – those with overt political agendas yet also open to post-structuralism and psychoanalysis – the conflict about the subject became an internal debate. Taking only one example, modern feminist scholarship's aim to restore women to their rightful place in history and culture found biography and autobiography essential to their project. But – they began to ask, nudged by poststructuralist theory – what was the status of the subject so restored, and what place might she occupy?

Nowhere was the political agency of subjects and the rights and wrongs of liberal humanism a more vexed question than among feminist scholars in the 1980s when humanist identity was on trial, accused of supporting an essentialised reference to a biologically, psychologically and culturally fixed femininity. Second-wave postwar western feminism had created the framework for the personal as political, and had initially encouraged all forms of life writing as a kind of collective testimony to the present and historical terms of women's subordination, but its own theoretical and political evolution produced strongly critical after-thoughts to this initial project. The desire for independent agency for First World women – Jane Eyre's cry from the rooftops of Thornfield, that 'women feel just as men feel' – also came in for criticism, seen as complicit with a Eurocentric 'cult' of individualism. And in gender's relationship to biography there were other more general concerns – not least that the work of women writers tended to be reduced to or collapsed into their lives by male critics as a way of diminishing their literary achievement – a reflection of the view that women could (and sometimes should) *only* write autobiographically inflected prose or poetry. Beyond this crudely reductive misogyny, many feminist theorists argued that texts had a life of their own, a public, general, depersonalised set of meanings; they were not simply a clue to the singular lives of their authors. Yet this separation of biography and writing, which, like other poststructuralist and deconstructive moves, tends to fragment and interrogate the idea of unified subjectivity, hung in a delicate balance with other feminist imperatives, especially the humanist project to restore personal agency to women. Banished through one theoretical door by day, the recalcitrant female subject was secretly admitted, perhaps a little chastened and subdued, through another by night because of 'political necessity'. Similar 'strategic' recourse to traditional humanist concepts of identity were, as Gayatri Chakravorty Spivak has argued, important for both women and for postcolonial subjects – and these issues were also key to debates in lesbian, gay and queer studies.[9]

Not so much exiled then as on permanent political and theoretical trial in these years, biography, when viewed as the genre which most uncritically fetishised the liberal humanist subject and its works, was deeply abjected in cutting edge English departments of the 1970s and '80s. Political and institutional changes reinforced this attitude. Literary history – of which literary biography was a subfield – and the New Criticism, which focused on the text alone and prohibited biographical analysis, had managed to rub awkwardly along together in what was, seen in hindsight, the less openly abrasive academic climate of the 1950s and early 1960s when English was still largely and complacently in the hands of old boys and new men. The expansion of higher education, and the more inclusive hiring practices in universities which followed, brought welcome diversity to institutions, but with it came more open ideological warfare in literature departments. What enlivened them with provocatively up-front political claims for literature and for theory, put paid, for a time, to what remained of genteel academic civility. Biography was sneered at for its anti-theoretical assumptions; its old-fashioned fascination with personality, life history, genius or heroism; for the belletristic tradition of its style; and even for its commercial possibilities. As a genre it often took the fall for other issues which it could be seen to represent in a very visible and discursively violent debate around the identity and future of English studies. By the mid 1990s some of this animosity had exhausted itself and started to resolve. Theory could still disturb and disrupt but it had lost its shock value and its novelty, ceding the last to a revived interest in literary and cultural history, much more open to and interested in past lives. It was no longer so clear to former combatants or newly minted scholars just where the progressive politics of literary studies were to be found. Indeed the seismic shifts in world politics from 1989 onwards gave liberal humanism, and the universalist versions of subjectivity and agency that defined it, an ethical boost in unexpected quarters, thus laying the ground for biography's return to favour in left-leaning English departments, as well as elsewhere.

No single cause provides a persuasive account of the present vogue for biography, which has clearly been brought about by a complex of changes in the cultural, social, economic and political climate that are not necessarily allied and may be quite contradictory. I have been tracing biography's fortunes in the academy, but much literary and historical biography of course is produced by freelance writers happily unattached to higher education, and, most importantly, published by trade presses. Enormous changes in the economics of publishing gradually eroded the elitist preference of the academy for university press publication; these same presses fighting for their lives were struggling hard to retain traditional monographs in their lists, and began complementing them with books with a wider appeal than University libraries, books they could also sell to the educated common reader for a decent profit. The quickening of the academic pulse, not least my own, at the possibility of a 'crossover' publication that would satisfy the institutional hierarchies but be piled high for Christmas at the chain bookstores has been an ironic effect of the hard times in publishing. At the same time it is clear that the new room made across publishing for biography and life story has proved an excellent way of widening the audience for historical and cultural writing, achieving one longstanding but hard to realise democratic aim of progressive academics. In Victorian Studies alone the current rich variety of biographical treatments on offer has broadened and deepened the understanding of the period's lived dimensions. Literary biography and theoretically framed critical studies are not now seen as inevitably at odds. These days, more often than not, they are read as complementary not antagonistic approaches.

There remains however a lingering view that biographies of long-dead authors serve as a kind of escape literature from the terrors of late modernity, a temporary holiday from the unhappy, complicated present into a simpler past, a reading experience likened to an encounter with the nineteenth-century novel with which it is now so often compared. 'Escape literature' itself seems to me a very problematic category for popular fiction genres: it is these genres, the gothic, the thriller, even the romance that are often the first to turn pressing social issues into narrative. And while Victorian fiction may seem to provide pleasurable thrills without danger, the further we get away from the Victorian novel, as I have suggested in the first essay in this volume, the less like an easy ethical read it becomes. The same goes, I believe, for Victorian lives. We may take Samuel Johnson's point that, while authors share the 'common condition of humanity' with 'hopes and fears, expectations and disappointments, griefs and joys, and friends and enemies like a courtier or a statesmen', the really interesting dramas of their affective lives are professionally driven, so that their 'deep involutions of distress, or sudden vicissitudes of fortune' were graded 'from book to book' rather than as a hero's, 'from battle to battle'. Even so, the distinction was surely made in order to give the former some of the dramatic public – and political – status of the latter. [10]

Both in his identification with his subject and his problems in researching him, the lows and highs of the literary life are the privilege and penalty of the literary biographer also, most often presented satirically, as farce rather than tragedy. In A. S. Byatt's *The Biographer's Tale* (2000), a comic novel framed as a little parable of the biographer's dilemma at the millennium, its postgraduate protagonist, Phineas G. Nanson, gives up literary theory in the middle of 'one of Gareth Butcher's famous theoretical seminars' on 'Lacan's theory of *morcellement*, the dismemberment of the imagined body'. [11] *Morcellement* interpreted by

Butcher starts out as a jokey figure for the work of poststructuralist theory. But as Phineas, at the prompting of a mentor who loathes theory, takes up biography as an alternative pursuit of 'things' and 'facts' instead of theoretical chimeras, 'the dismemberment of the imagined body' morphs quickly into an equally apposite analogy for the frustrations and limitations of the biographer. Guided by his theoretical gurus, Phineas has considered 'biography a bastard form, a dilettante pursuit. Tales told by those incapable of true invention, simple stories for those incapable of true critical insight', a debased feminine genre – as opposed to hard theory and high art – for 'lady readers who would never grapple with *The Waves* or *The Years* . . .'.[12] Yet even as he flees from it, Phineas finds he cannot put theory behind him – its way of thinking follows and influences him as he tries to put together the life of an elusive fictional biographer of the 1950s, Scholes Destry-Scholes, whose magnificent three-volume opus on the equally imaginary Victorian scholar, Sir Elmer Bole, has been forgotten. Victorian biography in the twenty-first century, Byatt suggests persuasively, cannot ever be an innocently pastoral return to some imaginary *status quo ante* for its subject, author or reader. In the end Phineas, governed in part by what he does and doesn't discover, abandons even biography, forfeiting the fantasy of being able to map a past life in full for a fulfilled life devoted to ecological science and heterosexual love. He can give up 'literature' it seems, and the desire to control interpretation, to dismember the text or reconstruct the life, but not writing itself. His tentative ambition at the story's end is to combine two practices which will 'exceed our power to describe, to imagine or understand . . .'. He will himself invent a postmodern popular form, writing 'useful guides' that would 'mix warnings with hints, descriptions with explanations, science with little floating flashes of literature, which still haunt me and will not be exorcised'.[13]

Byatt's slight but witty tale – structured as quest and romance like her more ambitious *Possession* – drives home the point that the assumptions and conventions about factual narrative and fiction have changed so radically since the modernist moment that we encounter life writing, and the subjects it treats, from a very different reading position and set of experiences with narrative both written and visual. Since both Marx and Freud, whose ways of thinking about both society and the self have become part of common sense consciousness even when their specific paradigms are rejected, the life stories of celebrated writers cannot fully create for us some imagined world in which 'genius' triumphs, or where men always make the history they intend. On the contrary, these new biographies – their dust jackets comfortingly blazoned with the mug shot of the great man or woman – are caught in the same web of psychic, social and discursive indeterminacy as any other text of our political moment. Indeed many of them start from this assumption, which is why biography has become such a lively and provocative genre for writers and readers. And the truth is that, whether in opposition to or in partial sympathy with new modes of thinking, recent biographies have all been touched by – hostile commentators might say infected with – the theorisations and politics of the second half of the twentieth century and the opening of the twenty-first, especially the social movements around gender, race and sexuality.

In *The Biographer's Tale*, Byatt focuses on a male biographer and his masculine subject, exploring *passim* the different historical versions of masculinity that they represent, and dramatising their virtual engagement in the biographical encounter. The rereading of men's lives through the lens of the present millennium seems to raise some of the hardest questions about the present interest in Victorian life writing. From the 1970s through the 1990s the feminist project of reinterpreting Victorian women provided the most interesting challenge. It too had its difficulties: heroic or meek, genius, crusader or good wife, richer or poorer, the trick was to try to construct life histories in which they were neither heroes nor victims, histories that acknowledged their subordinated status but refused to interpret them as 'relative creatures' to be measured or contrasted to male norms in straightforward ways. Victorian masculinity too has undergone analogous and sometimes complementary forms of revision by social and cultural historians – and by psychoanalysis. George Mosse has, for example, synoptically traced the construction and pursuit of that durable concept, the 'manly ideal' – with its emphasis on the physical and ethical purity of male bodies and minds – from the middle of the eighteenth century to the beginning of what he sees as the beginning of its breakdown as late as the 1950s. And Herbert L. Sussman, in *Victorian Masculinities* has argued that these ideals have more to do with the register of fantasy than with achievable practice.[14] Masculinity, like gender itself, has become plural rather than singular: not so much a binary system as a less than reliable rough guide to sexed subjects.[15] Men used not to be, but somehow have become, 'more' relative, even paradoxically so, measured against an unspoken criteria that has adopted, even if it doesn't admit it, a more culturally femocentric set of ethical norms through which behaviour is measured. (Byatt humorously makes her would-be biographer Phineas small but perfectly formed, the homunculus of a new man in the process of being born, still craving masculinity and desiring women but finding it – and them – in new practices and places.) The male reader is now regularly supposed to care as much about how a great writer, scientist or political figure treated their wives, mistresses, mothers and daughters as about their work. Yet even spun and tweaked to meet halfway the new niceties of readerly sensibility, biographies of Victorian men, one suspects, appeal to us *because* robustly unapologetic patriarchs are what pre-twentieth-century history can offer us as a holiday from the highly moralised terms of our own period's sexual politics – men forgiven their laddish or authoritarian ways in advance for not living in our present enlightened moment.

Secrets and Lies – The Psychopathologies of Biography: *Life of Johnson*

Like the lives it chronicles, biography, of all literary genres, novels included, seems the most immediately vulnerable to moral and psychological judgement. At one end of the spectrum the form and its practitioners are over-idealised. In the mid-eighteenth century, as the genre was trying out its modern form, Samuel Johnson, emphasising its altruistic action on the human heart, if not the lofty disinterestedness of the biographer, described biography as beneficially producing that 'act of the imagination' that allowed us to feel sympathetic identification with the 'joy or sorrow' of others.[16] Precisely a century and a half later *The Biographer's Tale* has it both ways, half affirming, half satirising biography's supposedly unselfish contribution to knowledge: 'What can be nobler . . . or more exacting, than to explore, to constitute, to open, a whole man, a whole opus, to us?' Byatt's Professor Ormerod Goode intones, urging Phineas to take up biography as a higher literary task.[17] Not surprisingly, such idealisation provokes a reaction, perhaps especially from writers and scholars with an investment in the genre, who recognise a less benevolent side to its making and consumption, and who are not slow to portray the biographer's motives, aside from the ordinary desire for fame and fortune, as nastier and nuttier than they first appear – a diagnosis that sometimes extends to biography's audience. In a memorable and mischievously muckraking reflection on biography and the role of the biographer – a full-frontal assault on its new pretensions – the journalist Janet Malcolm, herself a writer with a biographical bent, explores the 'transgressive nature of biography' that she thinks is rarely acknowledged by critics or readers, suggesting provocatively that:

> Biography is the medium through which the remaining secrets of the famous dead are taken from them and dumped out in full view of the world. The biographer at work, indeed, is like the professional burglar, breaking into a house, rifling through certain drawers that he has good reason to think contain the jewelry and money, and triumphantly bearing his loot away.[18]

Masked by a veneer of academic respectability, the 'voyeurism and busy-bodyism that impel writers and readers of biography alike are obscured by an apparatus of scholarship designed to give the enterprise an appearance of banklike blandness and solidity'.[19] Refuting the supposed differences between renegade and respectable capitalist in her elision of the professional thief and the banker – and merging the desires of biographer and reader as they both rapaciously pursue 'backstairs gossip' – Malcolm rounds off her gleeful exposé by infantilising this insatiably curious duo, representing them slyly as overgrown children 'tiptoeing down the corridor together, to stand in front of the bedroom door and try to peep through the keyhole'.[20] Writing and reading biography are caricatured as a form of scopophilia – the desire to know forbidden secrets as instanced in the desire to look – an illicit intrusion on the living subject and a somewhat more macabre activity in relation to the dead. Worst of all, much like the fictional Phineas, who started out thinking that biography was a debased, feminised genre in which Bloomsbury scandal substituted for the hard work of grappling with Woolf's prose, Malcolm believed that the biographer's much-hyped 'industry' contributed to the reader's belief that by reading the biography of a great author 'he is having an elevated literary experience'.[21]

But is this pathologising of authors, readers and genre in the interests of deflating biography's overblown ethical and aesthetic claims either persuasive or fair? The biographer and her readers are surely not, except in Malcolm's (and Phineas's) fantasy, engaged in some kind of intellectually debased *folie à deux*, a dark conspiracy to substitute the recounted life for the literature. The curiosity that drives the biographer to hunt out family secrets and sexual irregularities may be grounded in the child's desire to look, but even so, its objects are systemic elements of the genre rather than a psychopathology that can be evaded by the clued-up, self-knowing practitioner. Epistemophilia drives all narrative along, even when it is itself driven, as it sometimes seems, by the complementary urge not to know, to forget, to deny, to repress. Nor is privacy, a term that Malcolm deploys as if it were a lost right rather than an historically constructed idea, a sacrosanct category of social or subjective life. Privacy in every sense, professional as well as personal, *is* inevitably challenged by biographical writing, as it is by autobiography, memoir and other types of public discourse, but why exactly, one might ask, should it not be?

This is a question which other critics take on with more nuance. What Malcolm does highlight, if in too lurid colours, is the complicated ethics of the biographer's practice. What are the rights, if any, of the hapless biographical subject? Critic John Barrell echoes Malcolm when he suggests that the 'paradox of modern literary biography' is that 'readers will

happily read about famous writers as long as they don't have to be troubled much about what they wrote', but his criticism is focused on how literary biography is written, at the censorship and will to power of the
biographer over his subject, the way in which the biographical project
gets skewed, rather than on the prurience or pretensions of readers.[22]
Barrell, writing on Richard Holmes's *Coleridge: Darker Reflections*
(1998), argues that the rule seems to be that 'Coleridge's poetry may be
quoted where it appears to throw light on his private life. His prose writings may be discussed only so long as that discussion does not interrupt
or retard the narrative', and so long as writing can be translated in the
melodrama of personal life 'as a struggle with circumstances, as another
episode of Coleridge's psychic life, as another qualified success snatched
from the jaws of yet another abject failure'. Modern literary biography,
Barrell warns, is on the wrong track when too exclusive an emphasis on
the '*vie privé*' implies that 'writing has significance chiefly as an exhala-
tion from . . .'[the author's] 'most private anxieties, and is to be read
mainly as a key to understanding them'.[23] Instead of being driven by the
drama of a writing career from 'book to book', as Johnson imagined the
genre, it becomes largely case history: psychic 'battle to battle'. There is,
Barrell argues, an inversion of literary biography's reason for being when
readers are asked to be exclusively interested in the screwed-up, opium-
addicted Coleridge, rather than the author of the sober, influential *On the
Constitution of Church and State*. This point seems particularly persuasive. If the work becomes the secondary referent and ravaged celebrity
masculinity (or femininity for that matter) becomes the primary rather
than the complementary text, then literary biography does have an empty
centre. Barrell asks for the priority of the literary to be restored, as well
as for a less manipulative practice on the part of the literary biographer.

The temptation to let the disordered life dominate literary biography
has, nevertheless, a long and surprisingly distinguished legacy, and if we
follow its trail we come back to questions raised at the beginning of this
essay about the way in which, at different historical moments, biography
positions and imagines male literary subjectivity. Holmes's spectacularly
disturbed Coleridge is only one of biography's disordered, unstable,
writing men; it is as if, paradoxically, the genre becomes early on not only
the occasion for constructing exemplary masculine lives, but, together
with the novel, the discourse where the incoherence of the psychic life of
men can be safely expressed. Samuel Johnson's career was jump-started
by his much-admired *An Account of the Life of Mr Richard Savage*, one
of the early examples of modern biography, together with James
Boswell's *Life of Johnson* (1791). It was one of several written about the
messy life and death of the drunken, charismatic eighteenth-century poet,

Johnson's friend, who believed himself to be the bastard son of an aristocratic lady.[24] How the biographer figures, and figures himself, in such an account has always been an issue. Johnson, for example, wrote himself out of the scandalous urban exploits that, in fact, he shared with his friend Savage. David Glover argues that in his *London Journal 1762–1763*, James Boswell's pursuit of a kind of stable, essential character for himself finds him constantly tacking 'between contrasting styles of masculinity in order to believe in his own self-worth'. Writing the *Life of Johnson*, the 'account of an exemplary life' whose 'achievements' and 'virtues' were 'so extraordinary' that Johnson's posterity as a literary icon would be assured, provided Boswell, as much as his famous subject, with a secure identity and literary posterity.[25] At the very starting point of the tradition of modern literary biography, a symbiotic relationship between male biographer and male subject is established which aims to confirm the present and future viability of masculine – and literary – subjectivity. If however, we take Johnson's life of Savage and Boswell's *Life of Johnson* together, biography does not do this entirely through the characteristic exclusion of the less virtuous and admirable elements of masculinity, as Mosse has argued about the development and maintenance of the 'manly ideal'. Savage's transgressive masculinity and Johnson's inspiring triumph over obstacles and setbacks become written into the complementary relationships between male literary subjects and their male biographers. These are subtended, as I hope to show, by different and sometimes competing philosophies of art and concepts of masculinity across the last two and a half centuries. Such a symbiosis is not, however, a smoothly functioning operation, but one which often exposes while it attempts to close the fissures and fantasies in the past and present ideas of masculine and literary subjectivity.

In Johnson's *Savage* and Boswell's *Johnson*, biographies of contemporaries and friends, the biographer's and the subject's approach to questions of subjectivity and authorship are bound within the same historical moment. In contrast, biographies of long-dead literary figures have no such temporal coherence, and require more complex historical negotiations between the world of the biographer and that of his subject. Motives for writing the biography of a long-dead writer vary widely. The sympathetic identification that Johnson sees as the effect of biography on its readers is in the first instance the act of imagination that the biographer performs, for without some element of it the finished work can seem flat or even persecutory – why bother, the irritated reader asks, if you are bored by or dislike your subject and his world view? Over-identification with a life or its times can have an equally unsatisfactory outcome; like badly done karaoke, both the subject's voice, and the biographer's attempt to lip sync in time to it, only emphasise the impossibility of effacing the historical gap through mimicry. This blurring of perspective has been a particular temptation in recent literary biographies of nineteenth-century figures; Alison Light points out that biographical nostalgia is anything but temporally located, but yearns to float free of time. She argues that

> Holmes's *Shelley: The Pursuit* (1974) and his two volumes of *Coleridge* (1989, 1998), Peter Ackroyd's *Blake* (1995), Andrew Motion's *Keats* (1997) [. . .] in their different ways [. . .] evoke the Romantic longing for a life and a self which could be emancipated from the world, freed by their work from the mess of history, politics, traditions and ossified personal relations. For such biographers, biography is itself a species of romance, fuelled by the utopian desire to evoke a transcendent, yet coherent personality, shaped by, and yet bigger than, the circumstances in which it found itself.[26]

The romantic ideology of the self, its version of humanism, is secured by the transcendence of the literary imagination which becomes at once a property of the self and the work of art. That is the step too far that these biographies make, for, Light implies, when the historically specific romantic subject, whose individualism and idealism belong to the high hopes and disappointments of his time, becomes indistinguishable from the biographer's nostalgic longing for this impossible unity and transcendence, then literary biography as a genre becomes itself personified as a de-historicised subject. It is the effect of this particular biographical identity crisis at its most extreme that I want to explore in relation to Peter Ackroyd's *Dickens*.

Literary Biography – Genius in Genre Trouble: *Dickens*

Strange things can happen to literary biography even when the work is paramount and the biographer less snoopy voyeur than self-appointed hagiographer. Peter Ackroyd's monumental and gripping *Dickens* is an example of the danger for the biographer of an over-idealising identification that occasionally tips into its opposite, revealing the biographer's envy and competitiveness.[27] Ackroyd's biographical writing is formally experimental, even postmodern, offering readers the pleasures of fiction alongside those of 'traditional' biography. Yet in *Dickens*, these 'fictional' elements – speculative rhetorical flourishes in the main body of the text, and *amuse bouche* interchapters, surreal dreamlike fantasies that operate like cartoon episodes in a realist film text – seem less to transform the genre than to provide distracting, semi-readable garnish. And despite its undeniable brio, eloquence and detail, there seems to me something peculiarly airless about Ackroyd's approach to his subject, an approach which prioritises the deep psychic connection between the author's childhood and his fiction. The biography pays lip service to the colourful, complex social and political world that Dickens inhabited and influenced, but its evocation of the period has more to do with a determined campaign to justify Dickens's stature as artist in terms of a late romantic aesthetic still operating in the early to mid Victorian period, an aesthetic which acknowledged his formidable gifts but was reluctant to grant him, or other novelists, that elusive accolade. We might see this as one of the common impulses of historical biography – a retroactive repair of injustices to the subject. Ackroyd however, is curiously reluctant to celebrate Dickens's gifts as they have been celebrated from the perspective of twentieth-century critics or theorists like Mikhail Bakhtin (1895–1975), who made Dickens an exemplar of a new kind of novelistic practice, praising the way in which his fiction includes and orchestrates the heterogeneous voices of Victorian England. Perhaps Ackroyd's reluctance arises because this way of reading Dickens leads inexorably to those structuralist or poststructuralist theories of language and literature which disengage the author from his work.[28] Rather, *Dickens* is driven by theories of art and authorship derived from romanticism, but adapted to give the novel the aesthetic status and transcendent authority that it did not have in the first half of the nineteenth century.

It might seem that this project has a simple historical logic which would 'return' Dickens to his time, allowing us to see his career and aspirations as he and his contemporaries might have done, but in Ackroyd's ideologically rigid treatment it ends up skewing that history in ways that seem counterintuitive. *Dickens* is determined, even at times desperate, that nothing to do with the wider world interrupt the narrative of the man and his 'genius' for too long. Journalism, for example, so important an element of Dickens's career at all stages, suffers badly in this respect. A chapter which tells us about the setting up of *Household Words* in 1850, surely as key an event as any in Dickens's professional life, swings back by page three to Dickens's hopes for his children, and the simultaneous composition of his most autobiographical work, *David Copperfield*.[29] Ackroyd sees Dickens's long involvement with journal editing and journalism as a diversion from the fiction that makes him a transcendent artist, and his discussion of it seems rushed and parenthetical. His febrile comment on Dickens's innovative career as editor of two leading popular journals, far from making clear its considerable impact on Victorian print culture in the 1850s and 1860s, expresses astonishment that the 'greatest author of his age' did the arduous, hands-on job of editing a weekly periodical, a job that 'any number of nineteenth-century journalists could have accomplished'.[30]

At the level of the personal the biography is also highly selective in what it chooses to interpret. Dickens's weird relations with women dead and alive – with his wife Catherine, her younger sister, Mary, and Ellen Ternan – although treated at considerable length, receive little helpful illumination, because they must be made to contribute to or be radically excluded from the congratulatory dyad that Ackroyd has set up between genius as a form of authorial subjectivity and the literary evidence for it. 'Genius', both as an abstract and subjective noun, as in someone's 'genius' and a 'genius', is central to Ackroyd's thinking, but while he never defines it, relying on its continued common currency at our own *fin de siècle*, it often seems in his hands an anachronism retrieved from a dusty conceptual archive undisturbed since at least Dickens's own lifetime. Its insistent repetition in *Dickens* constitutes a rejection of the intense scrutiny and criticism to which 'genius', along with other transcendent concepts of the author and authorship, have been subjected from the 1960s onwards.[31] Classical in origin, 'genius' comes in the late eighteenth and early nineteenth century to designate not only a quality of mind but a form of artistic subjectivity.[32] A fully acknowledged source that governs much of Ackroyd's thinking about authorship is Thomas Carlyle's 'The Hero as Man of Letters' (1841). Carlyle makes his quintessentially modern hero 'a product of these new ages' and 'one of the main forms of Heroism for all future ages'.[33] In his turn, Carlyle credits Johann Gottlieb Fichte's 1800 lectures 'On the Nature of the Literary Man' as the origin of his model, adapting the surface and depth structure of 'Appearances' and the 'Divine Idea of the World' that Fichte uses, as well as his characterisation of the '*true* Literary Man' as 'Priest' or 'Prophet' of the 'Divine Idea'.[34] The 'Man of Letters' worthy of Carlyle's capitalisation is in essence Fichte's, who, Carlyle explains, 'is sent hither specially that he may discern for himself, and make manifest to us, this same Divine Idea: in every new generation it will manifest itself in a new dialect'.[35] In 'The Hero as Man of Letters', ' "originality", "sincerity", "genius", the heroic quality we have no good name for', is handily subsumed as a type of 'heroism', but elsewhere in his writing, he falls back on 'genius' as the embracing term.[36] Ackroyd too, clearly thinks 'genius', if more battle-scarred a category than he will admit, still has enough resonance today that it need not be unpacked for the general reader. 'Genius' has a lot to answer for in *Dickens*, taking on an ever more overreaching explanatory meaning as the book proceeds.

Ackroyd explains that Carlyle never rated fiction – a cheap infantilising illusion, 'magic lanterns to amuse grown children' – highly enough for Dickens to be a candidate for his pantheon.[37] Ackroyd, for whom the novel is a form of high art, argues not only that Dickens belongs in

Carlyle's canon, but coercively insists that it was where Dickens himself wanted to be: the biographer's and the author's desire must be made to coincide. If one reads Carlyle's definition of the 'Man of Letters' 'shorn of its Idealistic elements', Ackroyd suggests, it 'is precisely the position which Dickens was moving towards; and precisely the role which he seems to have wanted to assume'.[38] Dickens, like so many other men and women in the period, was both strongly influenced by and took issue with his friend Carlyle, something Ackroyd admits, but as a more uncritical Carlylian than his subject, he wants them to be twinned heroes both 'trying to find and to express the "Time-Spirit"'.[39] What that might be for them seems curiously – but perhaps predictably for a popular biography published in 1990 – configured to prejudices that became commonplace in the two decades of Thatcherite hegemony. Ackroyd approvingly, although with more than a hint that this view might provoke reaction from some of his readers, designates the correspondence of Dickens's and Carlyle's attitudes to the Victorian world as their 'common distaste for the more overt forms of philanthropy (especially to other races), for model prisons, and indeed of most conventionally "liberal" activities and ideals'.[40] Driving home this point later in the book, Ackroyd briefly notes the pair's vociferous support for the notorious Governor Eyre, whose brutal suppression of the 1865 rebellion in Morant Bay, Jamaica, moved the British Government to suspend him and liberal Englishmen to demand that he be put on trial, an issue that divided metropolitan Britain. Here, Ackroyd dismisses the critique of Eyre as that of 'orthodox liberals', arguing that Dickens's outspoken racism, which led him to support the American South in the Civil War, and Eyre in 1865, was a sign of his 'unsentimental' approach to racial issues, and had, in any case, the merit of consistency: Dickens had held such opinions from his youth.[41] The 'radicalism' therefore that Ackroyd identifies and praises in Dickens and Carlyle had no necessary alignment with socially progressive Victorian thinking, but represents as much their dissent from, as their agreement with it. Ackroyd's way of dealing with Dickens's views on race and empire not only deflect a serious discussion of them but align Carlyle and Dickens's contempt for mid-nineteenth-century liberalism with the declining reputation of twentieth-century liberalism in the 1980s.

For Ackroyd to present Carlyle and Dickens as a double act of Great Victorian writers, he must make the claim – hugely inflated if one thinks of the competition – that 'Carlyle was the single most important philosophical writer of his period'.[42] However, to endow Dickens with the same high status as imaginative writer requires more than the biographer's mere assertion, even backed by Carlyle's upbeat version of Fichte, which, for all its optimism about the future role of literary men, tends to reinforce Carlyle's exclusion of popular fiction on the grounds that it was debased entertainment. Wittingly or unwittingly, Ackroyd annexes other romantic philosophies that better support his case, silently moving towards a more Hegelian insistence on the unity between appearance and spirit. In his 1820 *Introduction to Aesthetics* Hegel discusses several ways in which the sensuousness of the work of art, both in its mode of being and the way in which we must apprehend it, can speak to the spirit without an absolute distinction between the two. The 'work of art', Hegel suggests, 'stands in the *middle* between immediate sensuousness and pure thought'.[43] The 'subjective productive activity' of the good writer cannot take place in two stages as separate activities – a 'prosaic' thought or 'theme' which is then put into 'poetical images, rhyme and so forth'. This would inevitably produce 'bad poetry' because it 'would be operative as *separate* activities what in artistic production has validity only as undivided unity'.[44] Hegel comes nearest to defining Ackroyd's immanent idea of great art and Dickens as great artist when he says that the

> productive fancy of an artist is the fancy of a great spirit and heart, the apprehension and creation of ideas and shapes, and indeed the exhibition of the profoundest and most universal human interests in pictorial and completely definite sensuous form.[45]

This, taken out of the historic and aesthetic criteria through which Hegel ranks great art, is *Dickens*'s Dickens to a tee.

The unified nature of the creative act and the sharp distinctions between philosophy and art in Hegel's work are both useful clues to Ackroyd's unwillingness to consider Dickens as a thinker or philosopher. They support too his suggestion that there is a division of intellectual labour in which Carlyle becomes the invisible philosophical hand in whatever passes for ideas in Dickens's writing. For Hegel, philosophical abstraction was the antithesis of art. His belief in the decline of art in his own time was partly to do with its cross-contamination with philosophy, a modern leakage that produced that impure, separated practice from which bad poetry springs. This division has implications for the ethics attached to Ackroyd's aesthetic. Although he sees the public preoccupations of the two writers as closely allied, only Carlyle seems to own these ideas in such a way that he can be judged morally responsible for them. For it is even misguided, Ackroyd argues at one point, to label Dickens's social preoccupations as 'radical' or in any sense political, not because he didn't have strong opinions, but because 'the unique nature of his perceptions' endows him with aesthetic immunity.[46] Ackroyd's impulse to keep Dickens (or rather *Dickens*) safe from the ethical analysis of his philosophy or politics, leads to a dubious use both of the idea of the work of art's totality, and of the distinction between philosophy and art. If Dickens's art comprehends the social and the political, Ackroyd's analysis implies, it cannot logically support an independent critical analysis of it.

Yet in reading Dickens through what I am designating as a Hegelian lens, Ackroyd does creatively extend the generic forms and the time-line that early nineteenth-century theorists would allow to genius. Dickens is crowned with the kind of aesthetic imprimatur that Hegel granted only to classical authors and which Carlyle, whose 'modern' literary heroes were eighteenth-century figures – Rousseau, Johnson and Burns – also refused to his nineteenth-century contemporaries. In championing the hybridity of nineteenth-century forms, and in twinning Carlyle and Dickens as its joint practitioners, Ackroyd retains the idealisation of 'genius' but hands it to the period's gifted, experimental, and often reactionary populists:

> Both writers marrying philosophical or social analysis with the vivid scene or detail, both of them moving away from that strict separation of genres which had marked eighteenth-century writing, both of them uniting the most unlikely opposites – a private self-communing speech with public rage and denunciation, an almost apocalyptic vision with a strict determination to tell the 'truth', a Gothic stance with the need also to be 'real' and to be 'immediate'.[47]

(Ackroyd's quotation marks presumably signal to the reader that these terms may only have unproblematic purchase within their Victorian context.) By making Dickens and Carlyle joint innovators of style, genre and authorial persona – representing in a particularly meaningless and misleading set of abstractions, 'the true lineaments of the 1830s and 1840s, that period of passion and responsibility, of faith and scepticism' – Ackroyd attempts to resolves the dissonance between the 'romantic' and the 'Victorian' in both writers, and to play down the turbulence of these decades of schismatic political and philosophical divisions. His joint encomium has another, even more urgent, object, for it serves to reverse, by implication, Hegel's entropic view of art's inevitable decline, now rewritten as a celebration of Victorian literature's generic and philosophic vitality.

The drive for coherence and unity in *Dickens* extends to what is puzzling and contradictory in Dickens's personality; the strategies used to force that coherence draw on the conceptual unity of appearance and spirit, art and artist in German romantic thought and English versions of it, but end up, I want to suggest, as caricature. The 'Prologue' to *Dickens* is headed by Carlyle's well-known elegiac description of Dickens: '. . . deeper than all, if one has the eye to see deep enough, dark, fateful silent elements, tragical to look upon, and hiding amid dazzling radiances as of the sun, the elements of death itself'.[48]

Missing out the opening to that passage in Carlyle's letter to John Forster, Dickens's friend and biographer, 'His the bright and joyful sympathy with everything around him', Ackroyd rewrites the surface/depth model a few pages later in his own voice, telling us that Dickens was an often sorrowful and cold man beneath his surface bonhomie and sociability.[49] The resolution to this antinomy becomes the very art in which it is found, for his 'particular genius' was to 'turn his life into an emblem of that period – instinctively, almost blindly, to dramatise it'.[50] The assertion that Dickens's life (rather than his work) is somehow emblematic of the Victorian period, rather than having a complex relationship to it, becomes, in Ackroyd's hands, an oversimplified and reductive way of solving the problem of how to present the social in biography, pre-emptively evading the always tricky (but always interesting) questions that the articulation of a single life to its times must raise. Although when he chooses, Ackroyd can be very thoughtful about social issues in Dickens – the author's depiction of the lower middle class for example – so much that is disturbing in Dickens's work and his life and of interest to modern readers, has been glossed over or airbrushed out of *Dickens*. Far too often, through its transcendent claims for its subject, its unwillingness to go too deeply into the sources and objects, social and personal, of Dickens's coldness or rage, the biography appears filiopietistic and defensive rather than exploratory.

If German romanticism, unreferenced except through British writers like Carlyle, infuse Ackroyd's account of genius, a very different German theorist of a later generation ghosts his biographical reading of the novels. Dickens's fraught and often traumatic youth dominates Ackroyd's analysis of both the life and writing. Often light, subtle and persuasive in its tracing of the transformation of personal trauma to fictional text, Ackroyd's interpretations depend on a common sense Freudianism awkwardly grafted on to romantic ideas of childhood. *Dickens* never resorts to technical psychoanalytic language. Binding romantic and psychoanalytic theory together without commenting on their possible incompatibility as analytic tools means that the methodology that informs and structures the study becomes in itself a form of pastiche. When method is presented in this way as a common sense 'truth', the reader is offered no position from which he can critique it. Ackroyd's too heavy stress on childhood experience as the key to Dickens's recurring themes and figures, together with his unwillingness to discuss his approach with his readers, imposes on the narrative a non-negotiable priority, one which blocks the possibility of other more social, cultural or political interpretations.

I have been describing Ackroyd's biographical practice as particularly controlling of its interpretation, too retroactively protective of its subject, and by implication, of the biographer. But *Dickens* includes other elements which initially seem to undercut the benevolence and authority of the biographer. If Carlyle and Dickens are literary and temperamental brothers, there is a younger and much more insecure sibling who appears at the margins of this picture. Within Ackroyd's creepily adulatory tone one can hear the hiss of a peculiarly rivalrous subtext. The modern biographer, the peripatetic professional Londoner and minor novelist, presents himself, parodically, as sympathetically but competitively aligned with a subject of whom he is in almost disabling awe. In this mode, the biographical project is dramatised as an attempt to catch and hold not the reader's, but Dickens's, attention. This disconcerting effect is made perfectly explicit in one of the odd inter-chapters that Ackroyd inserts into *Dickens* about a third of the way through the biography and immediately after the chapter which discusses the relationship between Carlyle and Dickens. These inter-chapters, Ackroyd's clumsy bow to the postmodernity of modern biography, are at once fey and awkward – in some, the characters in Dickens's novels meet, for reasons which are never quite clear. Not listed in the table of contents, numbered in roman numerals rather given status as ordinary chapters, but not exempt from sequential pagination, their formal relationship to the biography is deliberately ambiguous. Mini psychodramas, they leave the realm of fact to call the reader's attention to the independent life of the characters in Dickens's novels, and to the biographer's phantasmatic relationship to his biographical subject. In the second of these strange vignettes, the biographer and the author are back in 'the time of Pickwick, and of Oliver Twist, and of Nicholas Nickleby'; they are walking together in London – down Kingsland Road, in fact, 'towards the great church of Shoreditch'.[51] But after answering a few sycophantic questions, Dickens abandons his annoying interlocutor with an abrupt 'Good day to you . . . I must be on my way'. 'Eventually I was able to catch up with him and to walk beside him; he merely nodded to acknowledge my presence.' Pushed to converse again, Dickens reminisces about the shops that used to be there in his childhood. 'You remember so much,' says the fawning biographer. 'I remember *everything*,' replies Dickens, grandiloquently: a man apparently unequipped with an unconscious, or at least in denial about the impossibility of not forgetting. Not a surprise then, when this omniscient being gets away from the mortal biographer: 'We walked together a little more but gradually his footsteps grew faster, leaving me further and further behind'.[52] In Ackroyd's reverie, Dickens is still young, with the future before him, but the wannabe biographer is younger still, a weedy neophyte not yet in full stride: patronised, dismissed, outpaced. Divine author, aspiring Boswell scurrying alongside, failing to catch up, the burlesqued self-deprecation of the authorial voice: the scene falls somewhere between self-parody and bathos – laced through, one feels, with a frustration that can't find an appropriate register of expression. Troping on a recurring motif in Dickens's novels, the vignette parodically condenses the unequal relations between men of different ages and social status. In a disavowal of the biographer's hubris, Ackroyd is represented here, in his own fantasies, as yet another lampooned subaltern. Yet if one steps back a little, there is something false about this picture. It is Ackroyd, after all, in his popular histories, who has become the modern chronicler of London and Dickens. In this scenario, it is his recall and invention that is operative; he can become at once the eager young acolyte and the orchestrator of Dickens's life.

And of his death. In the Prologue, Ackroyd imagines us at the author's funeral, and by shifting from Carlyle's association of Dickens and death to Dickens's own preoccupation with mortality, he leads us to the conceit that we are being dragged to this mawkish, macabre funeral scene because: 'There are times, when looking at Dickens, or when looking at the people who mourned him, the years between his time and our own vanish. And we are looking at ourselves.'[53] The celebration of dead genius is of course the occasion of literary biography, and by making us imaginatively present at the scene, recognising in the corpse our own features, Ackroyd as funeral director asserts both his own authority and a version of the altruism with which Samuel Johnson credited the biographer. One can't but feel that the scene also functions as a knowing referent to the theories of subjectivity and authorship that Ackroyd is contesting throughout *Dickens*. Literalising 'The Death of the Author', Ackroyd challenges the ground of Roland Barthes's theoretical deposition of the writer's privileged place as a transcendental subject, replacing it with a death scene meant to evoke the affective moment of romantic subjectivity's reincarnation. Dickens and his work are conflated in this vignette: the identification a modern reader might feel with a novel and its characters is extended, seamlessly, to the novelist himself and those several generations that loved and admired him. The denial of historical distance, ascribed to a universal 'we', but emanating from the biographer, operates both in the realm of cliché and of the uncanny – estranging what we might recognise as partly familiar in an historical figure, by making too great a claim for that familiarity, an effect that surfaces elsewhere in the biography. More than a trope of universal recognition, it implies a necrophiliac intimacy between the subject of the biography – from Ackroyd's perspective an ever freshly dead writer, always about to be, or just having been, buried and mourned – and the modern self.

In Simon Callow's brilliant, slightly camp and very over-the-top one-man show *The Mystery of Charles Dickens*, the script written by Ackroyd and based on *Dickens*, the identifications of biographer, novelist and characters have been dramatised. Callow acted out, made explicit, the psychic moves involved in writing literary biography.[54] What is merely embarrassing in Ackroyd's experimental intertexts where characters and author and author and biographer interact, worked wonderfully as theatre. Callow was always himself *and* Dickens – and never quite the characters. The physicality of Callow's performance, its high point the rendition of Dickens's disturbing public reading of his fiction, embodied the melodramatic elements of both Dickens's and Ackroyd's personas and imaginations. *Dickens* as theatre, shorn of its transcendental pretensions to unity, also allowed the audience to see how subjectivity – of writers, biographers or characters – is a more elusive, phantasmatic and unstable thing than Ackroyd's biography will allow.

I've been dwelling on the oddness of Ackroyd's *Dickens* in part because I think that its undeniable power as a compelling narrative should be taken together with its pretensions, its exclusions, and its queasily unsettling and downright embarrassing moments. Its very unevenness is symptomatic, I think, of the mixed attraction and repulsion felt towards the lives of nineteenth-century literary men. As I have argued, Ackroyd's portrait begs many key questions about its subject, but it does not, to be fair, entirely 'clean up' Dickens in any ordinary filiopietistic way. Conventional, nostalgic and mainstream in many of its emphases, it also 'queers' Dickens for us, not primarily in a sexual sense, although it confirms, even while trying to play down, the strangeness of the author's sexual and affective life. Rather, the 'queerness' appears in its anachronistic treatment of its subject, Ackroyd's puzzling attempt to make an important writer, whose late twentieth-century reputation is secure enough without it, a transcendent giant of literature, not in terms of the aesthetics of the present which is only too willing to see social novelists as great writers, but within a hermeneutic that belongs to the late romanticism of the early Victorian period. This posthumous accolade in *Dickens* produces a readerly unease about writer and biographer – creates them both as eerie and oddly atemporal figures.

'Queer' is a term in process, one whose etymology is haggled over by literary critics, but for the purposes of my argument David Halperin's embracing view that 'Queer is by definition *whatever* is at odds with the normal, the legitimate, the dominant. *There is nothing in particular to which it necessarily refers*' is a provocative starting place.[55] For

Halperin among others, 'queer' is always the opposite not only of heteronormativity but of all other hegemonic or dominant positions. This sort of 'queer' is clearly not what Ackroyd intends when he argues that Dickens is simultaneously against his times (a radical in reaction alongside Carlyle); at one with them (embodying them unconsciously and blindly as part of his genius); and transcending them – also through his genius. Yet Halperin's way of defining queerness makes room for new forms of opposition, as Fichte's aesthetics did for new forms of art. A Dickens who is reified *as* his age, who is made to insist that he 'remembers everything' and to 'be' his social and subjective texts, is a construct who is denied the crucial incommensurability, the psychic and social fracture, between self and other. This is not, however, Dickens's grandiose conceit, but Ackroyd's. Such an anachronistically unified, idealised and idealist subject is, for this modern reader at least, a genuinely scary apparition blown in from an idea of the past in Ackroyd's imagination, a grotesquely inflated humanist subject more at odds with late modernity's 'normal' than the more recognisable, perhaps now almost 'orthodox', oppositional, transgressive subject posited by Halperin. It may not be quite true, however, that Ackroyd fully believes in this cartoon version of the romantically aggrandised Dickens and his doppelgänger, the all-knowing biographer, although an alternative version offered to the reader is also expressed in the language of late romantic excess. In the 'Prologue' to *Dickens*, Ackroyd directs us to Dickens's own fascination with the 'seascape' to describe both the ceaseless 'surface' activity of his life, with its storms and cross-currents, and its below surface depth of 'lost objects' that, by implication, cannot be turned into language or story: 'If we dive down deeper, dive into the unfathomable depths, what then do we see of him?' Ackroyd asks. 'Lost objects which have drifted down, now flattened beyond recognition. Darkness and silence. Strange phosphorescent images. Is this what Carlyle meant – a man whose radiance contained the presence of death itself?'[56] The watery image is a favourite not just of Dickens but of many other eighteenth- and nineteenth-century writers.[57] The 'radiant' 'presence of death' both as the end and origin of storytelling has a psychoanalytic resonance too; a clue to something romanticism and psychoanalysis both tried to identify, albeit in different modes, as grand but flawed androcentric humanity, a melancholic being constructed through 'loss', or, as a follower of psychoanalyst Jacques Lacan might say, through 'lack' – through the phantasmatic threat to masculinity itself. And here is where we can see the cracks in Ackroyd's attempt to weld together two incompatible theories of the self. He finds in Dickens what psychoanalysis would regard as the infantile fantasy of full and undifferentiated subjectivity, of a wholeness that no one can achieve, but he discovers as well some other unspoken life beyond and below discourse. This unspeakable aspect of subjectivity, figured here as shards of the shipwrecked self no diver can reach or identify, a realm that can be imagined, but which no subject or author can access, is of a different order than the unconscious space where Dickens's childhood traumas are stored, neatly stacked, one imagines, ready to be retrieved for his fiction. The pumped-up grand illusions of *Dickens* seem to be responding to an unspecified threat to the idea of the author as hypermasculine subject, and offers a clue, however tentative, to Ackroyd's wish to make us believe in Dickens as a reconstructed late romantic subject, a man whose sublime 'genius' we can neither query or fathom, an archaic figure larger than life. From one point of view *Dickens*'s Dickens seems to be locked in an idea of the Victorian past, in an imagined world that still believed in romantic heroism. However his transcendence is also figured as Christ-like. At the fetishised scene of his funeral, we, his mourners, his readers, identify with him, his dead/alive likeness acting as our mirror.

Ackroyd's way with Dickens has at least one very interesting precedent. David Glover points out that Carlyle, in his best biblical manner, recreates Samuel Johnson as literary hero in similar 'lofty' terms, invoking Shakespeare, and arguing that great men like Johnson arose from 'the *in*articulate deeps' – a term which conveys both Carlyle's identification with Johnson's humble origins, and that oceanic something beyond, before or below discourse that Romantic philosophers, post-Freudians and deconstructionists point to in different ways. At odds with Boswell's social and conversational Johnson, Carlyle's Johnson is a tragic figure, in Carlyle's words, 'a giant, invincible soul: a true man's'. These identifications, as Norma Clarke and Glover argue, are oedipal in character, in Carlyle's case literally so, in that his stonemason father was for Carlyle 'among Scottish peasants what Samuel Johnson was among English authors'. This identification aids in Carlyle's construction of a literary 'brotherhood' and a version of literary heroism that, Clarke suggests, imaginatively excludes the encroaching threat of literary women.[58] For Ackroyd, the oedipal identification with Dickens as both the 'true man' and giant among authors is figurative, and, like all oedipal relations, involves murderous and rivalrous thoughts, which render the heroic brotherhood of writers across time, like the idealised masculinity it represents, deeply unstable. It may not be surprising then that like Hegel and like Carlyle, Ackroyd finds it impossible to discover literary heroes or an idea of authorship adequate for his own modernity. Projecting that hero back in time, and then suffering from the anxiety of influence his imagined presence poses, does not solve his problem with the present, but rather compromises his project at every stage, drowning *Dickens* in nostalgia, evoking a subjectivity that never was, writing a life as an elegy, a form of discursive mourning that creates its own loss.

Biofiction – The Novel Lives of Henry James: *The Master; Author, Author; The Line of Beauty*

With a sigh of relief, I want to leave the theatre where Ackroyd's melodrama of Victorian authorship promises to run and run, and turn to another provocative staging of Victorian literary biography. We do not now automatically think of Henry James (1843–1916) as an eminent Victorian. He was not always, but has come to be, too deeply connected to twentieth-century ideas of the modern, now seen as much the progenitor of our 'own' modernity, post World War II, as the modernist writers who followed him. They, of course, were as quick to reject his most complex last works as already out of date as James himself was eager, as a young reviewer in 1865, to turn his devastating critical lens on *Our Mutual Friend*, the product of Dickens's 'late' period.[59] Yet although he outlasted Victoria's reign by some fourteen years, and became a British citizen only the year before his death, James was chronologically, and in other ways too, at least as 'Victorian' as he was by birthright and upbringing 'American'. As a literary figure, as well as in his writing, he challenged national boundaries, modes of writing and the temporalities of the modern. For all of my adult reading life, which I date from my college years in the late 1950s, James – love him or hate him – was the Anglo-American *modern* novelist one was expected to have read. Throughout the 1970s and 1980s I taught him as an American 'realist' writer to my worldly English students. He never failed to shock them, and worse, to upset their belief in their own contemporaneity. His fiction, so elegantly full of psychic violence, so riddled with sex, money and death, and so brutal in its repudiation of the happy ending, confused their sense of historical distance, of the singularity of their own carefully fashioned identities. If James's acute psychological realism could touch my students' raw nerves – I finally gave up teaching *What Maisie Knew* as its account of a child tossed between parents and stepparents pressed too painfully on their own experience and the thin-skinned feelings of late adolescence – then where and when was their unique modernity? On the other hand, James himself as authorial persona, promiscuous only in his ready acceptance of social invitations, had almost zero appeal to students who had been drawn to study American Literature because they admired the lives and work of Henry Miller or Jack Kerouac or even

Sylvia Plath. I was relatively young then too, a product of the 1960s, and James's life, insofar as it seemed a lived life at all as opposed to the life of and in the mind, had very little resonance for me, except for the single fact of his expatriation to Britain, an experience which I had shared and with which I could therefore, ruefully, identify.

We might be forgiven for thinking that James's own story had been so completely dispersed into his texts and characters, so reflected on in his own tripartite autobiographical writings and his wonderful voluminous correspondence, as well as so completely recorded in one of the century's most monumental biographical projects (Leon Edel's five volumes published between 1953 and 1972), not to mention Fred Kaplan's *Henry James: The Imagination of Genius* (1992), that it did not require further attention or documentation, least of all a new genre to promote it.[60] Yet two gifted novelists – one Irish, one British; one tragic, one comic – have each made Henry James the protagonist of a historical novel, the fictional genre that James thought it least possible to execute successfully. This reinvention, moreover, has been accompanied with the sort of publicity that typically greets the rediscovered lost manuscript, and the coincidence of subject matter has inevitably produced comparisons and triggered professional rivalry. These ironies would not have been lost on James, whose interest in the foibles and frictions of literary culture, in literary ambition and in the gap between the figure of the celebrated writer and the work, is the subject of some of his best and most poignant short stories. In James we have the Man of Letters in almost pure form, a man whose 'one great passion', he is alleged to have told Hugh Walpole, was the 'intellectual life'.[61] What has happened to our early twenty-first century world, and the idea of the author within it, that Henry James, the iconic writer whose life was lived, if ever one was, from 'book to book', now seems to embody an exemplary drama of selfhood, to hold the secret to something crucial about the past and present of 'modern' male subjectivity?

The return of James the man to the forefront of our consciousness has been prepared for by a couple of decades of revisionist criticism of James's writing. In his perceptive Introduction to *The Cambridge Companion to Henry James* (1998), Jonathan Freedman argues that the present millennium has become 'the moment of Henry James', and he points out how unlikely this renaissance might seem.

> At a critical moment so leery of traditional notions of literary and cultural value, so impatient with gestures of authorial self-aggrandizement, so suspicious of the prerogatives of class privilege, few writers would seem *less* likely to survive than one thoroughly embedded in the highest of high literary culture, driven by desire for canonical status, fascinated by the intensities of the drawing room and the mores in our MTV-mediated age of instantaneous

apprehension. The thickness, the opacity, the ambiguous range of reference of Jamesian prose demands attention, focus, and that rarest of contemporary commodities, *time*.[62]

In answer to his own question, Freedman notes that James has proved an author of surprising resilience to critical fashions, though each shift in critical perspective rewrites him in their own image. 'Each successive wave of theoretical and critical practice – New Criticism, deconstruction, feminism, marxism, New Historicism – staked their claims and exemplified their style of interpretation by offering powerful re-readings of James.'[63] Freedman himself chooses 'family, nation and the literary' as the three themes in James which highlight present concerns, but rather than settling comfortably for a James who responds to the crises of late modernity, he recommends James to us for his 'oddity' – his 'queerness' in the non-sexual sense that James himself uses the term – and for the way 'he challenges us continually to rethink our own sense of the relation between past and present . . . without ever ceasing to understand that this process is a process, not a dogma'.[64] In making that very anti-ideological point, in offering us James as a restless interrogatory sensibility endlessly at odds with his own time, and yet always a a writer who resists becoming our contemporary, Freedman is of course doing just what he warns against: constructing James as just the man for an era in which certainties at every level seem to have vanished, a 'moment' which having lost its taste for grand narrative and theoretical purities, has found in literature a renewed ethical resource, and in the literary life, whatever its failures and discontents, an exemplary humanity.

James's malleability as an exemplary writer for different conjunctures may be one key to his present popularity. If, at his own *fin de siècle*, Henry James was worried about the decline in his readership, his career in the nineties and noughts of ours continues to be on the up and up. His work remains largely in print, and, even more important, his fiction goes on being successfully translated to the small and large screen. Through adaptation, he now reaches a wider public than even he had dreamed of; via television and cinema he has posthumously achieved that dramatic success that eluded him in his lifetime. The last decade and a half has seen a number of new studies of James. Cambridge University Press has been his most consistent patron with the equivalent of a book a year from the early 1990s through 2004, works which range from studies on sexuality and queerness through to questions of gender, philosophy, nation and race, authorship, publicity and popular culture.[65]

The revival of critical interest in James may have, in some respects, prepared the ground for his metamorphosis into a fictional character, but both Tóibín's and Lodge's takes on James are supplementary and at times antagonistic to the James that emerges from recent criticism. And the novels also do more than borrow the 'facts' of James's life to construct a freewheeling meditation on it. Biofiction, the term coined to describe the hybrid genre, can be interpreted in various ways, as highlighting the tension between biography and fiction, as well as marking the overlap between them. Whatever one's ethical view of 'authenticity' as a gold standard for life writing, it is now an almost clichéd assumption that autobiography and memoir inevitably construct and invent their authors as quasi-fictional characters. Biography, although it may seek to modify and correct self representation, takes the same liberties. The novelisation of biography represents only the next logical stage of that process. But the 'bio' in biofiction also references a more essentialised and embodied element of identity, a subject less than transcendent but more than merely discourse. It implies that there is something stubbornly insoluble in what separates the two genres and that prevents them from being invisibly sutured; the join will always show. Biofiction is as vulnerable as any other kind of historical fiction to what James described as the 'single false note' which would unavoidably creep in to the 'almost impossible' attempt to invent or represent 'the old *consciousness*', but novelists today, even James's devout admirers like Lodge and Tóibín, are much less invested in the strict adherence to social or psychological realism, the 'knowledge and the imagination, the saturation, perception, vigilance, taste, tact' that James thought necessary to 'achieve even a passable historic *pastiche*'.[66] Perhaps James even did them a good turn by making historical fiction as written to his specification of artistic integrity so impossible a genre to get right. Agreeing with him, late twentieth-century novelists with another aesthetic to guide them were freed up to try for something both less exacting and very different.

The titles of their novels, Tóibín's *The Master*, and Lodge's *Author, Author*, both affirm and ironise the position of James as 'great writer'/great man. Where they remain faithful to their subject, if in radically dissimilar ways, is in their fascination with James's dedication to the writing life above everything else. In *The Master*, Tóibín constructs a curiously private, remote, almost asocial James – the James of his fiction's interiority and solipsism – very different from James the weekend guest, diner out and compulsive correspondent. Tóibín, as Adam Mars Jones has put it, emphasises the 'negative dynamic' both present and thematised in James's life and his work, summarised as 'failure, avoidance, renunciation and withdrawal'. As Mars Jones reminds us, James as writer was the master of the 'missed opportunity, the faulty choice'.[67] Michael Wood's review of *The Master* in *The London Review of Books* is titled

'What Henry didn't do'. Wood's thoughtful appreciation of the way in which The Master 'situates James's tender and timid yearnings in love in a whole life of losses and evasions', emphasises how what Martin Ryle has suggested is the novel's overriding theme of 'abstention' worked for, not against, James's writing.[68] Tóibín, using the strategies of memoir and of fiction to move backward and forward in a life, mercilessly probes the disturbing pattern of James's intense but always attenuated relationships with women and men, relatives and friends. *The Master* makes us understand and feel the attraction, the pain, but above all the logic of such a stance: ambivalence as a way of life, personal decisions always inflected against too great an intimacy with, or responsibility for, others. The economy of the writing is one of *The Master*'s triumphs. The novel's real time covers a relatively brief period from the mid 1890s through 1901 – interestingly it does not go beyond the Victorian era – but its associative organisation lets Tóibín range very widely over James's life, from his young manhood in New England to his final years in Rye, making vivid an extraordinary range of scenes and characters. Without needing to imitate James's sentences, indeed without doing that much to his own laconic fictional style except, as Mars says, to widen its lexicon so that James's own psychological vocabulary is subtly naturalised within it, *The Master* evokes what we think of as James's sensibility, his open-ended sense of the complexity of motives and causation.[69] For me, and I believe others also, it does something else quite astonishing that I associate with my experience of reading James: it leaves the reader to identify with James's predicament, his remorse, his forms of denial, as well as the disappoinment of his friends and would-be lovers. Yet somehow we are left to moralise the failure of affection or of emotional courage at our peril – to feel, again, as one does when reading James, that to moralise is inevitable, and in one register ethically right, but also to miss the point. And while Tóibín does speculate as to what relationships and incidents find their way into James's fiction – as Mars Jones says, the least successful element of the novel because the most facile and, I would add, already too familiar in the critical and biographical literature – he does not make the mistake of rationalising James's choices and inhibitions into a necessary stance whatever their personal costs to himself and others, justified somehow by the higher calling of writing. These untied ends are what make the novel a memorable literary experience in itself; they turn us back, as they must, to James's own work, where 'answers' are even less forthcoming.

In the 1960s through the 1970s when I was in my twenties and thirties, a young Marxist just encountering feminism and Freud, James was a guilty pleasure. His refusal to let characters off the hook or to punish them with anything more than the effects of their choices, although those effects were often fatal, was what made his work generically realist but also potentially utopian. If Daisy Miller or Milly Theale died, their deaths were not the exemplary instances of a fixed system of punishment and rewards common to the early and mid Victorian novel up to and including George Eliot, nor were they the victims of the pessimistic determinism of French and American literary naturalism. I was content to see James's psychology and epistemology within its historical context, neither entirely irrelevant to, or comfortably in tune with my convictions. (When one's own historical conditions and beliefs seem to promise the possibility of progressive change, as mine did then, it does not seem so urgent to appropriate the ideological frameworks of a past moment.) Today it is easy to see why Tóibín's James might have a strong appeal both as a man for his own and for our time. The very negativity that Tóibín highlights, that insistent note of abstention, has a melancholy correspondence to the post-lapsarian mood of the noughts. Not that *The Master* goes in for such crude presentism. Rather it evokes its period without cluttering it with stage props, and the rewards of this writerly reticence is that Tóibín succeeds in making his fictional case study both historically particular and of wider relevance.

Each novel takes as a key trauma James's public humiliation at the opening of his play *Guy Domville* in January 1895 at the St James Theatre, when, called on stage after a performance he had failed to witness, he was hissed and booed. His embarrassment was heightened by the fact that on the night of *Guy Domville*'s disastrous London opening, the nervous James had gone instead to the Haymarket to see Wilde's *An Ideal Husband* – hugely successful, but in James's eyes, as imagined by Tóibín, 'feeble and vulgar' – returning to the theatre only at his own play's close.[70] *The Master* uses this scene in the first chapter to adumbrate two intertwined themes in his novel. On one level the debacle serves as the literalisation of James's fears that the 'great flat foot of the public' had voted against his kind of serious fiction and drama, that 'nothing he did would ever be popular or generally appreciated', on another it highlights the supreme irony that he, who had so carefully avoided doing anything in his private life to place him 'in the annals of the unmentionable', had through this professional 'defeat and exposure' ended up there anyway.[71] *Author, Author*, structured more fully around James's disastrous flirtation with the theatre, leads up to and falls away from the scene at the St James. As Lodge describes it, the farce of James's full frontal exposure is much more simply the nightmare fantasy of authorship realised, the dramatic revenge of the always volatile and unpredictable literary marketplace on ambition. Lodge's James is obsessed with reputation to the exclusion of almost anything else; this is a novel that has surprisingly little to say about his fiction, or even, except at the very end, about the 'intellectual life', choosing instead to weave the story of James's failed theatrical career with the history of two of his literary friendships and their accompanying rivalries and discontents. In *Author, Author* the story of these friendships – with the well-married but worldly George Du Maurier, the illustrator and author of a hugely successful popular novel, *Trilby,* and Constance Fenimore Woolson, whose middlebrow fiction sold better than James's – dramatises aspects of James's emotional inhibition but focuses most particularly on his hunger for recognition. If Tóibín's James is sometimes too humourless and agonistic a figure, then Lodge's James overcompensates by being too relentlessly social and competitive, represented as forever straining for stable financial and literary success in an increasingly international print culture which withheld it, saving rewards for popular genre fiction and its applause for more accessible talents like Wilde's. In places, *Author, Author* reads like a list of James's more successful contemporaries, annotated with James's reservations about them. For all its factual detail, Lodge never brings either this historical milieu or the longer scenes with Du Maurier or Woolson to life; the dialogue is wooden and the relationships themselves often seem imaginatively untransformed from their historical sources. Without the life of the mind or the private life as more than superficial topics, what remains feels repetitive and one-dimensional. As with happy families in Tolstoy, the anxieties of authorship prove too like each other for them to be the main substance of a biographical novel. Just as James erred in thinking he could write for the theatre, Lodge, one of Britain's most gifted comic novelists, and a skilled literary critic, has chosen a genre, historical fiction, for which he has no natural talent. James's working-class servants – Minnie Kidd, Burgess Oakes and others – are neither plausible pastiche nor effective caricatures. As his use of them in the text, and his appended notes on research for the novel make clear, Lodge intended them to have lives and desires of their own, to be more than handy vehicles for comments on above-stairs life. However, he cannot find a register or rhetoric that grants them that autonomy, and they end up as copies of copies, parodic faithful servants, or cartoon cockneys. Nor does Lodge's laudably anti-sentimental James survive his reduction to the catalogue of his professional insecurities. Lodge affectionately rather than cruelly exploits those moments when he sees James as cutting both a comic and slightly pathetic figure. His overt aim is to deflate the reverence and high seriousness of James's filiopietistic following. But somehow James's character or his life resists being cut and pasted into a comic novel, and this lack of adaptability extends unfortunately to Lodge, who cannot stretch *his* generic talents, try as he will, to write anything else.

Both novels worry at the question of James's sexuality. *The Master* explores James's homoerotic feelings throughout; they are allowed to rise in conversation and reverie and in a series of imagined and inconclusive encounters – one with his lifelong friend Oliver Wendell Holmes when they share a bed as young men; one with a manservant, Hammond, set up by his friend, Lady Wolseley, to seduce him during a trip to Ireland; one in Paris, with the Russian writer, Paul Jowkowsky; and lastly, one with a young sculptor, Henrik Andersen, who visits him at Lamb House. Tóibín chooses James's friendship with Edmund Gosse rather than Du Maurier as the vehicle for exploring James's response to the repercussion of the Wilde scandal. (James's imaginative sympathies are with the abruptly deracinated fate of Wilde's young sons, forced to live abroad under another name.) Yet for all of its thematic and narrative prominence, Tóibín develops his speculative treatment of James's unrealised and only half-acknowledged sexual desires as only one element, if a central one, in a wider pattern of behaviour whose causes remain overdetermined. *The Master* plays up, rather than down, James's complicated affective relations with women; with his mother, his sister Alice, his cousin Minny Temple and with Constance Fenimore Woolson. Tóibín never tries to represents James in the way that provocative recent criticism has done, as the avant garde of modern queer fiction. But *The Master*'s interpretation of James, so structured around the transmutation of loss into writing, suggests what Lodge's goes to some pains to deny, that touch of queerness, in both the sense that James uses it, as 'strange, out of the ordinary', and also in its modern sexualised sense, each inflection connected to the elusiveness of the subjectivity he lived and portrayed. Tóibín, in recent interviews, has resisted biographical interpretations of his novel which imply that *The Master* sets up an implicit analogy between the prohibitions and penalties of late Victorian and Edwardian sexual mores and the difficulties of growing up gay and Catholic in post World War II Ireland, and indeed the novel, even with its Irish interlude, doesn't lend itself to that kind of coded reading. Lodge, on the other hand, wants to see the whole issue off. His no-nonsense dismissal of the James and sexuality question – a brisk mix of biological and social determinants: low libido, a disgust at the physicality of sex, Victorian standards about sex outside marriage – is actively hostile to further psychological investigation. In his reluctance to play voyeur by 'sexing up' the seemingly celibate author's life through speculation about unrecorded desires or acts with either sex, Lodge makes of him someone who can read about sex in French novels and represent the power of desire in the lives of his characters, but who is easily shocked by the naughty nineties, emotionally and libidinally behind his times, straightforwardly repelled by Oscar Wilde's personality and judgemental if not gleeful about his public downfall.[72] Lodge – who has of course written at length about the tragi-comic effects of Catholicism on his postwar generation – is evidently so unhappy with the image of a closet gay James that he makes his protagonist, in annoyed meditation, articulate his rejection of such a suggestion: 'they sometimes assumed his taste must be for men or young boys which Henry found still more offensive' – as if that were, in fact, the end of the matter.[73] The act of negation here seems to be more to do with the reaction of the modern novelist than his late Victorian subject. In *Author, Author*, James's squeamishness about sex of any kind is articulated with the shrinking market for serious art. Lodge's contrast of 'Kiki' Du Maurier's casual vulgarity, and the seam of degeneracy that he has James react against in Wilde, has an implicit parallel in Du Maurier's and Wilde's ability to please less discerning audiences.

No Whig version of progress from an age of repression to one of joyful liberation underpins either novel, both of which, if in different ways, perceive masculine authorship as under threat and revision. That threat is seen off in certain silences and refusals in both novels. It is interesting and rather surprising that James's interest in the women in his life and their inspiration for his fiction does not lead Tóibín, the more psychoanalytically attuned of the two, or Lodge, the professional literary critic, to make the theoretically commonplace point that the process through which they become textualised in his fictions might involve the identification of the male author with them. The figure of Oscar Wilde provides, in *The Master, Author, Author*, and to some extent in Ackroyd's *Dickens* where he also turns up, a limit case, and not an admirable one, for the expression of transgressive sexuality, and authorial publicity. Yet even with Wilde as a warning of the lower depths of abjection in which writers might find themselves, neither Tóibín or Lodge exploit to any great extent Michel Foucault's widely influential critique of the repressive hypothesis, which emphasises the ubiquitousness of sexual discourse as a form of surveillance and control in the nineteenth century. Indeed, in an old-fashioned way, as with so much narrative Victoriana, there is in both books just a whisper of wistfulness, although never full blown nostalgia, for a period when sexuality was still surrounded by codes and prohibition, as if the liberalisation of those codes has perhaps made it harder not easier for writers, both intellectually and in the marketplace.

The healthy demand for Victorian literary biography and biofiction suggests either that the death of the author, the disappearance and dispossession of what Barthes called 'his civil status, his biographical person' has been greatly exaggerated, or, conversely, that the threat has breathed new life into the idea of the author. As I have argued through-out this essay, the humanist subject cannot come back unaltered from the moment of theory. Barthes himself concedes that 'perhaps the subject returns, not as illusion, but as *fiction*. A certain pleasure is derived from a way of imagining oneself as individual, of inventing a final rarest fiction: the fictive identity.'[74] If, as in Barthes' proleptic boast, the author as absolute monarch became one of the 'disappeared', then is the per-verse wish to find his traces in the text perhaps met, if in vulgar fashion, through making him a character in a novel, where his presence satisfies both the epistemological terms of his banishment and the psychological demand for his return?

Last Victorian, first modern, both at once: James, like Dickens, becomes in these biographical treatments from two modern novelists, the site of anxiety about the futurity of authorship, now and then. Andrew Bennett suggests that for 'the Romantics . . . the judgement of future gen-erations becomes the necessary condition of writing itself'. 'Originality', also their invention, 'generates deferred reception'. An original work (for the romantics always a poem, now a novel) 'is both new and before its time . . . it is before its time precisely *because* it is new'.[75] Posthumous appreciation becomes the *sine qua non* of value – the guarantor not just of an author's work, I would argue, but in these recent representations of Victorian novelists of the literary itself, whose life as a discourse is often represented as more threatened in the millennial marketplace than it was seen to be at the opening of the twentieth century. Death, it turns out, is the one necessary event for our Victorian authors, so that Literature, which they embody in different guises, can be assured. *The Master* partly recognises and partly evades this paradox through its nar-rative strategy, setting up, in its opening pages, James's characteristic impulse to transmute loss – the death of his mother and aunt, the missed opportunity of a sexual encounter – into writing. Death is very present in Tóibín's novel, which dwells not only on Alice James's end, and Constance Fenimore Woolson's suicide, but also on death and dying in the American Civil War, the conflict that James and his brother William both avoided. But the novel refuses to end with the author's death, pre-ferring to leave James alone in Lamb House, having said goodbye to his brother, sister-in-law and niece, about to be born again in writing his last great fictions, a less than elegiac, more utopian ending.

In contrast, *Author, Author* uses James's last days as a frame, begin-ning and ending with his illness and death. As if to compensate for the intellectual thinness of the rest of the novel, this last chapter includes some of James's own thoughts on philosophy, the afterlife, and writing, and is also interleaved with an italicised commentary from Lodge as first person novelist/biographer/critic. In the manner, if not the style, of nineteenth-century fictional closure, he disposes of the fate of his characters, hurriedly bringing us up to speed on the bumps and bruises of the last decade and a half of James's life. *Guy Domville*, Lodge reminds us, was not a glitch in an otherwise ascending career curve, but a sign of the ebbing away of James's contemporary audience. Lodge cites the relative lack of enthusiasm and economic return for what we now think of as James's greatest books, and notes briefly that a second professional and emotional crisis was precipitated by the critical and financial failure of James's New York Edition of his works. More intimately and less pompously than Ackroyd, but with something of the same rivalrous and controlling impulse, Lodge finds it

> *tempting therefore to indulge in a fantasy of somehow time-travelling back to that afternoon of late February 1916, creeping into the master bedroom of Flat 21, Carlyle Mansions, casting a spell on the little group of weary watchers at the bedside, pulling up a chair oneself, and saying a few reassuring words to HJ, before he departs this world, about his literary future.*[76]

Highlighting his recent canonisation after a few decades of relative obscurity, and the students and academics who read and comment on his '*scrupulously edited, annotated*' fiction Lodge notes the audience of '*millions*' who not only read his books but '*encounter his stories in theatrical and cinematic and television adaptation.*'[77] A '*different and more pleasing fantasy*' entertains a mock-heroic version of the author as transcendent:

> *the spirit of Henry James existing out there somewhere in the cosmos, knowing everything I wished he could know before he died . . . totting up the sales figures, reading the critiques, watching the films and the television serials on some celestial video player or DVD laptop, and listening to the babble of our conversation about him and his work, swelling through the ether like a prolonged ovation.*[78]

It remains ambiguous whether, in forcing James to accept as ironic accolade, these profit-making, posterity-assuring transformations of his work into popular forms for mass audiences, Lodge's fantasy repairs or reinforces the abjection of the opening night of *Guy Domville*. Either way, taking the place of the hapless producer who misguidedly drew the unfortunate James through the curtains in response to the cry 'author, author', Lodge invites his character to stand before the admiring millions and '*take a bow*'.[79]

The futurity that Lodge stage manages for James depends not only on the transmutation of fiction into other genres and media but his even more problematic critical reinvention. And while Lodge sends up as farcical James's adoption by queer theory – his sexually squeamish James would presumably not be amused by the discovery of '*metaphors of anal fisting in the Prefaces to the New York Edition*' – he does not invite us to reflect that James might have been equally appalled by the sexually explicit rendering of his work in Jane Campion's adaption of *The Portrait of a Lady* or Hossein Amini's *The Wings of the Dove*.[80] In making the ironic point that we never get the posterity we desire, the disembodied James that inhabits Lodge's playful ether has to undergo a form of virtual lobotomy that excises aesthetic judgement as well as anxiety, allowing him to appreciate uncritically almost every bit of his comeback. There is no suggestion, for example, that James, with his rage for privacy as well as his desire for fame, and his expressed belief that the historical novel was a debased form, might be offended by his fictional figuration. The futurity of writing that Lodge describes is hooked to the constant and productive mutability of literary forms, to the inevitability of technology and globalisation to alter texts and audiences beyond anyone's predictive capacity, and to the handily complicit willingness of the authorial spirits of the past to suspend their critical prejudices so that they may enjoy posthumous celebrity in our late modernity. Tóibín's horizons and ambitions seem at once more modest and more conservative. The ending of *The Master* anticipates only the 'day's work' ahead, and by omission downplays the turmoil and disappointments of James's last years, laying out a lonelier, but less troubled, writing future. As he moves around Lamb House, before beginning his dictation, James 'relishes the silence and the emptiness . . . going into the rooms as though they too, in how they yielded to him, belonged to an unrecoverable past' joining 'all the other rooms from whose windows he had observed the world, so that they could be remembered and captured and held'.[81] In this passage, the social and the solipsistic as paradox are both evoked and left unresolved. Yet 'the world' as 'remembered, captured and held', which, in that closing sentence, seems to trace the biographer's process as well as James's, represents an even more powerful fantasy of authorship and futurity than Lodge's burlesque turn as master of ceremonies. *The Master* retains a traditional if always secular faith in the integrity of writing, perhaps in the vehicle of fiction in particular. In Tóibín's acceptance of the melancholy position for masculinity and for authorship as a scene that must and can be written, he makes of James the archetypal writer for his own time and ours, indeed the hinge through which we can understand something of the connection between those two very discrete temporalities.

For other devoted Jamesians, the late twentieth-century landscape is as violent and corrupt as James's own time, and its future even less predictable. Alan Hollinghurst's Booker Prize-winning novel, *The Line of*

Beauty, adapted in 2006 for television by Andrew Davies, is as much a tribute to James as either Lodge or Tóibín's biofiction, but James's presence is dispersed through story, character and writing.[82] It is set in the mid to late 1980s, in the euphoric rush of Thatcherism's triumph, and in the early years of the AIDS pandemic. Its provincial protagonist, Nick Guest, like so many of James's naïve and idealistic young heroes and heroines, comes to Europe, here London, and gets entangled with corrupt cosmopolitan society via his involvement with the Fedden family, the posh parents of a college friend who take him in. Nick has embarked on a PhD dissertation on Henry James and style at the end of the nineteenth century, but he gets distracted from it in his pursuit of pleasure, in his case gay, interracial, cross-class sex. The novel warns against an abstracted aestheticism, even as it praises 'the line of beauty', not in the valuable Guardi on the walls of the Tory politician Gerald Fedden's Kensington town house, where Nick becomes a longstay houseguest, but in the more ephemeral curve of a young man's 'plump buttocks', during stolen sex in the gated garden of the exclusive square. Hollinghurst is Britain's most prominent and successful contemporary gay novelist. The influence of James has always been apparent in his meticulously observed, affectively fine-tuned and beautifully written portraits of an age, which promote an emotional literacy and a polymorphous perverse morality for the present day. *The Line of Beauty* is his most political novel to date and, by his own admission, the first in which he has fully confronted the AIDS crisis. At the novel's end, Nick, perhaps inevitably, gets caught up in the financial and sexual scandal descending on Gerald Fedden. Nick has been having an affair with a university friend, the multi-millionaire Wani Ouradi, now dying of AIDS, with whom he has been working on various projects, including a glossy 'art' journal OGEE. Their relationship is exposed in the national press by Fedden's unstable and vengeful daughter Catherine, and is cited as additional proof of the Fedden circle's immoral lifestyle. In the face of this general family catastrophe, Nick becomes the Feddens's scapegoat and is summarily ejected from the house of his Thatcherite patron.

Neither pastiche nor biofiction, *The Line of Beauty* remembers James by thematising both the persistence and the fragility of his legacy in the present, in representations that can be both graphic and funny as well as sombre. At one point, about halfway through the book, Nick

> was reading Henry James's memoir of his childhood, *A Small Boy and Others*, and feeling crazily horny, after three days without as much as a peck from Wani. It was a hopeless combination. The book showed James at his most elderly and elusive, and demanded a pure commitment unlikely in a reader who was worrying excitedly about his boyfriend and semi-spying, through

dark glasses, on another boy who was showing off in front of him and clearly trying to excite him.[83]

At the same time, James is obliquely associated for Nick with his emerging sexuality. Earlier in the novel, identifying himself as a 'James man' to a Trollope fan at a party, feels to Nick, like 'coming out'.[84]

James is never a stable referent in *The Line of Beauty*, which is what makes his presence in the novel so alive and imaginatively creative. We are not meant, I think, to make simple analogies between Nick's fate and that of James's innocent provincials – such an easy correspondence is part of Nick's disturbing *naïveté*. Hollinghurst's partly mock-heroic use of Nick's own fantasied association with James extends to the book's denouement. Towards the end of the novel Nick has a Jamesian moment when, in the luxurious publishing offices provided by Wani, he finds himself dictating letters to the secretary, Melanie:

> In Wani's absence he'd grown fond of dictating, and found himself able to improvise long supple sentences rich in suggestion and syntactic shock, rather as the older Henry James, pacing and declaiming to a typist, had produced his most difficult novels . . . . Today he was answering a couple of rich American queens who had a film-production company perhaps as fanciful, and nominal as Ogee was, and who were showing an interest in the *Spoils of Poynton* project – though with certain strong reservations about the plot.[85]

This bathetic fantasy is interrupted by a visit from the sister and girlfriend of his first London lover Leo, who have come to tell him of Leo's death from AIDS, a blow which, as Nick's downfall rapidly accelerates, contributes to his superstitious conviction that his next AIDS test will show that he also, in spite of the precautions he has taken, will be infected. As he takes his final leave of Fedden's house in the last page of the novel, his mind is occupied with his fantasy of being forgotten by all who knew him.

From a Jamesian perspective, we might read Nick's haunting if melodramatic sense of his impending death as predictive, in line with the fictional deaths in Europe of the young American sculptor, Roderick Hudson, or that of the curious American girl Daisy Miller, who dies of a fever after she insists on seeing the Coliseum at night, and is taken there by the amoral Italian gigolo who knows he can never marry her. Roderick and Daisy in their different ways are, like Nick, in love with beauty. These deaths in James's early fiction are both salutary and slightly punitive; it is hard not to think that the author is not himself ambivalent about the stubborn hubris and greedy passion for life of his heedless, innocent Americans. But Hollinghurst seems to step back a pace from this move, from making Nick at once the sacrificial victim of a deeply corrupt and hypocritical society, and a casualty of his desire to be a cosmopolitan but essentially trusting person, with all the ethical and physical risks that entails. It is always the crudest and most corrupt characters in *The Line of Beauty* who see AIDS as the just punishment for homosexuality; as a very contemporary and idiosyncratic moralist, Hollinghurst's expressed difficulty with the topic may in part have been the problem of avoiding a plot line that does just that, in spite of itself. Throughout, the novel's free indirect narration keeps Nick's addiction to consoling fantasies, as well as to coke and sex, at arm's length – he is always the last to guess the truth of his situation – and his sense of his own ending might just be, one feels, another of these. In James's most subtle fictions, early and late, from *The Portrait of a Lady* through *The Ambassadors* and *The Golden Bowl*, protagonists are made to go on living past the end of innocence.[86]

Nevertheless the possibility of Nick's death is there, for him and for the reader. Hollinghurst is only able to write this bleak prospect for his protagonist as an historical novel, if one of the very recent past, a time remembered by the living gay author from a point in the future when the AIDS pandemic, in Britain at least, has a more hopeful outcome. Even so, it is Hollinghurst's darkest, least politically optimistic work to date. It casts a shadow too on the association with James. The threatened loss of Nick's futurity, and his identification with James as novelist – he never sees himself as one of James's sacrificial lambs but always as the author-observer – marks out another difference between the reader's and Nick's sensibility. It also makes Hollinghurst's tribute to James more complicated and contingent than in either Tóibín or Lodge, who take James's 'greatness' as a writer as somehow axiomatic for our time if not for his. In making the vulnerable and only too mortal Nick the standard bearer of James's literary and ethical imagination in late modernity, an identification that doesn't serve Nick all that well, Hollinghurst both reaffirms and questions James's relevance for our times.

What David Lodge has called *The Year of James* has extended itself into 2006 via the television serialisation of *The Line of Beauty* and, in the same month, two extracts from Lodge's literary revenge on his perceived rival – he has not yet been able to bring himself to read Tóibín's *The Master*. Published in the Saturday review of *The Guardian* as trailers for the book, these comic takes on the bad joke that the zeitgeist has played on James's admirers, imitators and would-be chroniclers, Lodge in particular, are an uncomfortable read in which a less than controlled spite against Tóibín bubbles up through the ironic surface of the witty narrative.[87] The Henry James bonanza has not yet run its course, and his manifestation, more poltergeist than seemly ghost, seems willing to go on rattling furniture and feelings in the house of literature.

Conclusion

The renaissance of Victorian literary biography and its crossover into biofiction rode the wave of the new popularity of life writing, but it has, I believe, a more local and a more general significance. As I have been working on this essay, I have had the recurring thought that Carlyle was more prescient than he knew in making writers into modern heroes. Their durability as exemplary figures if not model citizens has been extraordinary, extending into a time when print culture itself is seen as under threat from new technologies. Past heroes, together with the concept of heroism itself, have taken some deservedly sharp knocks in a long twentieth century littered with disasters and wrong turns. As it was with Carlyle, it is the deep disillusion with public political life that directs our gaze, in our search for figures to admire, to those odd individuals who lived 'from book to book' and whose writing we continue to read with pleasure and profit. Seeking them in pre-modernist authors also seems to reflect a political pessimism. Romantic and Victorian writers can be seen as still belonging to a modernity we recognise as anticipatory to our own, but one in which we feel retrospectively less implicated. It is not surprising either, that our social novelists – Jane Austen for the early years of the century, Dickens for its middle decades, and James for its last quarter – are the writers who stand out in this way. They are writers alike only in that they have no grand narratives to sell us. They do not stand in the vanguard of anything except writing itself; they are secular writers with generally conservative politics – this is true no matter how cleverly Dickens and James are tweaked by present day critics – with an imaginative investment in the representation of the everyday and a commitment to an ethics of personal relations.

This is a time, as Paul Gilroy has recently suggested, of 'postcolonial melancholia' in relation to the state of politics, a state, he argues, that must be worked through to find new forms of hope rather than fear in multicultural societies.[88] It would certainly not be Gilroy's favoured response to it, but in such a moment, when what has been lost cannot be given a name, imaginative literature, perhaps fiction especially, has become not only the discourse where, uniquely, the utopian imaginary can elaborate its social and personal vision, but a structural space which represents the utopian itself. The Victorian world, with all its faults, is now popularly seen to have done one thing well by nurturing and extending that space, to have provided the conditions which allowed important writers and their work to come into being. And, *pace* Barthes, to desire and find those authors in the work through their traces in writing has proved to be not quite enough. It seems that readers do require an extra-textual, embodied subject, a life that can represent a kind of prequel or sequel to the work, something, anyhow, supplementary to it. The author may still be imagined as in privileged control of the work if nothing else in their lives – that paternal power of authors over the text has proved harder to shift than a couple of generations of theorists believed, and is, however qualified, still in some sense the *raison d'être* of literary biography. Whether experimental or traditional in form, literary biography of major novelists inevitably places its subjects within the world of quotidian representation that the social novel itself employs. Biography and memoir arise as secular forms alongside the novel – fraternal and a bit rivalrous. In choosing three modern novelists, Ackroyd, Tóibín and Lodge, as my exemplary 'biographers', I have accentuated the closeness of the forms and the degrees of identification and rivalry between biographer and subject, but I would suggest that these idiosyncratic examples highlight common questions of representation and identification for literary biography more generally.

For each of these biographers, albeit in radically different ways, their subjects and their work provide a stake in the futurity of fiction and authorship – and even heroism – in the new millennium. Ackroyd's often grotesque portrayal of Dickens as romantic genius, makes, nevertheless, an impassioned case for the social novelist as a both representative and transcendent man. Tóibín and Lodge have, as I have argued, a more agonistic relationship to James and to the future of the literary. It is more than coincidence perhaps that they each, quite independently, highlight the opening night of *Guy Domville*, that moment of public rather than private abjection in James's middle years, not simply to rescue him, in fantasy, from it, but to dramatise the past and present vulnerability of masculinity, writing and authorship. It is symptomatic too that the affective lives of Charles Dickens and Henry James cannot and are not represented as traditionally heteronormative, yet their deviation from that norm is not cast by any of these authors as a radical form of transgression. The sense in which these lives are queered does not meet David Halperin's oppositional definition but rather moves towards a recognition that 'queer' might represent a more paradoxical and contradictory masculine – and literary – subjectivity. Identity and literary innovation have a conservative as well as a radical genealogy. In these treatments we are seeing in practice the evolution of new forms of manhood, responding to, even sometimes hostile to, an extensive body of work on the history of sexuality in the nineteenth century and the focus of queer studies on Victorian masculinity. Even where biography or biofiction represents authors' lives as contingent and unstable identities, a view of identity perfectly suited to our times if not theirs – it provides the modern reader with that crucial thing that a sense of futurity seems to require, a figure who can be ritually resuscitated, murdered, mourned and praised. That is paradoxically true even if we accept the idea that these literary lives are in some sense, like our own, a fiction: this knowledge may make the author, as called up by many biographies today, easier to relate to. After all, nobody's perfect.

At the opening of this essay I suggested that we should see the rise of life writing and biography as a productive and creative response to the challenge of postmodern cultural forms and the influential constellation of theoretical writing that, for a few decades, raised a strong argument against liberal humanist conceptions of the subject. Some part of that critique has entered the common sense of the culture, but other parts have been rejected. Biographers of Victorian writers today have the opportunity to move between the very different paradigms of agency that mark out the nineteenth century and our own, entertaining the paradox as part of the writing itself.

In a letter to Lytton Strachey, that inventive biographer of eminent Victorians, written on Christmas day 1928, Sigmund Freud, born in 1856, comments fretfully on the project of writing biography at all. He has been moved, he says, by Strachey's very speculative and psychoanalytically freighted, *Elizabeth and Essex*, while Strachey's earlier work on eminent Victorians had only given him an essentially 'aesthetic' enjoyment. 'You are aware,' he writes,

> of what other historians so easily overlook – that it is impossible to understand the past with certainty, because we cannot divine men's motives and the essence of their minds and so cannot interpret their actions. Our psychological analysis does not suffice even with those who are near us in space and time, unless we can make them the object of years of the closest investigation, and even then it breaks down before the incompleteness of our knowledge and the clumsiness of our synthesis. So that with regard to the people of past times we are in the same position as with dreams to which we have been given no associations – and only a layman could expect us to interpret such dreams as those.[89]

As Anthony Storr, discussing this letter points out, this reservation did not make Freud himself 'refrain from indulging in psychoanalytic speculations about historical figures who interested him'.[90] We could hear Freud's doubts about the biographical project simply as a corollary to James's realist strictures about the impossibility of the historical novel, but that is by no means the only way, nor even the most productive way, to hear either set of cautions. James's reservations were voiced at a time when he himself was planning to write an historical metanovel, which in its story of a young man who enters the nineteenth century past also comments on the difficulty of that imaginary encounter. This uncompleted, always about to be resumed, project, titled *The Sense of the Past*, lay beside him as he wrote the novels of his late phase; he was still intending to return to it in 1915.[91] We might interpret the generic and epistemological worries of Freud and James as provocations rather than impediments. That is certainly how their anxieties have been heeded by biographers and novelists today, whose new versions of Victorian lives at once amplify and ironise the dissonances within present ways of thinking about subjectivity, history and life writing.

Notes

1. Samuel Johnson, 'Biography' in *The Rambler*, 60, Saturday, 11 October 1730 in Richard Holmes (ed.), *Johnson on Savage* (HarperPerennial: London, 2005) p. 112.
2. Sigmund Freud to Lytton Strachey, 25 December 1928, cited in Michael Holroyd, *Lytton Strachey*, 2 vols (London: Heinemann, 1973) vol. ii, pp. 615–16.
3. The displays have recently shifted. Life writing now occupies much of the third floor, and in spring 2006 the long ground floor sweep was devoted to 'London', including a big section on 'London Lives'.
4. Roland Barthes, *The Pleasure of the Text*, Richard Miller (trans.) (New York: Hill and Wang, 1975) p. 27.
5. Jacqueline Rose, 'Feminism and the Psychic', *Sexuality in the Field of Vision* (London: Verso, 1986) p. 23.
6. Jenny Uglow, *Elizabeth Gaskell: habit of stories* (London: Faber & Faber, 1993); Jan Marsh, *Christina Rossetti: a literary biography* (London: Jonathan Cape, 1994); Juliet Barker, *The Brontës* (London: Weidenfeld & Nicholson, 1994); Lyndall Gordon, *Charlotte Brontë: a passionate life* (London: Chatto & Windus, 1994); Julia Markus, *Dared and Done: the marriage of Elizabeth Barrett and Robert Browning* (London: Bloomsbury, 1997); Frederick R. Karl, *George Eliot: a biography* (London: HarperCollins, 1995); Rosemary Ashton, *George Eliot: a life* (London: Allen Lane, 1996); Kerry McSweeney, *George Eliot: a literary life* (Basingstoke: Macmillan, 1991); Kathryn Hughes, *George Eliot: the last Victorian* (London: Fourth Estate, 1999).
7. Iain Finlayson, *Browning* (New York: HarperCopllins, 2004); Clyde de L. Ryals, *The Life of Robert Browning* (Oxford: Blackwell, 1993); Sarah Wood, *Robert Browning: a literary life* (Basingstoke: Palgrave, 2001); Peter L. Shillingsburg, *William Makepeace Thackeray: a literary life* (Basingstoke: Palgrave, 2001); D. J. Taylor, *Thackeray* (London: Chatto & Windus, 1999); James Pope-Hennessy, *Anthony Trollope* [1971] (London: Phoenix Press, 2001); Victoria Glendinning *Anthony Trollope* (London: Hutchinson, 1992).
8. Tennant's *Felony* also deserves analysis as part of the phenomenon, but the focus of this essay will be on male authors' representation of Victorian male writers.

9. See Spivak's discussion of the need for, and the problems with, 'strategic essentialism': the first in, Gayatri Chakravorty Spivak, *In Other Worlds: essays in cultural politics* (New York: Routledge, 1987) p. 205, and the second in a later interview with Ellen Rooney. In the interview she points out that 'Identity is a very different word from essence. We "write" a running biography with life-language rather than only word-language in order to "be."'. Gayatri Chakravorty Spivak, *Outside in the Teaching Machine* (New York: Routledge, 1993) p. 4.
10. Samuel Johnson, 'Literary Biography', *The Idler*, 102, Saturday, 29 March 1760, in *Johnson on Savage*, p. 126.
11. A. S. Byatt, *The Biographer's Tale* (London: Vintage, 2001) p. 1.
12. A. S. Byatt, *The Biographer's Tale*, p. 5.
13. A. S. Byatt, *The Biographer's Tale*, p. 257.
14. See George L. Mosse, *The Image of Man: the creation of modern masculinity* (New York: Oxford University Press, 1996) and Herbert L. Sussman, *Victorian Masculinities: manhood and masculine poetics in early Victorian literature and art* (Cambridge: Cambridge University Press, 1995).
15. For a longer account of the evolution of modern masculinities see David Glover, 'Masculinities', in David Glover and Cora Kaplan, *Genders* (London: Routledge, 2000) pp. 56–85.
16. Samuel Johnson, 'Biography', *Johnson on Savage*, p. 111.
17. A. S. Byatt, *The Biographer's Tale*, p. 5.
18. Janet Malcolm, *The Silent Woman: Sylvia Plath and Ted Hughes* (London: Macmillan, 1995) pp. 8–9.
19. Janet Malcolm, *The Silent Woman*, p. 9.
20. Janet Malcolm, *The Silent Woman*, p. 9.
21. Janet Malcolm, *The Silent Woman*, p. 9.
22. John Barrell, 'Inside the Head', *London Review of Books*, 22:21, November 2000.
23. John Barrell, 'Inside the Head'. See also Richard Holmes, *Coleridge: Darker Reflection* (London: HarperCollins, 1998).
24. Samuel Johnson, *An Account of the Life of Mr. Richard Savage, Son of the Earl Rivers* in Richard Holmes (ed.), *Johnson on Savage* (London: HarperPerennial, 2005) pp. 301–5.
25. David Glover, 'Masculinities', pp. 73–4.
26. Alison Light, 'Writing Lives' in Laura Marcus and Peter Nicholls (eds), *The Cambridge History of Twentieth-Century English Literature* (Cambridge: Cambridge University Press, 2004) pp. 759–60.
27. Peter Ackroyd, *Dickens* (London: Minerva, 1991). All references to this edition.
28. M. M. Bakhtin, 'Discourse in the Novel' in Michael Holquist (ed.), *The Dialogic Imagination* (Austin, TX: University of Texas Press, 1981) pp. 301–8.
29. Peter Ackroyd, *Dickens*, pp. 610–45.
30. Peter Ackroyd, *Dickens*, p. 622.
31. See especially Roland Barthes, 'The Death of the Author' (1968) in Stephen Heath (ed.), *Image-Music-Text* (London: Fontana/Collins, 1977) and Michel Foucault, 'What is an Author?' (1969), in D. F. Bouchard (ed.), *Language, Counter-Memory, Practice* (Oxford: Basil Blackwell, 1977).

32. For the evolution of the idea of genius as a masculine attribute see Christine Battersby, *Gender and Genius: towards a feminist aesthetics* (London: The Women's Press, 1989).
33. Thomas Carlyle, 'The Hero as Man of Letters: Johnson, Rousseau, Burns' in Carl Niemeyer (ed.), *On Heroes, Hero-Worship and the Heroic in History* (Lincoln: University of Nebraska, 1966) p. 154.
34. Fichte quoted by Carlyle, 'The Hero as Man of Letters', pp. 156–7.
35. Thomas Carlyle, 'The Hero as Man of Letters', p. 156.
36. Thomas Carlyle, 'The Hero as Man of Letters', p. 155. But see Carlyle, *Past and Present* (1843), book 4, chapter 7, for a more unambiguous use of 'genius'.
37. Thomas Carlyle, *Past and Present*, book 4, chapter 7, cited in Peter Ackroyd, *Dickens*, p. 320.
38. Peter Ackroyd, *Dickens*, p. 319.
39. Peter Ackroyd, *Dickens*, p. 320.
40. Peter Ackroyd, *Dickens*, p. 320.
41. Peter Ackroyd, *Dickens*, pp. 1025–6.
42. Peter Ackroyd, *Dickens*, pp. 321–2.
43. Friedrich Hegel, *Introduction to Aesthetics* in T. M. Knox (trans.) and Charles Karelis (intr.) *Hegel's Introduction to Aesthetics: being the introduction to the Berlin Aesthetics Lectures of the 1820s* (Oxford: The Clarendon Press, 1979) p. 39.
44. Friedrich Hegel, *Introduction to Aesthetics*, p. 39.
45. Friedrich Hegel, *Introduction to Aesthetics*, p. 39–40.
46. Peter Ackroyd, *Dickens*, p. 146.
47. Peter Ackroyd, *Dickens*, p. 322.
48. Cited in Peter Ackroyd, *Dickens*, p. xi.
49. Thomas Carlyle to John Foster, cited in W. Forbes Gray, 'Carlyle and John Forster: An Unpublished Correspondence', *Quarterly Review*, 268, January–April 1993, p. 280.
50. Peter Ackroyd, *Dickens*, p. xv.
51. Peter Ackroyd, *Dickens*, p. 324.
52. Peter Ackroyd, *Dickens*, pp. 324–5.
53. Peter Ackroyd, Dickens, p. xv.
54. *The Mystery of Charles Dickens* opened in London's West End in 2000. It has toured England and the United States, played briefly on Broadway and, lately, been shown on TV. It is available on DVD.
55. David M. Halperin, *Saint Foucault: towards a gay hagiography* (Oxford: Oxford University Press, 1995) p. 62.
56. Peter Ackroyd, *Dickens*, p. xv.
57. See the Thomas Hood poem, 'Silence', that is the epigraph to Jane Campion's film *The Piano*, discussed in 'Retuning *The Piano*', p. 150.
58. For this discussion see David Glover, 'Masculinities', pp. 74–8, and Norma Clarke, 'Strenuous Idleness: Thomas Carlyle and the man of letters as hero', in Michael Roper and John Tosh (eds), *Manful Assertions: Masculinities in Britain since 1800* (London: Routledge, 1991) p. 41.
59. James wrote that *Our Mutual Friend* was 'the poorest of Mr Dickens's works. And it is poor with the poverty not of momentary embarrassment, but of permanent exhaustion', cited in Peter Ackroyd, *Dickens*, pp. 1021–2. In the late 1880s and early 1890s James would write a series of short stories

that play with the theme of the 'exhausted' or played-out great writer. See 'The Lesson of the Master', 'The Middle Years' and 'The Death of the Lion' in Henry James, *Selected Tales* (London: Penguin, 2001).

60. Leon Edel was a one-man James industry. His five-volume *Henry James* (London: Hart Davis, 1953–72) was compressed into a two-volume *The Life of Henry James* (Harmondsworth: Penguin, 1977). Edel edited the four-volume *Letters of Henry James* (London: Macmillan, 1953–74). There is not yet a complete edition of James's letters. I recommend Philip Horne (ed.), *Henry James: a life in letters* (London: Penguin, 1999) for an excellent synoptic view of James's writing life.
61. Cited in Philip Horne's 'Introduction' to *Henry James: a life in letters*, p. xx.
62. Jonathan Freedman, 'Introduction: The Moment of Henry James', in Jonathan Freedman (ed.), *The Cambridge Companion to Henry James* (Cambridge: Cambridge University Press, 1998) p. 1.
63. Jonathan Freedman, 'Introduction', p. 1.
64. Jonathan Freedman, 'Introduction', pp. 18–19.
65. Cambridge University Press has seemed determined to corner the James industry. Titles from 1991, excluding the *Cambridge Companion* cited above, are: Judith Woolf, *Henry James: the major novels* (1991); Merle A. Williams, *Henry James and the philosophical novel* (1993); Edwin Sill Fussell, *The Catholic Side of Henry James* (1993); Kevin J. Hayes (ed.), *Henry James: the contemporary reviews* (1996); Sara Blair, *Henry James and the Writing of Race and Nation* (1996); Gert Buelens (ed.), *Enacting History in Henry James: narrative, power, and ethics* (1997); Richard Salmon, *Henry James and the Culture of Publicity* (1997); Beverly Haviland, *Henry James's Last Romance* (1997); Hugh Stevens, *Henry James and Sexuality* (1998); Colin Meissner, *Henry James and the Language of Experience* (1999); Robert B. Pippin, *Henry James and Modern Moral Life* (2001); Tessa Hadley, *Henry James and the Imagination of Pleasure* (2002); Andrew Taylor, *Henry James and the Father Question* (2002); Eric Haralson, *Henry James and Queer Modernity* (2003); Alfred Habegger, *Henry James and the 'Woman Business'* (2004).
66. My summary of James's critique of the project of writing an historical novel is drawn from two sources: Henry James, 'American Letters', *Literature* (1898) and Henry James to Sarah Orne Jewett, 5 October 1901 in Philip Horne (ed.), *Henry James: a life in letters*, p. 360.
67. Adam Mars Jones, 'In his master's voice', *The Observer*, Sunday, 22 February 2004.
68. Michael Wood, 'What Henry didn't do', *London Review of Books*, 26: 6, 18 March 2004. Martin Ryle hit upon 'abstention' as the theme of *The Master* in a conversation on 4 March 2006.
69. Wood, in his review cited above, comments on Tóibín's use of style that: Language is taken away from James rather than given to him, which brings him closer to us than he might otherwise be. Not that Tóibín's language is jarringly contemporary or slangy. It is just not an imitation; it is lighter and less ornate than the Master's own.
70. Colm Tóibín, *The Master* (London: Picador, 2004) p. 16.
71. Colm Tóibín, *The Master*, p. 20, p. 19.

72. David Lodge, *Author, Author* (London: Secker & Warburg, 2004) pp. 57–62 and pp. 284–5.
73. David Lodge, *Author, Author*, p. 58.
74. Roland Barthes, *The Pleasure of the Text*, p. 62.
75. Andrew Bennett, *Romantic Poets and the Culture of Posterity* (Cambridge: Cambridge University Press, 1999) pp. 3–4.
76. David Lodge, *Author, Author*, p. 375.
77. David Lodge, *Author, Author*, p. 375.
78. David Lodge, *Author, Author*, p. 382.
79. David Lodge, *Author, Author*, p. 382.
80. David Lodge, *Author, Author*, p. 382.
81. Colm Tóibín, *The Master*, p. 359.
82. Alan Hollinghurst, *The Line of Beauty* (London: Picador, 2004).
83. Alan Hollinghurst, *The Line of Beauty*, p. 312.
84. Alan Hollinghurst, *The Line of Beauty*, p. 54.
85. Alan Hollinghurst, *The Line of Beauty*, pp. 396–7.
86. In Andrew Davies's adaptation of *The Line of Beauty* for BBC2, broadcast in May 2006, this ambivalent ending is left in place, with perhaps less foreshadowing of positive (i.e. fatal) results since we don't have access to Nick's dark thoughts. The results of Nick's third blood test which is shown, is, as in the novel, in the future.
87. Reviewing Lodge's *The Year of Henry James* (London: Harvill Secker, 2006) in the *Times Literary Supplement*, 9 June 2006, p. 40, Henry Hitchings concludes that Lodge's
    story of professional disappointment is also an act of self-exculpation and self-consolation, and it never takes account of the very real possibility that *Author, Author* was simply not as accomplished as *The Master* – or indeed as his own best work.
88. Paul Gilroy, *Postcolonial Melancholia* (New York: Columbia University Press, 2005).
89. Michael Holroyd, *Lytton Strachey*, vol. 2, pp. 615–16.
90. Anthony Storr, 'Psychiatry and Literary Biography', in John Batchelor (ed.), *The Art of Literary Biography* (Oxford: Clarendon Press, 1995) p. 74.
91. The novel, with James's notes for its completion, was published posthumously in 1917. Henry James, *The Sense of the Past* (New York: Charles Scribner's Sons, 1945).

Historical Fictions – Pastiche, Politics and Pleasure

In the early years of the swinging sixties, I and my young contemporaries, like twentieth-century generations before us, called all repressive attitudes towards sex, whatever their actual national or historic origins, 'Victorian'. The scorn with which the term was used implied that the 'Victorian' view of the world was so outmoded that to invoke its taboos amounted to a ludicrous and pitiable attempt to return to the world of one's great-grandparents. 'Victorian' was regularly applied, for example, to the resurgent postwar moralism espoused by our parents, a conservative turn which was nothing if not contemporary in its impulse. Yet while 'Victorian sexuality' may have been, for us, an oxymoron, the persistent presence of 'Victorian' as the unhealthy antonym to the sexual freedom demanded – among other liberties, social and political – by progressive postwar generations, indicated a lingering belief in its residual cultural power, as well as, perhaps, a reluctant fascination with the world it evoked. For the dominant sense that the 'Victorian', defined as a socially coherent world view, was definitively *over* – twice dead after the social and political transformations of two world wars – provided a psychological as well as cultural distance that rendered the Victorian period harmless in its ability to affect the present, and, as a consequence, ripe for reassessment and renarration, a readiness marked by renewed interest in its ideas, its inventions, its political aspirations and its imaginative literature.

These conflicting attitudes towards the Victorian had unexpected, and positive, cultural effects. The postwar drive to complete the de-Victorianisation of Western societies, exemplified by the call for freedom of expression, liberated our ways of knowing the nineteenth century. The state's embattled and eroding suppression of sexually explicit literature were 'Victorian', we thought, in its fully punitive sense, even though the key obscenity trials that defined such censorship and kept it in the public mind were all directed at twentieth-century fiction: *Ulysses* (1922), *Lady*

Chatterley's Lover (1928), *The Well of Loneliness* (1928). Through the 1960s, as the courts in Britain and the United States reluctantly reversed their positions on what were by then modernist classics, thus implicitly widening the scope for the legal distribution of literary erotica, the re-publication of Victorian pornography became possible also, its texts sometimes offered in paperbacks with lurid covers, but prefaced with an antiquarian gloss and a thin veneer of scholarship. When, in 1964, critic Stephen Marcus outed *The Other Victorians*, alerting readers to the presence of an 'exotic subliterature that fermented far beneath the "respectable" surface of mid-Victorian society', sex was reintroduced into our ideas of Victorian society, but the exposure of its seamy underside only confirmed the repressive hypothesis we had grown up with, proof positive of the Victorians' collective duplicity and double standards.[1] Nowhere was this more visible than in the Victorian literary canon – the novel especially – still present in our school and university curricula, and in spite or perhaps because of its own silences and inhibitions, still stubbornly popular with general readers. *The Other Victorians* capitalised on this popular presence in its emphasis on sex as a form of *writing* – and by implication reading. It introduced an idea that would give a new twist to the way in which sex and the Victorians were conjoined, shifting the attention from practices to representation, from forbidden fucking and secret lives to sex imagined – sex in the head – and transcribed – sex on the page.

My interest in fictional Victoriana in the last half century begins at this oddly contradictory conjuncture, when the libertarian impulses of the 1960s, so invested on the one hand in driving a final stake through the heart of Victorian values, reanimated them on the other through its prurient curiosity about the period. (Something of the same investment can be seen at work in the 1790s, that revolutionary decade which saw the remarkable flowering of the gothic novel just as the rise of the rationalist philosophies attacked religious and supernatural beliefs as mere superstition.) The strange belatedness of the literary imagination, the way in which it often lags behind the real-time of belief systems while making its own thrifty use of its remnants and discards, is one element in the continuing popularity of fictional Victoriana. Sexuality may be the leitmotif of these fictions, but other themes emerge as they too become emblems of a past whose power over the present had been broken. When the end of class society in Britain was declared in the postwar decades, Victorian class culture became another available antiquarian topic for fiction to explore, its taboos and excesses almost as exciting and exotic as Victorian sexuality. And as Britain's industrial heart declined and disappeared, so writers turned their gaze, with something less than nostalgia, onto the nineteenth-century culture of work.

Above all, however, these novels were a symptom of a surprisingly passionate reinvestment in the language and structures of Victorian print culture, especially its fiction and poetry, a reignited affair with a rich and reliable old flame, long neglected and foolishly abandoned for the cosmopolitan delights of literary modernism.

As I suggested in the last essay, Henry James's famous, forbidding judgement on the historical novel as a literary project 'condemned . . . to a fatal *cheapness*' because of the difficulty of thinking '*with your modern apparatus*' about the consciousness of persons 'whose own thinking was intensely-otherwise conditioned', acted as a challenge rather than a prohibition to ambitious writers of Victoriana in the last quarter century.[2] Acknowledging the difficulties of making pastiche read like what James called 'the real thing', they responded to his warning by putting his realist criteria in quotation marks, knowingly embracing the cheap and fraudulent as part of the pleasure of historical pastiche – the best if not the most real thing about it. In John Fowles's *The French Lieutenant's Woman* (1969), the Victorian story is told and interpreted by a loquacious modern pedant, who constantly interrupts its freshly antiqued language and dialogue to offer helpful asides on the period. Or pastiche goes operatic, an over-the-top performance in several literary genres by different characters and literary figures – poetry, letters, journals, stories as well as retro Victorian narration and dialogue alternating with a thoroughly modern comic novel – as in A. S. Byatt's *Possession* (1990), whose subtitle *A Romance* explicitly rules out any expectation of traditional realism. In case modern readers think romance is a love affair rather than a literary form, *Possession* glosses it through epigraph, that helpful convention of nineteenth-century fiction, citing a well-known gobbet from the Preface to Nathaniel Hawthorne's historical novel, *The House of the Seven Gables* (1851), which defines Romance as expressing 'the truth of the human heart' in opposition to the 'Novel' which aims for 'minute fidelity, not merely to the possible, but the probably and ordinary course of man's experience'. In case we are still looking for 'truth' of some sort, the second epigraph, from Robert Browning's 'Mr. Sludge, "the Medium"' comments satirically on the 'helpful lies' of the writer of fiction and biography.[3] History is here somewhere, if only in its fictional lies, but its precise temporality, like its 'truth', is uncertain. Historical fiction has to be a Romance, argued Hawthorne, as 'the Romantic definition lies in the attempt to connect a bygone time with the very present that is flitting away from us'.[4] Never historical fiction's easiest mode, mimetic realism becomes merely another style to be parodied in Byatt's Victorian excursions. Victoriana sometimes dispenses with historical narrative altogether, as in the novel with which this book begins Brian

Moore's *The Great Victorian Collection* (1975), a surreal meta-commentary on the impossible desire to possess the Victorian past, set in 1970s California. David Lodge's *Nice Work* (1988) locates its characters in his home town Birmingham, codenamed Rummidge, explicitly referencing Victorian industrial fiction, drawing on its narratives, themes and forms to write a wholly contemporary satirical novel. Borrowing postmodern styles, but adapting them to retro genres and themes, the hallmark of innovative historical fiction in the last third of the twentieth century was a juxtaposition of heavily ironised late twentieth-century commentary and the self-conscious cleverness of the Victorian reference, as imitation, citation or rewrite. The readers of these novels and others like them written between the late 1960s and the new millennium, have been encouraged to enjoy the alterity of their narrative modes and points of view, and to appreciate their apparent destabilisation of what might constitute 'history' or the 'historical' in the historical novel. This highly reflexive style is starting to seem less than current, part of the discursive fashions and cultural debates of the *fin de siècle*. Clear swings in formal strategies are hard to track across a genre that has become so capacious and lucrative that it contains several mini-genres, including pastiche Victorian crime fiction and mass-market romance. For reasons that I will try to address at the end of this essay, middlebrow Victoriana, which depends neither on over-elaborate pastiche nor an intrusive authorial presence, has been making a comeback at the high end of the market in the last few years. For the discussion which follows, which ranges over the shifting history, politics and aesthetics of postwar fictional Victoriana, I have singled out key novels by John Fowles, David Lodge, A. S. Byatt and Sarah Waters, all critical and commercial successes which highlight historical fiction's uneasy relationship between the present and the Victorian past.

Smartening up the Sex Novel – Victoriana goes to College: *The French Lieutenant's Woman*

With his 'internationally bestselling *The French Lieutenant's Woman*, a novel of Victorian sexuality', John Fowles put the postwar fictional reprise of the Victorian on the global cultural map as 'serious' art with a popular appeal. Its protagonist is a young, middle-class, intellectual Englishman, Charles, drawn to Sarah, the mystery woman of the title, made sad, mad and notorious the length and breadth of Lyme Regis, the effect of her supposed seduction and betrayal by a callous French officer. Pastiche passages alternate with commentary on them by the book's pedantic modern narrator whose own history remains untold. Fowles's novel took its overt premise from the common sense which labelled the Victorian period as a society whose class-governed rules of behaviour imperilled and punished those who broke them, a society and individuals tormented by imposed sexual conformity, but with a freshly exposed seam of transgression running through it. *The French Lieutenant's Woman* both made waves and rode them, heightening the revival of literary Victoriania. Even without help from the hit film starring Jeremy Irons and Meryl Streep in 1981, it sold solidly throughout the 1970s as the blurb, cited above, from the eighth reprint of the Triad Granada paperback in 1978, clearly shows. Its startling success helped to reverse the declining critical fortunes of the historical novel, a genre out of favour with the modernist sensibilities of an interwar literary avant-garde. For with a few notable exceptions – Robert Graves's *I Claudius* (1934) and Mary Renault's postwar classical cycle – historical fiction for adults had become an undemanding staple of middlebrow and lowbrow fiction: mildly salacious novels in costume with a particular appeal to the woman reader.[5]

Interestingly, Fowles chose to trope on this generic stereotype rather than rejecting it entirely, cleverly gathering a new audience without alienating readers faithful to the genre itself. He borrowed shamelessly from the language of popular romance, especially from the suggestive naughtiness couched in lavender prose of the middlebrow interwar sex-novel. (We might include here such late examples as the Margaret Mitchell blockbuster *Gone With the Wind* (1940), or Radclyffe Hall's earlier, more daring and criminalised *The Well of Loneliness* (1936).) In deliberate contrast to the unexpurgated D. H. Lawrence, James Joyce, Norman Mailer and Henry Miller, sailing off the shelves of the bookstores in the late 1960s, sex as a described event is barely present in *The French Lieutenant's Woman* – what the novel has instead is sex as fantasy, sex as unanswered and impeded desire, sex as a kind of everpresent, quasi-pleasurable, but always agonistic discourse. The novel has a lot to say about this kind of compulsive thinking, but it is a disappointing read for anyone looking for explicit erotic detail. Writing sex can, however, take many different forms. What Fowles brings off in the pastel prose of the pastiche sections of *The French Lieutenant's Woman* is perhaps no more than Mitchell or Hall achieved in something of the same vein, or that Victorian writers themselves were expert at – Emily Brontë in *Wuthering Heights* for example. *The French Lieutenant's Woman* libidinises longing and frustration, so that the description of the Victorian man and woman's psychic struggle with forbidden lusts substitutes for the full frontal literary fornication that was becoming *de rigueur* in twentieth-century prose. On the other hand, writing as a self-conscious practice in this novel, as with others I will consider below, is deeply connected to the erotic manoeuvres that are *The French Lieutenant's Woman*'s leitmotif and narrative occasion.

This artful circumspection, interrupted by the narrator's rambling commentary and digressions, is the novel's rhetorical coup, at once setting *The French Lieutenant's Woman* apart from what were being established by experts as the 'high' literary erotics of Joyce and Lawrence, but distinguishing it also, through its metacommentary, from middlebrow historical fiction. Fowles is best known as a novelist for whom sex is a central concern – perhaps too central: during the years when his wife Elizabeth was his confidant and first reader she regularly persuaded him to tone down the language and limit the number of sex scenes.[6] Yet sex – as a topic and narrative pretext for the novel – is less an obsession in *The French Lieutenant's Woman* than, like its heroine, an elusive and tantalising lure, its realisation and its aftermath deferred by the authorial persona's hovering presence in the pastiche sections and his visible manipulation of his plot. We are never allowed to forget, for more than a few pages, that the sex-effect in the novel, as well as its retro characters, is produced by language.

The story in *The French Lieutenant's Woman* borrows many of its sensational components from the twentieth-century bodice ripper, but instead of history lite, bound seamlessly into the narrative through a bland authorial voice or expository dialogue, history is dragged in with a capital H, courtesy of its teacherly voiceover that reminds us both of our temporal and philosophical difference from the Victorian world and of the author's ever-present control of the narrative. The idiosyncratic but anonymous narrator with his intrusive social facts, obvious historical comparisons and heavy-handed digressions, is, as an early reference to Brecht suggests, designed to alienate the reader from the seductive identification with the story and its protagonists. He is, however, so deliberately unsympathetic a presence – easily imagined as an aging autodidact, with the reader as captive audience – that he can never compete with the intricate narrative for our attention. Yet through his carefully calibrated crankiness, Fowles does introduce a crude but crucial new virility into what was becoming a largely feminised form, by presenting his story from the doubly masculine perspective of the unnamed narrator and Charles, the leading character. The achievement of *The French Lieutenant's Woman* proved surprisingly hard to replicate. Although it opened the door to much greater formal experimentation with the historical novel, its success suggesting that the audience for historical fiction would respond to more substantive and more argumentative accounts of the past, perhaps no faux Victorian novel really compared with it in terms of critical approbation and sales until A. S. Byatt's *tour de force Possession*, in 1990; Sarah Waters's lesbian Victoriana at the end of the decade was another, and initially rather surprising, success story. Michel Faber's eight-hundred-page blockbuster, *The Crimson Petal and the White* (2002), was also critically well received; regularly, if mistakenly, called 'Dickensian', it recounts the picaresque adventures of Sugar, a Victorian prostitute, as told by an anonymous modern narrator-cum-pedagogue, who guides the reader through the London slums, echoing Fowles's storytelling strategy, but including the kind of sexual detail that appears in the subliterature cited in *The Other Victorians*.[7]

The undisguised pedantry of *The French Lieutenant's Woman*, whose narrator often seems to be addressing a seminar of attentive students rather than common readers, signals the way in which the novel constructs its imagined audience as undergraduates and its unfolding narrative as a learning curve. It set up the possibilities for fictional Victoriana as having a pedagogic as well as a purely pleasurable function, one that flatters its expanded audience with its seriousness, encouraging later practitioners in this vein to develop variations on its theme. As universities, in line with Tory policies, continued to expand student numbers in the 1980s, English departments acquired new prestige and some unwelcome notoriety for their promotion of theoretical work. Theory and its discontents becomes the touchstone for the representation in literary Victoriana of the sometimes symbiotic, sometimes rivalrous relationship between imaginative writers and the academy. Authors like Byatt and Lodge – themselves formidable critics with distinguished academic careers – have always been more engaged than enraged by theory, interested and sometimes partisan commentators on the ferocious opposition it encountered, setting it to work as well as sending it up in their fiction. *Nice Work* is the third of Lodge's academic novels to track the transformation of English as a transnational discipline. Taking its cue from Fowles, perhaps, it is the most overtly didactic of this trio, its omniscient narrator and the characters conducting in indirect discourse and in dialogue a book-long exposition of the economic and cultural plight of Britain in the 1980s. In *Nice Work*, Lodge thematises the culture wars of the decade by making the real-life rancorous debates about literary theory at Cambridge – 'featured', as Lodge says, 'in the national and international press' – an episode in the personal history of Robyn Penrose, the novel's heroine.[8] Robyn's undergraduate career was spent at trendy Sussex University in the early 1970s, a time, in Lodge's account, 'immediately after the heroic period of student politics' when left wing students looking for a cause were struck with a sense of 'belatedness'.[9] As a young postdoctoral scholar at Cambridge who believed that 'critical theory had at last moved to its rightful place, centre-stage, in the theatre of history', Robyn takes part in 'the great debate about the future of the English Faculty' staged in the University Senate.[10] At Cambridge Robyn is exposed to 'structuralism and postructuralism, semiotics and deconstruction, new mutations and graftings of psychoanalysis and Marxism, linguistics and literary criticism', new ideas which incite a 'civil war' in the English Faculty, and feel to Robyn like 'revolution'.[11] Robyn's attachment to theory, here imagined as the substitute for an earlier generation's single-minded passion for left wing politics, is balanced with her self-definition as a feminist and a fighter for social justice. Mirroring the move that the novel itself is making, her interest in contemporary theory and her fascination with nineteenth-century realism are represented as both paradoxical and logical – the late 1980s is the moment when theory and historicism find a new détente. The same constellation of interests, without the left-leaning politics, is realised by Byatt in *Possession* whose acknowledgements for the 'use of copyrighted material' include the Institute for Psycho-Analysis for two extracts from Freud, and Tavistock Publications for a chunk of Lacan's *Écrits*. Maud Bailey, the novel's 'modern' female protagonist, is like Robyn Penrose a theoretically sophisticated feminist literary scholar who focuses on nineteenth-century poetics, and especially the work of her ancestor, the imaginary poet Christabel LaMotte. These novels instantiate the way in which the humanist and anti-humanist, and the realist and the anti-realist impulses of theory and imaginative writing begin to develop a productive rather than an adversarial relationship. In *Possession*, Maud, the theorist, forms a professional alliance that blossoms into romance with Roland Michell. Roland, whose name rolls together medieval, Victorian and poststructuralist associations, is a rigorous scholar who has studied theory, but defines himself as a traditional textual critic, His PhD, *History, Historians and Poetry? A Study of the Presentation of Historical 'Evidence' in the Poems of Randolph Henry Ash*, with its historicist preoccupations and its interrogatory bracketing of 'evidence' echoes the novel's own destabilisation of history and truth. Yet at the novel's opening, his seemingly unfashionable critical approach has supposedly made him unemployable in British English literature departments; by its close, only a short time later, he is a sought-after hire in Amsterdam, Hong Kong, Barcelona, a sign perhaps of the return of cultural history and textual analysis to favour. At the end of the novel Roland reinvents himself as a poet: it is not clear that he will continue in academia at all, but Maud, in contrast, stays on. Academia suits her. She and women like her for whom literary history and theory are compatible resources are its future. There is a hint that the Victorian period has undergone a degree of feminisation, both in its objects of study and in those who work on it. In both *Nice Work* and *Possession*, a revived interest in Victorian literature and society is associated with the ascendancy of feminists as literary scholars and the priority of gender and sexuality in their work. This history goes back to the early 1970s, when feminism launched a full-scale rewrite of the literary canons and social history of the long nineteenth century, initially written within the framework of traditional humanism, but the next formation of academics – to which Robyn Penrose and Maud Bailey belong – are influenced, as these novels suggest, by semiotics, psychoanalysis and deconstruction.

Rather than dismissing it as a debased form, the cluster of theoretical approaches that have become embedded in university English departments have benefited the reinvention of the historical novel. They have queried both the vertical and horizontal division of discourses, blurred distinctions between fact and fiction, disturbed the divisions between the popular, middlebrow and the avant-garde, and given genre fiction of all kinds new status as a literary form. If one looks beyond the opening up of its curriculum however, the evolution of the modern university in the last three decades has a distinctly darker side. Its increasing emphasis on productivity, specialisation and corporate and commercial identity tends to support – on behalf of 'standards' and professionalisation – some of the very categories that literary theory has been trying to undermine. And here lies some of the appeal of the mid-nineteenth-century for contemporary authors. The Victorian period was a time when domains of knowledge were slowly coming to be – but were not yet – fully institutionalised, and this anterior or even transitional moment is in part the attraction for authors, expressed in different ways in their pseudo-Victorian fictions. *The French Lieutenant's Woman*'s narrator is deeply nostalgic about the 'amateur' scholar and thinker; its protagonist Charles – not wealthy exactly but with expectations and financial independence – dabbles in geology and discusses Darwin with Lyme Regis's intellectual GP. In Brian Moore's *The Great Victorian Collection*, as in *Possession* and *Nice Work*, the modern university is in deep trouble – punitive and bureaucratic in Moore's Canada, cash starved in Lodge's Britain and under threat of colonisation by American academic entrepreneurs in both Lodge and Byatt. The Victorian world appears for some of these authors as an imagined past where knowledge and creativity operated in a milieu less regulated by the state and more integrated in its understanding of the world, even if more bounded by social convention and haunted by inequalities.

Fowles's narrator is a a twentieth-century academic manqué, and we the readers become his hapless pupils, as he instructs and bores in turn with nuggets of Victorian social and political history and his own opinions, the text dotted with occasional explanatory footnotes, Victorian style. His all-knowing voice is full of references to those eminent Victorians, Marx, Darwin and Freud. Marx, the most important, enters in his most humanist incarnation in an epigraph from *Zur Judenfrage* (1844) just below the book's title: 'Every emancipation is a restoration of the human world and of human relationships to man himself'; he is described early on as a variety of independent intellectual, 'that beavered Jew silently working . . . in the British Museum Library'.[12] Marx is part of the narrator's cultural capital; yet while he is a contemporary of the novel's educated characters, he is not part of their world. Brian Moore's tragicomic hero, the young Canadian history lecturer obsessed with Victorian things about which he knows a great deal, also has limits put on his knowledge. The conceits of the novel show that the author's own reading is more wide-ranging and cosmopolitan: Ideas from Benjamin, Freud and perhaps even Baudrillard are immanent in the surreal narrative of *The Great Victorian Collection*.[13] David Lodge rewrites Elizabeth Gaskell's *North and South* as a witty social and cultural commentary on Thatcher's Britain. Giving Phillip Swallow – his fictional academic alter ego from the earlier academic novels *Changing Places* (1975) and *Small World* (1984) – a minor role at last, Lodge invents a 'shadowing scheme' through which lecturers from the university and managers in local industry learn about each other, a plot line that permits Robyn Penrose to use the rude double meaning of the Silk Cut cigarette billboard ad to explain first year semiotics to her 'shadow' opposite, rough-hewn northern industrialist Vic Wilcox.

Shamelessly raiding Lodge's well established satires of Anglo-American academia and its transatlantic antics, A. S. Byatt makes all the modern characters in *Possession* English or American academics pursuing lost manuscripts, letters and missing biographical detail.[14] Her academic cast includes every strand of literary criticism, from young feminist Lacanians and deconstructionists to editors, biographers and more conventional feminist critics, most of whom, the retro romantic young hero and heroine aside, are fairly sketchy cartoon creations. In spite of Byatt's own dazzling ability to move across the critical and creative field – or perhaps because of it – in *Possession* there is a not-so-subtle competition between critical and creative talents that is expressed in both the plot and its enunciation. Roland begins to write poetry himself, good poetry, and this gift, which 'comes to him' magically towards the end of the novel, alters his relationship to himself, turns him from plodding traditional scholar to a different kind of subject altogether.[15] *Nice Work* takes its glamorous female semiotician seriously, or as seriously as a comic novel can, but in *Possession* the cards are subtly stacked against even the most sympathetic academic characters from the start: their preoccupations pale against Byatt's own rich, and above all literary, authorial voice, whose ear for the sound and sense of Victorian language goes beyond the reproduction of the formal rhythms of diary and letters, something she does well, but which many historical novelists can achieve, to the more challenging invention of their imaginative poetry and prose. *Possession* performs imitation as if it were a better, and certainly higher, criticism.

We can see the infighting between the interdependent but also autonomous arenas of writers and writing and criticism within the university as a symptom of the uncertainty about the financial health and cultural prestige of both domains in the last couple of decades, a crisis for which the conditions of Victorian cultural and intellectual life provide a useful foil – contrasting and correlative at the same time. But the faux fiction that I am concerned with has more serious ambitions on the order of those treated in the Victorian novels on which its life depends. Indeed they have, as it were, borrowed the seriousness and moral purpose of the Victorian world, even at times its tone, overriding both modernism's critique of the hollowness of that purpose and postmodernism's default cynicism.

If Victorian sexuality has been the dominant theme for narrative Victoriana in literature, film and theatre it has not simply taken the form of exposing the repressed and repressive Victorians as hypocrites obsessed with sexuality, nor, on the other hand does it necessarily confirm Michel Foucault's brilliant and influential inversion of the repressive hypothesis, which, at the end of the 1970s, argued that the proliferation rather than the suppression of the discourses of sex was what characterised the nineteenth century.[16] From Fowles through Waters – and with some exceptions like Faber's *The Crimson Petal and the White* – there has been instead more than a hint of nostalgia for a less sexually knowing and brazenly expressive society – a version of the old fart's complaint that the 'mystery', and with it the sexiness, has been taken out of sex. It is perfectly possible to read *The French Lieutenant's Woman* as a reaction against, not an advertisement for, the sexual revolution of the 1960s. Its maligned and self-accusing heroine, Sarah Woodruff, assumed to be the French Lieutenant's 'whore' by the Lyme Regis population, turns out to be a virgin whose only sexual encounter is with the stuffy, conscience-stricken protagonist, Charles Smithson. Her dilemma – and his – at the end of the story is whether she opts for a conventional marriage, or remains a 'bohemian' – not quite, but almost, a New Woman of sorts – living in the pre-Raphaelite, Rossetti household, and, arguably, bringing up Charles's child on her own. In this ending

Sarah keeps hold of her 'integrity', but sacrifices passion. The defense of her integrity is defined as a form of self-possession which at one level is simply her social and psychological independence, and at another much more perverse. Recognising this, in the second ending Charles

> saw his own true superiority to her: which was not of birth or education, not of intelligence, not of sex, but of an ability to give that was also an inability to compromise. She could give only to possess; and to possess him – whether because he was what he was, whether because possession was so imperative in her that it had to be constantly renewed, could never be satisfied by one conquest only, whether . . . but he could not, and would never, know – to possess him was not enough.[17]

The double ending of the *French Lieutenant's Woman*, often cited for its postmodern irony and open-endedness, works to frustrate readers' expectations of, and desire for, the romantic and sentimental genre; it acts as an interruption of our affective identification with certain clichéd tropes of love and family that is also a parody of the narrative prose that produced them. In the first ending the reconciliation of the lovers is made through the recognition that Charles has fathered a daughter, Lalage, and its falseness is signalled by its stylistic segue into stock romantic prose:

> At last she looked up at him. Her eyes were full of tears, and her look unbearably naked. Such looks we have all once twice in our lives received and shared; they are those in which worlds melt, pasts dissolve, moments when we know, in the resolution of profoundest need, that the rock of ages can never be anything else but love, here, now, in these two hands' joining, in this blind silence in which one head comes to rest beneath the other . . .[18]

The second ending, and the fact of two possible endings, marks the novel's deliberate intention not to offer the reader the romantic closure it has just satirised. This begins with an epigraph from Matthew Arnold's 1869 *Notebooks*, 'True piety is *acting what one knows*' coupled with a deeply secular and cynical one from Martin Gardiner's *The Ambidextrous Universe* (1967): 'Evolution is simply the process by which chance (the random mutations in the nuclei acid helix caused by natural radiation) co-operates with natural law to create living forms better and better adapted to survive'.[19] It ends with an assertion of individualism joined to a soft version of socialist humanism – citing a modified Marx – '*the actions of men* (and of women) *in pursuit of their end*' augmented by a throwaway reference to existentialism.[20] Independent agency, which both Charles and Sarah acquire in the anti-romantic ending, is not a simple good, but is represented as having been won at considerable emotional cost – it does not come free for either party. The close of *The French Lieutenant's Woman* is less a 'new' postmodern strategy than one recycled from Victorian realism, recalling the double ending of *Villette*, for which Charlotte Brontë reluctantly supplied the option of romantic closure to please her father. In its withholding of romantic felicity, Fowles's novel also evokes the uncertain end of *Middlemarch*. In the exculpation of its 'fallen' heroine from the abjection of 'ruin', it seeks to overturn the judgmental closures of Victorian fiction – the less than charitable ending in Elizabeth Gaskell's *Ruth*, for example, where the seduced seamstress must pay for her youthful fault by death while nursing her wicked seducer during a smallpox epidemic, or the even more retributive *The Mill on the Floss*, in which George Eliot drowns her heroine merely for compromising her reputation rather than physically losing her virtue.

There is something distinctly punitive nevertheless in Charles's realisation that Sarah is driven by her almost abstract desire to possess, in contrast to his more generous, normal, loving nature. The Victorian fictions which Fowles's novel reprises are narratives whose sexual and class politics *The French Lieutenant's Woman* can be seen both to critique, and, in a perverse way, reproduce. The unenviable role of fallen or working-class women in a profoundly class-ridden society is emphasised by the narrator throughout the novel, with little or no sympathy accruing to their female social superiors. Yet in Fowles there is a complex, but loosely causal link between Sarah's initial madness and her subordination as a woman – it is certainly one of the determinations of her obsession and melancholy. How much of this is due to the effects of libidinal repression and how much to the class snobbery and uptight morality of Victorian society – its moribund emphasis on and fixation with respectability – is left somewhat moot. In the final pages, Charles sees Sarah's withholding nature as more cruel than the effects of the social prejudice and false morality that he hates. On the whole, Fowles's novel is clearer about the evils of class society and the more straightforward social oppression of women than it is about the impasse between the sexes. Even when driven by mutual sexual desire, sexuality is a domain where Charles and Sarah's own levels of anxiety, denial and negativity seem paralleled by the equally convoluted and paradoxical position of the authorial consciousness, whose sympathies lie largely with Charles. And Charles himself, in the course of the novel, is made to listen to, if not buy into, a range of nineteenth-century views, moral, religious and medical, about female sexuality and madness. No more than Freud, and with something of the same ambivalence about women's demand for independence, can Charles, or his narrator, or Fowles, find out what the women they have constructed really want.

Yet the novel, even in its final unforgiving moments, has a kind of prescient clarity. Written on the very verge of the second wave of the

Women's Movement, *The French Lieutenant's Woman* is peculiarly alive
to the ways in which both men and women of Victorian modernity – and
the author's own – are trapped by unassimilable and mutually exclusive
desires and aspirations; their psychology and their world views seem to
separate rather than unite them the more they each strive for and espouse
a kind of equality. Sarah Woodruff is less a coherent or credible character in the novel than a cut-up or montage of types and anti-types of the
feminine arranged to suggest a new prototype for thinking gender. As a
writing strategy this identity, which shifts with each turn of the plot,
never quite works, but the ways in which it doesn't work are fascinating
if we look at them in relation to the feminist critiques which would be
launched in Britain and the United States in the same years.[21]

And, as other fiction in the genre written two decades later in the ebb
of second-wave feminism make clear, while feminism gives a language
and a living politics to the impasse between men and women in modern
European societies, before and after a formal equality is set in place, it
resolves none of the questions of sexuality, sexual difference and gender
that it so urgently and eloquently poses. For in those fictions in which the
late twentieth century is juxtaposed with the nineteenth, our own
moment is seen to suffer as much from the hypocrisy of liberation as the
Victorian did from the effects of repression. In Byatt's *Possession*,
Randolph Henry Ash, the composite nineteenth-century poet, has a wife,
Ellen, who, we discover at the novel's end, has suffered from an atavistic fear of sex so profound that she could never bear her, gentle, much-
loved husband to come near her. Though less redolent of casebook
pathology, the young twentieth-century lecturer, Maud Bailey, suffers
from a similar malaise, in its way as painful as Ellen's, who does not fear
intimacy even if she cannot express it physically. Maud confesses to her
would-be lover Roland in the last pages of the novel (although we know
it much earlier) that she is terrified of feeling altogether: 'When I feel –
anything – I go cold all over. I freeze. I can't – speak out. I'm – I'm – not
good at relationships.' Her cool good looks makes others see her as a
potential 'property or an idol' – a problem for all women who have
a vocation and, like her ancestor, Randolph Henry Ash's lover, the
minor Victorian poet Christabel LaMotte, Maud wants to protect her
'self-possession, her autonomy' so that she can 'go on *doing my work*'.
That work is defined as being about boundaries: 'I write about liminal-
ity. Thresholds. Bastions. Fortresses' says Maud, and Roland adds,
'Invasion. Irruption' to which she replies, 'Of course'.[22] Maud's object of
study and herself are figured here as identical. Awkward and unrespon-
sive, or at least not orgasmic in her infrequent sexual encounters, Maud's
hang-ups, Byatt implies, are as cruel a disability as Ellen's, at least in a

world where everyone is assumed to be sexually confident. *Possession* lives up to its subtitle – it is a romance in the generic and affective sense – and Byatt generously allows Maud to find heterosexual love and sexual satisfaction at last with Roland. Their future success in finding what Roland terms 'a modern way' to be together is set against the more compromised resolution of the Victorian story, the illicit affair between two Victorian poets which has a bittersweet conclusion, suggesting that, after all, the contemporary with its freedoms, its rampant individualism and its resources has its advantages.

Given its prominence in the final pages of *The French Lieutenant's Woman*, it is more than plausible, I think, to read Byatt's *Possession* as in part addressing and critiquing the misogynist discourse of possession in Fowles. Sarah's desire to possess involves some tortuous twists of both psychology and plot through which she misrepresents to the world at Lyme, as well as to Charles, her supposed transgressive relationship with the French Lieutenant. Her manoeuvres and manipulations are pathologised in the novel's second ending as the only and very controlling way in which she can imagine love, providing a good reason why Charles might do better to abandon her to her independent life, and take ship once more for America and a different future. In Fowles there are only two alternatives for women who crave psychological and financial autonomy through work – Sarah finds her employment as amanuensis to Dante Gabriel Rossetti 'so pleasant' it doesn't feel like work – one must accept the subordinate femininity of normative heterosexuality and motherhood or go for the unconsoled loneliness of autonomy. Byatt, in contrast, tries to distinguish between bad and good forms of possession and independence. When Roland finds a way to take 'possession of all' Maud's 'white coolness' she is liberated into both 'pleasure and triumph' and a more traditional heterosexuality, adjusted, as it always is Byatt's fiction, to twentieth-century egalitarian norms.[23]

Faber's *The Crimson Petal and the White* can also be read as an engagement with Fowles, with the sexual revolution and with feminism. Its protagonist Sugar who specialises in satisfying every desire no matter how depraved, and was brought up in a brothel by its madam, an embittered woman, is herself at work on a never-finished novel about a prostitute who becomes a serial killer of men. An appetitive reader, Sugar becomes the mistress of a man who makes soaps and perfumes, and in the least credible of its plot developments becomes nurse and governess and rescuer to his neglected little daughter and an ambiguous 'saviour' to his mad wife, whose insanity is overdetermined: sexual ignorance, Catholic fanaticism and a brain tumour all play their part. Misanthropic rather than misogynist, *The Crimson Petal and the White*'s women are the only sympathetic gender in the novel. William, the student rake turned bourgeois industrialist, becomes a subordinate character to Sugar, just as Sarah is to Charles in *The French Lieutenant's Woman*. In countering Fowles's suspicion of intelligent manipulative women with a more 'feminist', supportive take on them, and by folding Victorian pornographic language into his story (offering a few tidbits to male as well as female readers) Faber inverts without really altering the antagonistic structure of gender in Fowles's novel. As with Fowles and Byatt, Faber's female protagonist must be vulnerable but exceptional, in intelligence and beauty if not entirely in her ethical trajectory. Faber's literary skills are all in his detailed, nuanced accounts of Victorian settings and personal feelings; Sugar and William are narrative occasions for local descriptions of both place and affect, rather than characters whose psychological development is credible. In a last improbable twist of plot at the end of the novel, Sugar successfully absconds with the child, Sophie. Faber's resolution for them is nevertheless partly traditional, reinstating the good maternal – the ex-whore and her ward – in place of the novel's wicked and rejecting mothers at either end of the class spectrum.

All Work and No Play – Rewriting the Industrial Novel

In contrast to its obsessive interest for the Victorian protagonists in Fowles, in David Lodge's anti-sentimental *Nice Work*, sex and love in the 1980s is seen to be overrated – the enduring pleasure for its academic heroine and its middle-manager industrial hero alike is work. The 'nice work' of the title is an ironic refutation of the Gershwin song it cites, which argues in its introduction that 'The only work that really brings enjoyment/ Is the kind that is for girl and boy meant./ Fall in love – you won't regret it./ That's the best work of all – if you can get it.'[24] Robyn in *Nice Work* is bored by sex and romance, and her boredom is due neither to repression or acute disappointment. Her theoretical stance (which includes her belief that there is 'no such thing as the "self"' and 'no such thing as an author'), the industrial novels she writes on and teaches, and her own personal experience all suggest to her, in different ways, that it is not life's high point or a realisable goal.[25] Instead, Lodge argues, only half tongue in cheek, that work is and should be a libidinised enjoyment for the old and the new middle classes, whether it is running a factory or teaching the politics and semiotics of the Victorian novel. Lodge is here echoing the salience of work as a preoccupation and satisfaction in Mrs Gaskell's *North and South* (1854–5), a story in which gender inequality and class and regional differences are resolved both in terms of plot and affect by allowing the middle-class heroine, Margaret Hale, first to inherit and then to invest in the factory of the man she loves.[26] The Victorian work ethic was heavily fetishised, and not only by Victorian social conservatives like Thomas Carlyle, who never distinguished between the degrading or alienated labour of the poor and the intellectual 'work' of the middle-class author, but equally, with more nuanced distinctions between alienated and unalienated labour, by novelists and thinkers across the political spectrum. Work now and then is a touchstone for all the examples of fictional Victoriana I have cited. *Nice Work* makes sure we know what authors and books from the 1840s and 1850s are being referenced by citing or mentioning them, sometimes with their dates, in its opening pages – Elizabeth Gaskell's *Mary Barton* and *North and South*, Benjamin Disraeli's *Sybil: or the Two Nations*, Charlottë Brontë's *Shirley*, Charles Dickens's *Hard Times*, George Eliot's *Felix Holt*. About work and class, they are also the raw material of Robyn's labour, since analysing the structure and themes of the Industrial Novel in her writing and teaching is her vocation and avocation. (Her first monograph, *The Industrious Muse: Narrativity and Contradiction in the Industrial Novel* marks her out early in the novel as a productive academic.) Lodge makes the point that teaching is 'work' by intercutting Robyn's lectures on the Industrial Novel with Vic Wilcox's day at the factory, one a Marxist and feminist overview, the other the quotidian detail of the forces pressing on industrial life in Britain in the 1980s. The metropolitan money culture, whose workings are also given a synoptic airing in *Nice Work*, wins no ethical or aesthetic prizes in Lodge, but is treated with comic cosmic disdain. Robyn's brother Basil works in the City, and her ghastly sometime boyfriend, Charles, quickly follows his example, leaving poorly paid academia as fast as he can to sell shares on the Stock Exchange. There he has a brief affair with Basil's girlfriend, Debbie, a woman who has gone straight from her East End family of bookies to the hard work and the high life of a broker with no modification of her horrid estuary vowels.

Nevertheless, a resigned *realpolitik* pervades *Nice Work*, echoing Gaskell's belief in both *North and South* and *Mary Barton*, that organised resistance to the inexorable and impersonal nature of market forces is useless. While Lodge attacks Mrs Thatcher's decimation of 'the national system of higher education' in the 1980s, activist resistance to it in the pathetic 'one day strike' of the Association of University Teachers is represented as merely symbolic, and the wildcat walkout at Vic's factory, Pringle's, suicidal. They are as counterproductive as the long-term failed strike at John Thornton's factory in *North and South*, or both strike and Chartist petitions in *Mary Barton*.[27] When naïve, liberal

Robyn deliberately tells Danny Ram, one of the South Asian workers at Pringle's foundry, that he is about to be fired, this triggers a threatened strike. Vic makes her apologise to the worker, and angrily underlines his earlier explanation that a strike would be dangerously self-defeating for the largely immigrant work force.[28] Robyn's intervention wins tiny, grudging concessions on the part of management, but they too are little more than symbolic. It is Robyn's ideological stance born of ignorance, rather than Vic's unconcerned acceptance of labour market realities, which is behind the times, Lodge implies. Gaskell's economic liberalism is still operative, but not her middle-class female sympathy for the poor, which is as ineffective now as it was in the 1850s. What does survive in Thatcher's Britain, is Gaskell's belief in the national talent for honest industrial entrepreneurship. In *North and South*, the struggles to keep John Thornton's mill going when the trade cycle declines are contrasted with the get-rich-quick schemes of investors, which Thornton declines; his refusal to take such risks impoverishes him, but is narratively rewarded by Margaret Hale's support. While Robyn, following her left wing bibles – *Marxism Today* and *New Left Review* – argues that the economy is dominated by multinationals which will soon crush the little manufacturer, Vic replies 'Don't you believe it . . . There'll always be small companies'; at the end of the novel he is similarly rewarded by Robyn's offer to put her inheritance into just such an independent venture.[29] Lodge's anti-romantic solution turns back approvingly to the world of small business – the world, after all, from which Margaret Thatcher, the grocer's daughter, sprang, if not the one she brought into being. Turning from the more trans-Atlantic and European landscapes of his earlier academic novels, especially *Changing Places* (1975) and *Small World* (1984), *Nice Work* mounts an oddly conservative defense of Little Britain against both the United States and Europe – a high point is reached when Vic and Robyn go to Frankfurt and outwit some sneaky German industrialists. *Changing Places* acknowledged the seductive appeal and some of the virtues as well as the lunacy of 'Euphoric State', the West Coast campus where the bewildered British academic Phillip Swallow goes on exchange. Britain's University of Rummidge, Phillip's home institution, was, by contrast, represented as hopelessly provincial, staffed by scheming rivals and madmen in the manner of Kingsley Amis's *Lucky Jim*. *Small World*'s hilarious account of the globalisation of literary academia, as its faculties skip from conference to conference, is brushed but not bruised by Lodge's cynicism: like *Possession*, which imitates much of its tone in its 'modern' narrative, it is billed as a 'romance'. But by the late 1980s, with the British university system under siege – 'death by a thousand cuts' – Lodge, like many other academics, was out of love with Big Academia and busy defending the financially struggling but intellectually lively world of British higher education against the rich corporate giants of the American university system, who were ruthlessly head hunting faculty across the Anglophone world.[30] Yet Vic seems to win the argument he has with Robyn about university underfunding; his short answer is that the beleaguered economy cannot afford more public money for it. Referencing the Victorian fiction upon which *Nice Work* is built, Lodge turns a revisionary eye on what critic Raymond Williams, a crucial, cited source for Robyn's university lectures, has called the 'magical' endings of the novels of the 1840s, arguing as Robyn says in paraphrase of Williams, that 'a legacy, a marriage, emigration or death' were 'all the Victorian novelist could offer as a solution to the problems of industrial capitalism'.[31] As Margaret Hale does in Elizabeth Gaskell's *North and South*, Robyn Penrose inherits money from an avuncular family friend, a windfall which helps her decide to reject an offer from an American university in favour of Rummidge – Anglophone academia's small business – as well as back Vic Wilcox's entrepreneurial venture. Lodge's progressive attitudes towards gender embrace both Robyn's middle-class feminism and a fantasy of traditional domesticity, each played out through different class scenarios: Vic's new business will employ his bored wife and alienated children, saving his marriage and uniting his family, while Robyn is allowed to pursue her academic career as an independent working woman.

The changes that Lodge makes to the plot and message of *North and South* are telling ones, and few of them suggest that the 1980s have more viable solutions to the problems of the day than those imagined in the Victorian novel. Lodge's renarration of class and ethnic issues are particularly disheartening. The immigrant Irish, as scabs, or as the lowest element of the working class in Britain, make brief and unhappy appearances in Gaskell's novels as a degraded group in contrast to the much more sympathetic English poor. For Lodge, the non-white immigrant to Britain in the 1980s presents a larger problem of representation. The Irish in Birmingham in the late twentieth century are heavy-handedly caricatured in his earlier *Changing Places*; in *Nice Work* these scapegoats of the English Victorian imagination are replaced by non-white immigrants who stand in for all of the alienated or potentially troublesome working class – they seem, at points, to be all that is left of it. In the early pages of the novel,'[t]hree black youths with huge, multicoloured knitted caps pulled over their dreadlocks like tea-cosies lean against the plateglass window of the shopping-precinct café, drumming a reggae beat on it with their finger-tips until shooed away by the manageress' while inside Vic's wife and daughter, and other white women, drink cappuccinos and talk of the 'trouble in Angleside', the 'black ghetto of Rummidge' where youth unemployment runs at 'eighty percent and rioting is endemic'.[32] A Rastafarian leeringly offers to sell Robyn a joint at a stop light. At Pringle's, on the shop floor, the 'knockout' where the product emerges seems to Robyn 'like the anus of the entire factory', the castings like 'iron turds' presided over by a 'gigantic West Indian, his black face glistening with sweat, bracing himself with legs astride in the midst of the fumes and the heat and the din'. Robyn immediately revises the symbolism of the scene in her imagination so that it appears in abolitionist terms, with the West Indian as 'the noble savage, the Negro in chains'[33] but her self-edited response is satirised as knee-jerk liberalism, and the passage reads like a parody of the heroic chapter linking work and black labour in Herman Melville's masterpiece, *Moby Dick*.[34] Grotesque, threatening or near-anonymous, the plight of non-white British subjects may be, as Lodge suggests, deepened by Thatcherism, but *Nice Work* not only keeps them at arm's length but intensifies their difference from white Britons. *Mary Barton* and *North and South*, in contrast, devote a large part of their narrative to the representation of working-class life, exploring, with full recognition of the antagonistic interests at stake, the possibility of sympathy and understanding across class lines. In Gaskell's fictional imaginary these rapprochements are sometimes, but not always, senti-mental. In *North and South*, John Thornton, the hard master of the mill, painfully learns how to work with, rather than against, his work force through his embattled but productive relationship to Nicholas Higgins, one of the strikers, whose family and friends Margaret Hale befriends. Not even this limited interchange or détente seems possible or plausible in Lodge's rewrite. Simplifying the fine-tuned regional class distinctions in Gaskell, the white working class in *Nice Work* is virtuously repre-sented by the first-generation managerial class who have emerged from it, upwardly mobile Vic and his family, or less sympathetically, Debbie the cockney trader. Factory workers and the unemployed are more racially and culturally distinct even than Gaskell's English poor and the debased Irish, and are largely disempowered. The Asians at Vic's foundry and a black gardener at the University are anonymous figures, their only agency their threat – or lack of it – to order. Lodge's strategy for empha-sising how much is left to be done in a progressive agenda is to exagger-ate the marginality and powerlessness of these Britons, closing his novel with a scene on the university lawns of the imaginary Rummidge, where the 'young black' man pushing his mower and the students in his path do not exchange 'nods, or smiles, or spoken words, not even a glance'. The narrator comments on their 'mutual, instinctive avoidance of contact. Physically contiguous, they inhabit separate worlds. It seems a

very British way of handling the differences of class and race'.[35] The
irony of this remark leaves it poised between praise and blame. In this
vignette, Lodge echoes Disraeli's memorable comment in his novel *Sybil*,
one of two epigraphs to *Nice Work*, that England was composed of
'[t]wo nations; between whom there is no intercourse and no sympathy',
a view whose predictive description not only came from the Victorian
right, but was significantly at odds with the imaginative rendering of
cross-class 'intercourse' and 'sympathy' as well as conflict and antagonism, at the centre of *North and South* and *Mary Barton*.[36] Cross-class
romance, even that limited one between the successfully aspirant
working class and the downwardly mobile intelligentsia, seems,
strangely, more taboo in Lodge's 1980s than in the 1840s. Vic and
Robyn's affair is abortive, and even Charles gives East End Debbie her
walking papers. By merging the disparate agendas of Disraeli and
Gaskell, and writing class and racial difference in the 1980s as if it were
a reciprocal 'instinctive' aversion, something nationally conditioned and
biologically embedded, the novel implies that social antagonism, rather
than an historically specific problem of the late twentieth century, will,
like the poor, always be with us. In this respect Lodge shifts his novel,
consciously or unconsciously, nearer to Thatcherism if not to the right
of it. His political pessimism at the success of the Thatcherite putsch
leads him to repress the history of any resistance to it, or any alliance
between rebellious constituencies that is seen to have failed. University
staff strikers are ridiculed, and the solidary actions of the Thatcher years,
including the cross-class support for the Miners' Strike of 1984, the anti-
racial movement and rallies of the late 1970s and early 1980s are simply
ignored in this novel. The implication that there were no, rather than not
nearly enough, non-white students in British higher education, or that
Britain's multicultural society did not exist, rather than existing in contradictory and unequal ways, presents us by default with a political
image of modern Britain as more hopelessly divided than the bleakest
visions of nineteenth-century industrial fiction.

In both *Possession* and *Nice Work*, the political certainties of the old
left and even of a more durable traditional liberalism are seen to be crum-
bling. Certainly nothing of the supposed dignity of skilled manual labour
remains to be admired. When Robyn visits the dirty, deafeningly noisy
floor of Pringle's Foundry she thinks it is 'the most terrible place she had
ever been in her life'.[37] The degradation of manual labour – in Lodge a
seamless awfulness from the Victorian period to the present – is a way of
highlighting the relative privilege of Robyn's life, even if her job, like
those of the workers at Pringle's, is radically insecure. *Nice Work* does
end on a positive note. Its glimmer of optimism is located in a regional,

cross-gender, and cross-occupational unromantic alliance among the old and the new white middle class – in Lodge's novel represented by Robyn's sturdy utopianism, her commitment to teaching, and Vic's equally stubborn entrepreneurial and creative ambitions, as well as their ability as friends to learn from and support each other. Heartening as this may be in gendered terms, it is a strongly conservative view of social alliance and progress. In *North and South*, in contrast, there are three interacting social groups – genteel white women, white male industrialists and workers and their families (including women) – whose rapprochement makes the future possible. For Lodge, in the late 1980s, these liberal hopes are at odds with reality. Robyn may go on teaching them enthusiastically to her Rummidge students without doing any significant harm; the theory and the literature that Vic learns to enjoy in his shadowing of Robyn's 'nice work' may provide him with cultural pleasure but little else. A cynical and meritocratic philosophy is embedded in Lodge's satire, which anticipates and even approves, through its broad comic outline, the smooth transition from Tory government to New Labour, supported by a new and unpleasant note, for Lodge, of racism and xenophobia. *Possession*, in contrast, is both less politically engaged and less actively reactionary. Byatt does not even entertain Lodge's simple prejudices about the Thatcher years, for while she makes excellent fun of the greedy international race to track down Christabel LaMotte's revealing correspondence with her lover, Randolph Henry Ash, she has no overt quarrel with the new monied culture of Britain in the 1980s, which is glimpsed through minor characters as fun-loving and upbeat.

Pleasuring the Reader

However much the Victorian world, refracted through its imaginative writing, acts as a foil for arguments about culture and politics today, it is the rediscovered joys of Victorian literature that draws modern novelists back to the nineteenth century. In both the Victorian and the modern worlds of *Possession* it is romance, love, and poetry, together with the libidinised life of the mind, that makes life worth living. In a fascinating aside near the end of the novel Byatt intervenes as author to talk about the delights of reading: to tell us that while it is 'possible for a writer to make, or remake at least, for a reader, the primary pleasures of eating, or drinking, or looking on, or sex . . . they do not habitually elaborate on the equally intense pleasure of reading'.[38] Reading, like sex or thinking, has, Byatt suggests, its productive and unproductive practices, but these are located less in the nature of the text than in the mood, the receptivity, of the reader. *Possession* describes the 'perverse' nature of reading pleasure,

> the *mise-en-abîme* even, where words draw attention to the power and delight of words, and so *ad infinitum*, thus making the imagination experience something papery and dry, narcissistic and yet disagreeably distanced, without the immediacy of sexual moisture or the scented garnet glow of good burgundy.[39]

She endorses, in contrast, those characters – the soon to become poet Roland is one – for whom reading is primarily a sensuous experience, something 'violently yet steadily alive', 'heady', an affective, embodied, immediate, but not unthinking pleasure. Distinguishing between different kinds of readings of a single text, 'dutiful',' personal', 'impersonal', *Possession* opts best of all for an uncanny reading experience in which the text appears wholly new and already known, 'which make the hairs on the neck, the non-existent pelt, stand on end and tremble'.[40]

Byatt's discussion of the pleasures of reading might be imagined as in conversation with Roland Barthes's *The Pleasure of the Text*, almost certainly one of its silent referents. While *Possession*'s different categories of reading pleasure, which start with the subject, not the text, do not neatly map on to the distinctions that Barthes draws between the bliss (*jouissance*) and the pleasure (*jouer*) of reading, a common focus on the intensity and temporality of the reading experience is reflected not only in the meditation just cited but in the novel's structure and enunciation. *Possession*'s elaborate use of historical pastiche, its showy and skilful imitation of the public and private genres of writing – diary, letter, poetry, memoir, story – makes the experience of reading it hard to describe, producing a contradictory set of reading pleasures, that Byatt's discussion complicates without fully clarifying. Through its story and its use of pastiche, *Possession* implies that, discursively at least, the Victorians had it all – a kind of polymorphous perverse paradise of expression, a lubricious logocentrism which proves a compensatory sensuous resource in a time of restrictive sexual and social mores. *Possession* attempts to convey something of the expressive richness of Victorian discourse via bravura imitation, but these efforts cannot elicit, nor can they really be meant to, the response we might have to Victorian originals; the effect of their presence is rather to cool down than warm up the reading experience. In *Possession*, the sheer variety of Victorian literary styles, the elaborately spun web of parodies and pastiche serves only to draw attention to Byatt's very modern consciousness, her chameleon cleverness. The more virtuoso the passage of literary pastiche – Christabel LaMotte's poetry for example, written in imitation of at least three poets, Christina Rossetti, Emily Dickinson and Elizabeth Barrett Browning – the more the

reading experience becomes exclusively cerebral. The wittier the composite figures, the more plausible the mock poetry and prose, the more
whatever might be the 'Victorian' in the novel disappears into its simulation, so self-sufficiently enclosed within the text's own invented world,
that no Victorian 'outside' is present or necessary. The temptation to skip
these passages – while promising to return to them – is, in my case at
least, irresistible. (Barthes is reassuring on this point: all good readers
skip; to read every word is to be a plodding, passive reader.[41]) Only when
we return to the prose narratives of the Victorian and modern romance
plots, with their more traditionally told stories of desires foiled and fulfilled can we come upon anything remotely like the sensuous reading
pleasure that Byatt describes. However, Barthes points out that erotic
mimesis – sex on the page – is just what cannot induce the higher pleasure, the bliss, the *jouissance*, of reading, but represents instead a discourse of desire and of disappointment: the erotic, he mischievously says,
as deconstructed by psychoanalysis.[42] Pastiche poetry might be thought
of as a similar sort of tease and let down, a kind of instant reprise of
seduction, expectation and anticlimax. Within *Possession*, the more the
threads of the Victorian and modern plot are drawn together – its lost
letters found and mysteries resolved – the less comfortably we sit as
common readers, and the less clear it is which kind of pleasure, papery,
dry and perverse, or hot, moist and straight, we are being asked, or
allowed, to have.

Yet this very disordering of reading expectations may be a clue to
Possession's huge success with its audience, which surely rests on the different orders and intensities of reading it provides, its oscillations between
styles, genres and periods, between comic and sentimental address.
Traditional and innovative, comforting and disturbing, *Possession* might
be judged to aspire to both of Barthes's registers of textual enjoyment. At
its most conventional it can be seen as the

> Text of pleasure: the text that contents, fills, grants euphoria; the text that
> comes from culture and does not break with it, is linked to a *comfortable* prac-
> tice of reading.

At its most paradoxical it can almost be a

> Text of bliss: the text that imposes a state of loss, the text that discomforts
> (perhaps to the point of boredom), unsettles the reader's historical, cultural,
> psychological assumptions, the consistency of his tastes, values, memories,
> brings to a crisis his relation with language.[43]

Indeed Barthes's ideal reader is an 'anachronic subject' – a subject out of
time, but in control of his reading experience,

who keeps the two texts in his field and in his hands the reins of pleasure and bliss . . . for he simultaneously and contradictorily participates in the profound hedonism of all culture . . . and in the destruction of that culture: he enjoys the consistency of his selfhood (that is his pleasure) and seeks its loss (that is his bliss). He is a subject split twice over, doubly perverse.[44]

The same tensions between radical form and conventional content appear in Fowles's, Byatt's and Faber's portrayal of transgressive female sexuality through the figure of an elusive, exceptional woman. This figure is a woman with a history, a palimpsest of the representations of excessive female behaviour that runs from *Moll Flanders* forward, subsuming the seduced and abandoned heroines of the eighteenth-century novel through the self-defining individualists of the nineteenth century, including their neurotic or dangerous counterparts in George Eliot and in sensation fiction as well as the maddened heroines in Hardy. Treated today with more sympathy than censure, resistant and/or transgressive Victorian women quickly became a staple cliché of this genre of Victoriana, their redemption through work of different sorts reflecting their authors' implicit faith in the crude moral economy that replaces lust with labour. Almost all of the novels in this genre, from *The French Lieutenant's Woman* through Sarah Waters's *Fingersmith*, find this figure irresistible: from the late 1960s onwards she remains oddly durable in the hands of leading writers, even when her mild lesbian proclivities – hinted at in a brief voyeuristic peek in Fowles, homophobically expressed in Byatt – become a more complicated sexual and social identity in Waters. Fowles's Sarah Woodruff is, as I have said earlier, a syncretic figure: as a kind of tropic time traveller of the feminine, if not as a quasi-realist 'character' she makes narrative and political sense. Byatt's Christabel LaMotte, as a poet an awkward synthesis of Christina Rossetti and Emily Dickinson, with perhaps a touch of Barrett Browning without the politics, turns out also to be a woman-with-a-past who is narratively freed from its taint through her relationship with Ash. Christabel's betrayed and vengeful lover, the talentless painter Blanche Glover, in turn betrays the adulterers to Ash's wife Ellen, and later commits suicide in despair. This vignette, not in its particulars perhaps but in its component parts, reminds us of Mary Wollstonecraft's early strong attachment to her friend Fanny Blood who died young, and any number of other passionate female attachments in the century that follows. However, Byatt's negative depiction of Blanche as neurotic constitutes a silent refutation of the generative or artistically productive possibilities of woman-to-woman love documented and celebrated by historians of sexuality, beginning with Lillian Faderman's groundbreaking *Surpassing the Love of Men: romantic friendship and love between women from the Renaissance to the present* (1981). Even Byatt's 'modern' story has its gratuitous homophobic element, developed in the novel's comic vein through the American lesbian feminist academic Leonora Stern, who cheerfully but vainly pursues Maud Bailey. Leonora, pushy, proselytising but philosophical when refused, is easy to resist, about as sexy as that other jolly American 'professional' best friend, the journalist Henrietta Stackpole in Henry James's *Portrait of a Lady*. Byatt's romantic investment in good heterosexual sex, aligned in *Possession* to the straight sensuality of good reading, is a symptom of her sexual conservatism which guides her selective use of feminism in her treatment of both present and past, a feminism happiest when it is most traditional, celebrating female 'genius' and the poetic deployment of the feminine figure in the past, and professional excellence and success in women academics in the present.

There is a delicate balance between reward and punishment struck in the plot resolution of *Possession*. Christabel seems to do penance both for her affair with Ash and her abandonment of Blanche. While she suffers no guilt for her affair she blames herself for Blanche's cruel death. In the modern dénouement, a buried and unread letter from Christabel to Ash when he is dying, is, literally, dug up, a letter in which Christabel confesses to him that he has a daughter who has been brought up as her sister's child.[45] In it she tells Ash that the child has no interest in poetry, and does not love her strange and solitary aunt. Punishment indeed, and there is more: Christabel dies without knowing whether her letter has been read. The discovery indicates at first a poignant instance of the failure of the Victorian plot to achieve full sentimental closure. But in the Victorian ending to *Possession*, we are treated to a scene in which Ash, searching for Christabel, meets the child, Maia, and recognises her instantly as his own, an ending which resolves, for the reader if not the characters, a fantasy of full disclosure, reconciliation, family. Earlier, I suggested that *Possession* conducts a vigorous and persuasive intertextual argument with *The French Lieutenant's Woman* on the theme of possession, countering the misogyny that descends on the novel as Sarah morphs from pathetic victim to manipulative agent. In contrast to the sentimental satisfactions of *Possession*, the second, ferociously anti-romantic ending to Fowles's novel in which the question of whether Sarah has had Charles's child is left entirely ambiguous, looks ever more intellectually and politically interesting in its refusal of domestic felicity, and in its refreshing skepticism about whether men and women can, after all, come together on common ground.

The critical success of Sarah Waters's trio of 'Victorian' fictions, *Tipping the Velvet* (1998), *Affinity* (1999) and *Fingersmith* (2002) – the last shortlisted for both the Man Booker and the Orange Prize – suggests how firmly the faux Victorian novel, together with other historical fictions, has established its popularity with readers and its upmarket address. Waters's novels mark a decisive shift away from the self-conscious narrative strategies that worked so well for writers from Fowles through Byatt. For while Waters has written a PhD dissertation on lesbian historical fiction – research, she has said, that revealed the potential of an underdeveloped genre – it is the distinctive first person voices of her female narrators and characters which dominate her fictions; no authorial persona, pedantic or proselytising, intrudes. Well-researched, tightly plotted, stylishly written, these fictions owe a great deal in tone, structure, story and language to their nineteenth-century models and inspiration: Charles Dickens, Wilkie Collins, Charlotte Brontë, Oscar Wilde, Robert Louis Stevenson. But they wear these referents lightly. The use of pastiche is bold and self-confident – each novel marks itself out as 'modern' in its depiction of same sex relationships – imagining 'a history . . . the sort of history that we can't really recover'.[46] Nevertheless, unlike Faber's *The Crimson Petal and the White*, which keeps lesbianism at arm's length and in the brothel, Waters's books are built on the combined scholarship that historians of sexuality, together with feminist, gay, lesbian and queer studies, have uncovered. They are underwritten by the postwar social and cultural history of nineteenth-century London in particular, with its emphasis on gender, on the poor, on popular culture and on the pseudo-sciences, especially spiritualism. The novels fold those historical accounts back into nineteenth-century fictional forms: the picaresque, melodrama and ghost story of Victorian fiction, borrowing also from the pornographic subliterature revealed in *The Other Victorians*. Even *Tipping the Velvet*, the first and sunniest of the three novels, the one that Waters now regrets having dubbed a 'lesbian romp', has its darker aspects; these elements were cleaned up or passed over in Andrew Davies's excellent television adaptation, which exploited the music hall setting of part of the novel to great advantage, but drew the line at depicting the heroine's seamiest down-and-out-in-London moments. Desire, pleasure, possession and betrayal between women is explored in all three novels, most bleakly in *Affinity*, most successfully perhaps in *Fingersmith*, in which two girls, one from the criminal underclass, one the illegitimate child of a genteel woman, are switched in infancy. Both Susan Pinder and Maud Lilly, who become lovers, betray each other in the course of the convoluted plot but are reunited at the end. Lesbian romance in Waters's hands is never a simple democratic alternative to the battlefield of unequal heterosexual relations, a strong plotline in *Fingersmith* only, but is fraught with its own power relations and emotional violence. The very different narrative closures to each of the three novels suggest the variety of uses to which Waters puts the Victorian setting. *Tipping the Velvet* takes Nancy Astley from the dining room of her father's oyster parlour in Whitstable to the music hall, and the secret, vicious culture of wealthy lesbians, to its final scene, a socialist rally in the East End's Victoria Park six years later, where Nan, pledged to an activist partner, Flo Banner, finds herself using her dramatic skills to give a ringing speech denouncing capitalism.[47] *Affinity* ends, chronologically at least, with the despairing suicide of the emotionally unstable middle-class Margaret Prior, daughter of an eminent historian. Margaret becomes a prison visitor and falls in love with a manipulative and devious spiritualist incarcerated there, Selina Dawes.[48] A leading theme in *Affinity* is power struggles between women, all of them painful, some brutal and perverse. The prison, the home, and the spiritualist's parlour offer different settings for these scenarios, but no escape. *Tipping the Velvet* imagines Victorian lesbianism as a hidden practice with a subculture that has, in its most hopeful incarnation in the last section of the novel, a strong relationship to developing progressive politics; the demonstrations in Victoria Park remind this late twentieth-century Londoner of nothing so much as those summer events staged in the good old days of the Greater London Council in the early 1980s when the so-called loony left – loony because of its egalitarian policies on sexuality and race – was briefly in ascendance. *Affinity*, in contrast, portrays a Victorian dystopia: its narrative spirals downward into a fugue of depression along with its middle-class protagonist, portraying at every class level a female world of large and small tyrannies and injustices, where even the women who escape are bound together by forms of domination and submission.

Fingersmith has a more complicated sexual and cultural imaginary – Dickens and Collins are very visible in its underclass London scenes and in the gothic terrors of country house and asylum which are vividly evoked.[49] Its changeling plot emphasises nurture rather than nature in the development of Maud and Susan, but depends also, through the figure of Mrs Sucksby, on a distorted but still sentimental and biological version of maternal love. There are plenty of examples of nurturant and affectionate female relations in Waters, but women are as prone to cruelty as men. In all three novels the Victorian setting provides a space for Waters to emphasise the sadistic – if not necessarily the masochistic – side of masculinity and femininity. In the 1980s a major debate erupted among feminists generally and within lesbian feminism in particular about the nature of women's sexual fantasies, the limits of erotic literature and the ethical boundaries of same sex practices – what was the moral status, for example, of lesbian sado-masochism? The sexual imagination of women rather than men came under intense scrutiny, spawning conferences, books and demonstrations.[50] *Fingersmith* replays aspects of this debate in Maud Lilly's story. Partly raised in the madhouse where her mother had been incarcerated, Maud is taken home by her rich Uncle Lilly, a cold and bullying sadist, whose unrivalled collection of pornography attracts a coterie of male aficionados. Her resistance defeated by whipping and incarceration, precisely detailed, Maud is groomed to read her uncle's dirty books aloud to select male company, and to copy the precious texts. Her education consists of a heavy overdose of salacious literature. Not surprisingly she fears men and fancies women, and wants, above all, to escape her uncle's house, but her erotic imagination is indelibly influenced by her reading. In a surprise twist at the end of the novel, Maud finds her vocation in writing pornography herself. She is back in her dead uncle's country mansion, now hers, but with Susan, at last, as her lover. Like the historical novel in which she is imagined, Maud imitates with a difference the perverse erotic discourses through which she has been constructed, as a woman, and as a character. Ironic, but in no way punitive, this ending can be seen as a celebration and libertarian defense of the sexual and the literary imagination, and its appropriation by women writers today.

Fingersmith, via Maud's forced role as scribe and reader to her uncle, and her final career turn, highlights the question of reading pleasure, history, aesthetics – and sex on the page – in fictional Victoriana. For Waters the Victorian world is a space of invention, a supplement to what 'real' history, and even the most sensational and melodramatic of Victorian fiction do not tell us – a researched history fully imbricated with an imaginary one. More than many historical novelists, who regularly append bibliographies to their efforts, Waters leaves the distinctions between history and fiction open. In *Affinity*, Margaret's dead father, the eminent historian, 'used to say that any piece of history might be made into a tale: it was only a question of deciding where the tale began, and where it ended'. Margaret contrasts her own writing project 'which has so many separate lives in it, and is so curious a shape, and must be approached, so darkly, through so many gates and twisting passages' to his straightforward account of 'great lives, the great works, each one of them neat and gleaming and complete, like metal letters in a box of type'.[51] As Margaret decides, when she tries to think how she might tell the 'history' of Millbank Prison, it is the story of people through its gates that is the starting point, not raw statistics: the date of the building of the prison, which one learns in the morning but forgets by evening, is almost irrelevant. For Waters, although she says she starts with the plots, it is the subjective female voice, the confessional voice that Raymond Williams found, to his dismay, in *Jane Eyre* and identified as the innovative, and for him deeply problematic, element of the Victorian novel, that represents a vital continuity between writing in that Victorian moment and our own. There is much less anxiety and angst in Waters's use of the Victorian than in the self-conscious, self-referential fiction from Fowles through Byatt. Her research is embedded in the writing, which neither wears the academic qualification of the author on its sleeve, nor, as in Lodge or Byatt, is interested in singling out the university as the modern centre of knowledge about the Victorian. Theory and literary criticism underpins these narratives as generic emphasis, in settings, in themes: it does not parse the narrative for us, or cut it up into bite-sized lessons. One can, if one wants to look for it, see the influence of Michel Foucault's work in Waters's writing – the focus on the asylum and incarcerating institutions more generally, as well as a light-touch application of his argument that sexual discourse in the nineteenth century was not repressed but expanding. Equally, the serious issues of sexual politics and sexuality raised in each novel are developed without any pedantic aftertaste, which even skilful, part-pastiche efforts like Faber's feel they must retain. The pastiche ploys of the novels, especially their brilliant use of the sensational and gothic, mark their resistance to realist criteria or postmodern irony. Waters makes no distinction between entertainment and enlightenment; the 'modern' analogies I have been drawing are not underlined, but must all be the work of the reader who will derive others or none at all, bringing to the reading fictions their own particular histories and cultural capital.

Connecting a 'bygone time with the very present that is flitting away from us', was Hawthorne's tantalising definition of historical romance. His deliberately ambiguous notion of the disappearing present – is it 'flitting' before or behind us – does it matter? – makes the point that the temporal relationships in the historical novel are never as fixed as they at first look, and may, through their very attempt to connect two moments, disturb our sense of time altogether. It is interesting in this respect that Byatt and Lodge, through their modern narrators and stories, give the present a specificity so precise that it already is a past; only a few years on and *Possession* and *Nice Work* seem 'historical', not in their imitation of and reference to the Victorian – a less temporally defined imaginary space – but in their late twentieth-century particularity. Whatever the strategy of fictional Victoriana, however it references Victorian society and remembers its imaginative literature, there is something in the reference itself that still seems to hold our attention and produce a strongly affective readerly response. The rehabilitation of the historical novel and of the Victorian period as a setting capable of producing a reading experience that is potentially both cerebral and sensuous, have gone hand in hand. I have argued that there was a coincidence between this moment and the lifting of certain kinds literary censorship – that the libertarian impulse of the 1960s and 1970s paradoxically put the Victorian firmly behind us and made it an era open for all kinds of renarration and reinterpretation. The success of *Tipping the Velvet*, *Affinity* and *Fingersmith*, not to mention the élan of Waters's writing, surely rests both on the experimentation with the genre that has gone before, and the difference of these confident, readable novels from it. Waters deliberately makes it hard for her readers to distinguish between what is disturbing and what is comfortable in her writing, what disrupts or confirms subjectivity or historicity. She prompts us to ask what might be a correct or an incorrect response to literary erotics, or to the Victorian period, as simultaneously the site of social oppression, subjective development, and literary exuberance?

The political and aesthetic uncertainties of these most recent examples of Victoriana in fiction are a sign of the times, and while they give the genre new room to breathe and invent, they also reflect a contraction of the utopian imagination which has annexed the Victorian past, and its writing, as an example of oppression or a staging of progress. Towards the end of *The Pleasure of the Text*, Barthes has a little more to say about that perverse and interesting person, the 'anachronic subject' who seems to me intuitively not only the right kind of reader for fictional Victoriana but also, perhaps, a critic made in the image of the early years of the millennium, reflecting both its cynicism and its modest hopes. Barthes suggests that analysing the pleasure of any given text involves an encounter with a self which is an embodied, '*historical subject*; for it is at the conclusion of a very complex process of biographical, historical, sociological, neurotic elements (education, social class, childhood configuration, etc.)' that one is able to 'control the contradictory interplay of' both kinds of reading pleasure, the one comfortable, the other unsettling. The effect of this oscillation, when 'controlled' is neither 'consistency' or 'loss' but something nearer to Hawthorne's idea of romance writing and reading, in which the attempt to connect two points in historical time results in a question about the temporality of the present: 'I write myself', Barthes says, 'as a subject at present out of place, arriving too soon or too late (this *too* designating neither regret, fault, nor bad luck, but merely calling for a *non-site*): anachronic subject, adrift.'[52]

Notes

1. Stephen Marcus, *The Other Victorians: a study of sexuality and pornography in mid-nineteenth-century England* (London: Weidenfeld & Nicholson, 1964), bookjacket blurb.
2. Henry James, in 'American Letters', *Literature* (1898) and Henry James to Sarah Orne Jewett, 5 October 1901, both cited in Philip Horne (ed.), *Henry James: a life in letters*, p. 360.
3. A. S. Byatt, *Possession: a romance* (London: Vintage, 1990) unnumbered prefatory pages.
4. As cited in Byatt's epigraph to *Possession*.
5. For an excellent analysis of the interwar 'sex-novel', see Billie Melman, *Women and the Popular Imagination in the Twenties: flappers and nymphs* (New York: St. Martin's Press, 1988).
6. Elizabeth, Fowles's first wife, was initially a very active editor of his work, arguing successfully that 'one big love scene should be used in place of several smaller ones', and that 'hinted sexuality is much more exciting than the full treatment'. After 1971 he cut her out of the process, 'out of pique', and more full-frontal erotica returned to his work. See Eileen Warburton, *John Fowles: a life in two worlds* (London: Viking, 2004) pp. 251 and 330.
7. The four pages of critical excerpts that appear before the title page of the paperback cite Kathryn Hughes in *The Guardian*, suggesting that it is the 'novel that Dickens might have written had he been allowed to speak freely'. Conversely, *The New Zealand Herald* thinks it is 'like Dickens with an added dollop of very un-Victorian sex', implying the absence of sex, rather than its representation, in the period. Many critics praise its skill with pastiche and storytelling – *Kirkus Review* grants it 'the irresistible narrative drive of the Victorian three-decker'. While Faber is at times a very skilful stylist, I found the novel overlong, poorly plotted and tediously told by its intrusive narrator, who has none of Fowles's idiosyncratic interest. Michel Faber, *The Crimson Petal and the White* (Edinburgh: Canongate, 2003).
8. David Lodge, *Nice Work* (London: Penguin Books, 1989) p. 48.
9. David Lodge, *Nice Work*, p. 43.
10. David Lodge, *Nice Work*, p. 48.
11. David Lodge, *Nice Work*, p. 46.
12. John Fowles, *The French Lieutenant's Woman* (London: Triad/Granada, 1977) title page and p. 16.
13. See Introduction, pp. 1–2 and note 2.
14. For Byatt's fascinating account of the genesis of *Possession*, and its literary and philosophical influences, which include Swedenborg, Henry James and the proposals to dig up George Eliot's letters, buried with her, see 'Choices: on the writing of *Possession*', http://www.asbyatt.com/oh_Possess/.aspx.
15. Discussing the composition of Christabel LaMotte's poems in *Possession*, Byatt says that 'the nineteenth-century poems that were not nineteenth-century poems *wrote themselves*, hardly blotted, fitting into the metaphorical structure of my novel, but not mine, as my prose is mine'. They 'came to her' almost as Roland's modern verse does at the end of the novel. http://www.asbyatt.com/oh_Possess/.aspx.

Fiction

16. Michel Foucault, *The History of Sexuality*, vol. 1, 'An Introduction', Robert Hurley (trans.) (London: Allen Lane, 1979).
17. John Fowles, *The French Lieutenant's Woman*, p. 397.
18. John Fowles, *The French Lieutenant's Woman*, p. 393.
19. John Fowles, *The French Lieutenant's Woman*, p. 394.
20. John Fowles, *The French Lieutenant's Woman*, p. 398.
21. Eileen Warburton writes that 'both John and Elizabeth had read Betty Friedan's *The Feminine Mystique*, published in 1963. When they quarrelled on the subject, Fowles rebutted: "I don't believe all the feminist argument (Betty Friedan's) about unfulfilled women. There are just as many unfulfilled men because fulfillment is a comparative thing" '. *John Fowles: a life in two worlds*, p. 267.
22. A. S. Byatt, *Possession*, p. 506.
23. A. S. Byatt, *Possession*, p. 507.
24. 'Nice Work If You Can Get It', words and music by Ira and George Gershwin, recorded by Fred Astaire, 1938. From the 1937 film *Damsel in Distress*.
25. David Lodge, *Nice Work*, p. 40.
26. Elizabeth Gaskell, *North and South* (Harmondsworth: Penguin, 1970).
27. David Lodge, *Nice Work*, pp. 61–2.
28. David Lodge, *Nice Work*, p. 113.
29. David Lodge, *Nice Work*, p. 200.
30. David Lodge, *Nice Work*, p. 184.
31. David Lodge, *Nice Work*, p. 83. See Raymond Williams, *The Long Revolution* (Harmondsworth: Penguin, 1965).
32. David Lodge, *Nice Work*, p. 75.
33. David Lodge, *Nice Work*, p. 133.
34. Herman Melville, *Moby Dick*, Harrison Hayford and Hershel Parker (eds) (New York: W. W. Norton and Co., 1967). In Chapter 92, 'Ambergris', Melville celebrates the substance that is 'found in the inglorious bowels of the sick whales'. In Chapter 96, pp. 353–4, 'The Try-Works', Melville describes the industrial process by which the blubber is rendered in the over-heated bowels of the ship by the 'Tartarean' 'pagan harpooneers'. 'Their tawny features, now all begrimed with smoke and sweat, their matted beards, and the contrasting barbaric brilliancy of their teeth'. But Melville, unlike Lodge, cautions against an association of such non-white labour with barbarity, shit or Hell. His 'savages' are the unsentimental heroes of *Moby Dick*.
35. David Lodge, *Nice Work*, p. 384.
36. In *Sybil*, the eponymous heroine turns out not to be a working-class but an aristocratic woman. Disraeli's 'solutions' to the problem of the 'Two Nations' are reliant on upper-class hegemony and semi-feudal paternalism. Benjamin Disraeli, *Sybil: or the Two Nations* (Oxford: Oxford University Press, 1998).
37. David Lodge, *Nice Work*, p. 133.
38. A. S. Byatt, *Possession*, p. 470.
39. A. S. Byatt, *Possession*, pp. 470–1.
40. A. S. Byatt, *Possession*, p. 471.
41. Roland Barthes, *The Pleasure of the Text* Richard Miller (trans.) (New York: Hill and Wang, 1975) pp. 10–11.

42. Roland Barthes, *The Pleasure of the Text*, p. 58.

43. Roland Barthes, *The Pleasure of the Text*, p. 14.

44. Roland Barthes, *The Pleasure of the Text*, p. 14.

45. See note 13. Byatt, in 'Choices: on the writing of *Possession*' reminds us that there 'have been serious proposals to dig up George Eliot'.

46. Sarah Waters's comments on her faux Victorian fiction cited in this essay are drawn from interviews available on line: with Ron Hogan at www. booksense.com/people/archive/waterssarah.jsp and from an interview on Thursday, 24 October 2002 by 'Linda' on www.moviepie.com/filmfests/ sarah_waters.html and from her own website www.sarahwaters.com/ ints.htm.

47. Sarah Waters, *Tipping the Velvet* (London: Virago Press, 1999).

48. Sarah Waters, *Affinity* (London: Virago Press, 2000).

49. Sarah Waters, *Fingersmith* (London: Virago Press, 2003). *Fingersmith* has won the CWA Ellis Peters Dagger Award for Historical Crime Fiction and *The South Bank Show* Award for Literature. It was serialised on television in 2005.

50. For the flavour of this debate see Ann Snitow, Christine Stansell and Sharon Thompson (eds) *Powers of Desire: The Politics of Sexuality* (New York: Monthly Review Press, 1983).

51. Sarah Waters, *Affinity*, p. 7.

52. Roland Barthes, *The Pleasure of the Text*, pp. 62–3.

Chapter 4

Retuning *The Piano*

One of the most unsettling films of the 1990s, Jane Campion's award-winning *The Piano* abandoned the safe ground of classic adaptation, the favoured mode of Victoriana at the movies, for something altogether riskier and more inventive. A few weeks after its United States opening, a cartoon poking gentle fun at the media hype surrounding *The Piano* appeared in *The New Yorker* magazine. Reprising one of the film's most memorable scenes, the piano itself stands alone on the sweeping curve of a New Zealand beach. A thought bubble rising from the stranded instrument encloses a mental image of a comfortable Victorian parlour. The piano is dreaming, not of music, but of home.[1] By providing the piano with domestic longings and an interior life, *The New Yorker* cartoon parodied the film's own elaborate conceit that the piano was as much subject as object – one of a trio of nineteenth-century émigrés that include its owner, the mute Ada, and her young daughter, Flora. As the prosthesis that serves as Ada's lost or repressed 'voice', the piano supplies the missing sense that to others makes her human, a symbiosis that animates the instrument also, endowing it, for characters and audience alike, with figurative agency. In the film's extended play on the piano's metaphorical possibilities, place and time become more or less equivalent, so that the piano's perilous journey and miraculously safe arrival on the beach – only a little out of tune – is itself suggestive of its survival as a marker of cultural literacy that extends – but only just – into the present. Indeed *The Piano* manipulates the filmgoer's waning investment in the prestige that a hands-on knowledge of music and musicianship confers, making Ada's attachment to her instrument something that the narrative both cultivates and undermines. For like much recent Victoriana, *The Piano* conducts its flirtation with the past through alternating strategies of seduction and betrayal, inviting its audience to enjoy an erotic identification with its subjects while elaborating their ethnographic distance from them. The piano's orchestration of these dissonant

Figure 4.1   Holly Hunter (Ada) and Anna Paquin (Flora) from Jane Campaion's film *The Piano*

yet complementary perspectives underscores Campion's deft way with historical pastiche. The film is not only one of the most intricate examples of Victoriana to date, but a knowing, sophisticated metacommentary on it. This essay will explore the theme and variations that *The Piano* plays on both genre and history.[2]

Nearly but never quite tragic, and often very funny, *The Piano*'s dominant mode is melodrama, that 'modern' genre which emerged with the rise and rise of the subject in the late eighteenth century – the period when pianos also came into their own as cultural accessories for the bourgeoisie – and extending from the moment of romanticism through the uncertain present. The melodramatic imagination, as Peter Brooks has described it in a now classic analysis, captures both the narrative and moral tone of the film, which plays with the genre in the self-reflexive, semi-parodic style of postmodern texts generally.[3] Melodrama supplies a unifying frame for *The Piano*'s intertextual excursions, but its use in the film is itself historicised, highlighting the mutation of the melodramatic imagination across two centuries. Gothic, horror, sensation, romance, and domestic fiction are all narrative types which depend on the melodramatic from its late eighteenth-century origins onwards and have been imaginatively recycled by the cinema. All are cited, although primarily as literary rather than dramatic or filmic devices, in *The Piano*.

Indeed, denuded of Campion's twists and elaborations, the bare bones of the story, of a disgraced woman with a child, married off by a parent to a 'man I've not yet met' in a foreign place, are the very stuff of eighteenth- and early nineteenth-century gothic romance.[4] What follows from this set-up is also familiar narrative ground for the domestic and romantic in contemporary fiction and in film. The woman's marriage proves a disaster. The community of white European settlers and indigenous people she enters is uncongenial and alienating, and the environment by turns depressing and menacing. The young woman is seduced by, and then falls in love with, a more fanciable and sympathetic man of lower status, himself an outcast. Her husband responds with jealous violence, and tries to rape, imprison and hurt her. However in the end, partly through her own courage and perseverance, she ends up in a safe haven with her true love and her child, her story providing the necessary happy ending for melodrama, which Brooks, among others, thinks of as a bourgeois genre, the conservative progeny of the social and political conflicts that inaugurated modernity. Melodrama, in this reading, is a response to the moral uncertainty provoked by the physical and ethical upheavals of the French Revolution, whose unanswerable questions about social and psychic life required a theatre of cruelty which enacts and then simplifies them.

Yet *The Piano*'s plot – including its very provisional and ambivalent happy ending – is only the most obvious use that Campion makes of melodrama as the generic vehicle for historical reference. Ada's muteness – the narrative occasion of the film – is a literal rendering of what is, Brooks suggests, a typical leitmotif of melodrama, where muteness 'corresponds first of all to a repeated use of *extreme* physical and emotional conditions . . . evoking the extremism and hyperbole of ethical conflict and manichaeistic struggle'.[5] Seeming to say more than we need to know, melodrama is paradoxically the form for the expression of what is unsayable. In *The Melodramatic Imagination*, Brooks argued that there was

> a convergence between the concerns of melodrama and of psychoanalysis – and, indeed, that psychoanalysis is a kind of modern melodrama, conceiving psychic conflict in melodramatic terms and acting out the recognition of the repressed, often with and on the body.[6]

Elaborating this point, Geoffrey Nowell-Smith has suggested that the psychoanalytic category that melodrama most resembles is conversion hysteria, where the 'repressed idea returns converted into a bodily symptom'.[7] In the melodramatic film text, Nowell-Smith adds, music often becomes the vehicle for what the text cannot say. Brooks agrees with Nowell-Smith's alignment of melodrama and hysteria, emphasising the gendered effects of the analogy. For if 'the hystericised body offers a key emblem' of the convergence between melodrama and psychoanalysis, 'the place for the inscription of highly emotional messages that cannot be written elsewhere, and cannot be articulated verbally', then this body is typically 'a woman's body, and indeed a victimised woman's body, on which desire has inscribed an impossible history, a story of desire in an impasse'.[8] The equation between melodrama as a genre, and hysteria as a particular narrative within psychoanalysis, is doubly expressed in Campion's film: narratively through its mute heroine, a text-book conversion hysteric, who indeed uses music to 'siphon off' her undischarged emotion, and generically in the film's wider deployment of alternatives to speech. For Brooks, one of the leading paradoxes of melodrama is its touching faith in the ability to say all, its striving for a full expression which is always frustrated. The melodramatic text, he suggests, is one of impeded verbal articulation, which must resort to other forms, especially gesture and pantomime, for what is in excess of speech or which cannot be spoken.[9] *The Piano* with its mute, telepathic heroine who signs, writes and plays piano, its two languages and its subtitles, its set-piece Christmas pantomime and its graphic, silent sex witnessed by characters and viewers, is a check-list of such strategies. If genre itself can be formally imagined as a psychic subject, as Brooks and Nowell-Smith suggest, then melodrama is a typically female subject suffering, as Freud says hysterics always do, 'from reminiscences' – from a past that cannot be acknowledged or made sense of but is constantly cited through symptoms. However, melodrama as psychoanalysis, Brooks's first analogy, and melodrama as psychoanalytically defined illness, his later revision, are radically different things – the one promising a kind of cure, the other designating a set of symptoms. In *The Melodramatic Imagination*, Brooks praised melodrama's modern form as having 'the distinct value of being about recognition and clarification, about how to be clear what the stakes are and what their representative signs mean, and how to face them' – a defence of the genre read in terms of the success of a psychoanalytic hermeneutic.[10] Brooks is equally enthusiastic about melodrama's practical morality. Contrasting it with tragedy he argues that melodrama 'substitutes for the rite of sacrifice an urging toward combat in life, an active, lucid confrontation of evil'.[11] This endorsement, read today, seems to put a naively positive spin on the ethical effects of a genre whose moral impact may be less easy to assess; indeed Brooks's later formulation of melodrama as a set of symptoms rather than their cure is much less optimistic. If we adopt this second, less sanguine analogy, Victoriana can be seen as another subspecies of melodrama-as-hysteria, for historical pastiche today also appears to suffer from reminiscences – its obsessive recycling of the past less a confident reconstruction than a compulsive and displaced expression of the major impediments to such an enterprise in a world where linear narrative no longer commands simple belief.

The uncertain status of historical reference in the 1990s may account for Campion's impulse to overload *The Piano* with citations, some more obvious than others, and most, but not all, to nineteenth-century literary texts and culture. The richness of referentiality contributes to the film's fascination, but it deepens rather than dispels the problems of temporality and history it raises. If we pursue the comparison with hysteria one step further, it is as if each citation presents a new symptom of the crisis of historicity that the film cannot fully confront. As well as titbits of Thomas Hood's poetry and a pick-and-mix buffet of social and cultural history, the film seems to have swallowed whole a Penguin library of classic nineteenth-century novels in English, disgorging their parts into the narrative almost at random in a way that makes the techniques of much fictional Victoriana appear crude in comparison, a kind of rewriting by numbers, a set of clever but fixed correspondences. Suspended in *The Piano* are half-digested gobbets of James Fenimore Cooper's *Leatherstocking Tales*, Herman Melville's South Sea stories, *Typee* (1846) and *Omoo* (1847), as well as his *White-Jacket* (1850) and *Moby*

Dick (1851).[12] Pages torn from Nathaniel Hawthorne's *The Scarlet Letter* (1850) swim alongside Emily Brontë's *Wuthering Heights* (1847), Charlotte Brontë's *Jane Eyre* (1847) and *Villette* (1851), Henry James's *The Turn of the Screw* (1898) and *What Maisie Knew* (1897) and sensation fiction as a genre rather than a particular novel. In the film's viscous depths – the cinematography makes the New Zealand bush look more watery than the ocean that borders it – this transatlantic flotsam and jetsam, including recognisable fragments of Victorian thinking about empire, race, disability, childhood, civilisation and telepathy, remains separate but tantalisingly contiguous, a kaleidoscope of shifting references turning slowly together to form ever-changing patterns.

The popular and academic criticism that has discussed the extraordinary impact of *The Piano* on viewers, has noted, but not gone deeply into, this network of literary and historical citations,[13] a web so dense as to seem almost designed to discourage attempts at interpretation, presenting a tightly woven thicket of intertexts without an obvious point of entry. Reviewers and critics alike pick up on the references that Campion herself wanted to highlight – Emily Brontë as poet and novelist, and Thomas Hood of course; some likened Holly Hunter's severe dress to portraits of the American poet, Emily Dickinson. But these are only starters – and can mislead: Campion highlights *Wuthering Heights* as a source, but it is the tone, mood and genre that inspire her, a version of romance as something 'harsh and extreme', the 'gothic exploration of the romantic impulse'.[14] The *Piano* is not, for example, a remake of the story in *Wuthering Heights* in which Heathcliff gets the girl. Insofar as it cites the plot of *Wuthering Heights* at all, it effectively condenses the story of two generations, so that Stewart and George Baines share aspects of Heathcliff, Edward Linton and Hareton, and Ada begins as Cathy Earnshaw but ends, perhaps, more in the mould of the civilisable and civilising Catherine Linton. Even the transposition of the isolation of the moors to that of settler New Zealand involves an environmental inversion – the moors are open, while the New Zealand interior of *The Piano*, where most of the action takes place, is claustrophobic, more like the New World forests of James Fenimore Cooper's Leatherstocking novels. What Emily Brontë as novelist mostly provides is the emotional register of the film, its overripe late romanticism spiced with a hint of violence, both undercut perhaps by the mordant wit of its heroine. The palimpsest of competing and overlapping references works as a defence against, rather than a route to, a coherent reading. Crucial to the film's appeal, they stubbornly refuse to unlock its contradictions, another reason for thinking of this piece of Victoriana as using citation as symptom rather than cure. However, their insistent resonance within the film does lead us to a very interesting question: why is it that what we somewhat loosely think of as the 'historical' in costume film can trigger such extremes of feeling in its audience, emotions that are evoked by the way the 'past' and the 'present' are brought together? For while the strong feelings that *The Piano* elicited were ascribed by critics either to its provocative treatment of sexuality, or its problematic representation of the Maori, on further reflection the storms of affect seem rather to be precipitated by a collision between these two elements of the film – what we might call its 'cold' and 'warm' fronts – between, in other words, its unfinished and contradictory critique of colonialism and its eroticised and nostalgic reinvestment in its imagined history.

The controversies about the film's take on colonialism and race that attended its opening were twofold: some critiques were embedded in ongoing local political struggles of indigenous peoples in New Zealand, while others referred to more general and global debates about colonialism and its aftermath. Both of these responses were, in hindsight, predictable and comprehensible. While Campion clearly tried to guard against local criticism by the way in which she handled her use of Maori actors and Maori culture, as the narrative appended to the published script of the film makes clear, one could reasonably argue that the film meant to provoke a debate about the meaning of colonialism.[15]

I will return to the question of the film's take on the colonial past, but first I want to turn to that other, more puzzling fuss about the film's sexual narrative, a hostile reaction which although couched in the language of *fin de siècle* feminism, echoed an earlier more stringently prurient, and conservative, moment. Debates in the letter section of the *Boston Globe*, for example, remonstrating against the sexual exploitation of Holly Hunter's diminutive Ada by Harvey Keitel's George Baines, sound like a replay of much earlier outcries at Clark Gable's rape-or-was-it-seduction of Vivien Leigh in *Gone With the Wind* (1940), or the unease which greeted the sexual scenes in the film of *The French Lieutenant's Woman* (1981).[16] In each case the over-reaction of viewers duplicates the excess, the melodrama, of the film. And in each of the above cases the viewers' moral recoil had something, if not everything, to do with the historical setting of the films – a much wider license and a corresponding indifference seems to exist for films set in the amoral present. The Victorian *mise-en-scène* raises the sexual ante of the game of strip poker that George and Ada play – at first for the possession of the piano – from mere titillation to outright transgression. Their exchange is scandalous in direct proportion to its strong association with an imaginary time of prohibition and repression, rather than with loose late twentieth-century morals. The viewer is positioned first with Flora, and then with Ada's husband, Stewart, as the two spy on George and Ada, but while theirs is the voyeurism of children and jealous husbands in pursuit of illicit knowledge, ours is that of the modern subject discovering the sexual indiscretion of the historical past – the Victorian standing in for the infantile fantasy of a more absolute social law than that imposed in the libertarian present, a law which incites us to transgress, but just as surely brings down inevitable punishment. Yet we would be wrong to think that the disturbance that the film occasioned can be explained simply by reducing these key scenes to a generic sexual scenario, for just as quickly as we identify them as set pieces in a psychodynamic primer, they begin to generate variations on their theme. The film's explicit use of voyeurism, for example, could, in a film that is full of in-jokes, be read as a knowing wink to film theory which argues that the cinema itself is founded on human scopophilia, an insatiable desire to look at things supposedly barred to us. If we accept this analogy, which makes of us voyeurs all as we face the silver screen, we might judge ourselves to be equally complicit in the desire that costume cinema supplies in Technicolor, a desire to 'see' the past, an impulse that is almost as ubiquitous and as fraught with taboo and impediment as the atavistic curiosity that impels us to peep at the scene of seduction.

The cinema frames much more graphically, and I think more successfully, than the historical novels considered in the last two essays, questions about our need – and our ability – to know and possess the past. Film's enhanced capacity to arouse us highlights the accompanying affective and ethical implications of such desires and identifications. It also raises the important but often ignored issue of what or where the 'historical' is in Victoriana. If its references are contemporary symptoms which refer to a scenario that of its nature cannot be reconstructed, then the supposed 'real' history remains hidden. What is represented as history is what masks a traumatic moment which may not be a psychic or social event but simply a type of conflict. But supposing we don't go down the psychoanalytic path, instead approaching the uncertain status of historical reference in film and story from a more technical point of view, the 'past', even as a visual illustration clipped from a nineteenth-century novel, becomes strangely elusive. The more in our face the medium's representation of the past, one might argue, the more it seems merely a special effect of the technological present; from that perspective the literary and cultural references in the film are perhaps a way of splicing together the technologies of writing/reading and filming/viewing, technologies of production and reception that belong – at first glance anyway – to different centuries within modernity. And to complicate matters further, these sutures are rarely if ever performed between two historical points only – the nineteenth-century text and the filmmaker's present. In the case of *The Piano* they are sewn together by the cultural theories and interpretative schemas that come chronologically between these two moments. The ideas and perspectives that join the Victorian past to the late twentieth century – anthropology, psychoanalysis, and feminism – are also a semi-subliminal part of the film's web of citations. To open up the questions of genre and history with which this essay is concerned, I will be moving in and out of the texts and contexts from which the film draws, exploring as I do so, the peculiar geography and temporality of the virtual space – infinitely expandable and compressible – in which the modern narrative and its historical referents coexist, a space simultaneously located within the film's generic ambitions, its diegetic frame, and outside it.

Pianos and Women

The piano as sign and agent is as good a place as any to begin such an exploration, for, as *The New Yorker* cartoon slyly suggests, it is the film's somewhat precious but still effective device for bringing the mid-nineteenth-century world recreated in *The Piano* and our own into sync. As a consumer durable of the western middle-class home for over two centuries, now a fading but still recognisable contemporary register of class affluence and cultural aspiration, the piano articulates the pleasures and pretensions of nineteenth-century European colonisers with those of late twentieth-century filmgoers, especially the generation for whom piano lessons were still a familiar part of a girl's education – forming one of what the eighteenth and nineteenth centuries called her 'accomplishments'. A metonym for the ever widening bourgeois domestic culture of the last two hundred years, the piano in the parlour to be played by wives and daughters was a mark of nineteenth-century class mobility, but also of its contradictory condition that women of this class should think of the home, not the public world of work, as their natural sphere. Indeed an interesting paradox of modernity was that it fuelled women's desire for personhood, a desire sometimes channelled through the escape route but also the dead end of those arts specifically designed and marketed to make them content with a gendered, unequal division of labour and presence in public and private.

Early in the twentieth century, Max Weber put his finger on the piano's key function in the shaping of the feminised domestic culture of Northern Europe, noting its invention as part of industrial expansion and the new consumerism. 'Its specific public,' said Weber, 'consisted essentially of

amateurs . . . those belonging to sections of society which were confined
to their homes – monks in the Middle Ages and then in modern times,
women, led by Queen Elizabeth.'[17] In the eighteenth century it became,
thanks to its market of would-be amateurs, a large-scale industry; piano
building came to depend on 'mass sales'. 'The piano's present unshakeable position,' continued Weber, 'rests on its universal usefulness as a
means of becoming acquainted at home with almost all the treasures of
musical literature, on the immeasurable riches of its own literature and
finally on its character as the universal instrument for the accompanist
and the learner.' 'By its very musical nature,' he concludes, the piano is
'a bourgeois domestic instrument' whose ideal space is 'a modestly sized
room' and whose habitat is among 'Northern peoples, whose life, for
purely climatic reasons, is house-bound and centred on the "home", in
contrast with the South'.[18] Every note in Weber's brief reprise of piano
history rings true for its use in Campion's film. One can see how easily
the European North/South divide can be retranslated into the colonial
idiom, the South Seas now becoming that extra-domestic terrain in
which pianos – and possibly European women whose class identity they
confirm – are from one perspective, that of Stewart, matter-out-of-place,
irrelevant to the real business of empire, i.e. acquiring land and extract-
ing value from it, and from another, essential to that business, representing the less measurable but no less powerful value of metropolitan
culture that made colonial societies tolerable as well as profitable to
Europeans. The film suggests that there were enough pianos in settler
New Zealand, transported there by stubborn women less obsessed and
needy than mute Ada, to support a piano-tuner. Gripped by his desire,
George goes and fetches a blind one from some other part of the colony:
the presence of pianos and piano-tuners in the bush reminds the viewer
of the cultural and gendered imperatives of imperialism. When George,
in a moving and funny scene, caresses the piano as if it were Ada herself,
making visible not just his passion, but her autoerotic relationship to her
instrument and the confusion between women and things that their combined fetishistic status entails, the film gestures, in true melodramatic
mode, at what is surplus to a strictly economic or political critique of cultural imperialism. It is not clear in any case that the film intends any such
severe critique. It is significant that when Ada, at the end of the film,
abruptly decides to offload her piano as excess personal baggage, it is not
pianos as instruments or music as a cultural category that are dumped,
but only this one rather compromised piano together with Ada's
solipsistic and non-productive relation to it. But perhaps what is also
jettisoned is the audience's and the characters' allied relationship to Ada's
piano, their now hopelessly overdetermined associations with this

particular baby grand. By the end of the film, in any case, the piano's half-life as trope and joke has run out, and its death also signals the end of its generic usefulness. Narratively speaking, the piano has been the medium for Ada's tragic mode, musically expressed in Michael Nyman's tongue-in-cheek faux romantic score. It has, after all, twice pandered to Ada and her lovers – the off-screen music teacher seducer, Flora's father, and George – acting as a kind of perfidious duenna or nurse who colludes both with the unspoken wishes of her charge and the men who desire her. In the penultimate scene, when Ada follows the piano down into the sea, her foot caught in the ropes which held it to the boat, the piano is promoted from prosthesis and/or chaperone to become one of the twinned female figures of the eighteenth-century and early nineteenth-century gothic and historical novel, one of whom can be saved only if the other is sacrificed. In this role Ada's piano belongs to, and is too complicit with, older genres. Generically speaking the drowning of this piano is the (seeming) final subordination of tragedy and comedy, to make way for the triumph of secular melodrama whose positive outcome is 'modern' domestic romance. In the film's domestic coda, which takes place in the relatively civilised town of Nelson, where Ada settles with George and Flora, Ada becomes a piano teacher, socialising her musical talent by making her skill, not herself, the object of exchange.

Anthropology, Feminism, Psychoanalysis

The exchange of women, pianos and labour is therefore not only a preoccupation of the film but crucial to its interpretation of the narrative of modernity and civilisation. Making Ada mute and the piano her prosthetic 'voice' allows Campion to set up another one of her semi-private jokes, one that almost certainly has its sources in her undergraduate training in anthropology – a joke which will prove central to the film's disposition of its Victorian intertexts, its treatment of sexuality and its critique of colonial/imperial ideologies. In one of the landmark texts of twentieth-century theory, *Structural Anthropology*, Claude Lévi-Strauss makes a provocative argument about the origins of language, suggesting that 'marriage regulations and kinship systems' functioned 'as a kind of language, a set of processes permitting the establishment, between individuals and groups, of a certain type of communication'. In a move that he already knew would 'disturb' feminists, he went on to argue

> that the mediating factor, in this case, should be the *women of the group*, who are *circulated* between clans, lineages, or families, in place of the *words of the*

group, which are *circulated* between individuals, does not at all change the fact that the essential aspect of the phenomenon is identical in both cases.[19]

The ambiguity that lies between words as sign and value also exists, he insists, between women's function within kinship structure as sign – a mode of communication between men – and as value. As an example of the difficulty in understanding the double function of words and of women he points to

> the reactions of persons who, on the basis of the analysis of the social struc-
> tures referred to, have laid against it the charge of "anti-feminism", because
> women are referred to as objects. Of course, it may be disturbing to some to
> have women conceived as mere parts of a meaningful system. However, one
> should keep in mind that the processes by which phonemes and words have
> lost – even though in an illusory manner – their character of value, to become
> reduced to pure signs, will never lead to the same results in matters concern-
> ing women. For words do not speak, while women do; as producers of signs,
> women can never be reduced to the status of symbols or tokens. But it is for
> this very reason that the position of women, as actually found in this system
> of communication between men that is made up of marriage regulations and
> kinship nomenclature, may afford us a workable image of the type of rela-
> tionships that could have existed at a very early period in the development of
> language, between human beings and their words.[20]

Feminism has found Lévi-Strauss's formulation both tantalising and enraging, and has responded to it in different ways, sometimes challeng- ing its very premises, sometimes taking them almost too seriously or too literally. Campion refuses to identify her own perspective with feminism, but undoubtedly *The Piano* makes use of Lévi-Strauss both as inspira- tion and provocation, borrowing and revising his arguments and exam- ples. For a start, the communication between male equals which stands at the center of Lévi-Strauss's model of exchange, is the narrative premise of the film in the presumed transfer of Ada to Stewart by her father. But if such exchanges are the symbolic origins of language and civilisation then these systems as they appear in the film are represented as almost ludicrously dysfunctional. Every attempt at interchange is somehow dis- torted or impeded by differences of gender, class, race and capacity. In the world of *The Piano* communication between men and women, chil- dren and adults, men and men, Europeans and Maori, is conceived of as an almost intractable cultural problem. The film highlights instead the strangeness of language, its multiplicity and its limits, by using voice- over, sign language, music, mime, English subtitles and Maori. Moreover the interdependency of Ada and the piano, and the doubts Ada's mute- ness raises for Stewart and the other settlers about her human status, destabilises the kind of steady-state 'ambiguity' about subjects and objects that is crucial to Lévi-Strauss's argument – an ambiguity which is the effect of the split representation between woman-as-exchange and woman-who-speaks. Indeed the comic association of woman and piano in the film, where they both function in forms of ritual exchange and where it is sometimes unclear which of them 'also' speaks, lightly mocks both the distinction and necessary conflation between persons and things that is at the heart of Lévi-Strauss's theory.

Yet, as I have suggested, Lévi-Strauss's usefulness for Campion is not purely adversarial. *The Piano* can also be seen to exploit the unacknowledged levels of temporality embedded in *Structural Anthropology*. In Lévi-Strauss's model, the origin of language in the exchange of women is not meant to refer to marriage in modern industrial societies, but neither does it really apply, as at first it seems, to known pre-modern societies. All these societies already had elaborated language, so that language's supposed 'origin' in the egalitarian moment of exchange belongs not to the past as historical fact, but rather to an archaic, mythical moment of social/linguistic foundation somewhere in an imagined prehistory.[21] Indeed Lévi-Strauss's argument covertly depends on another less visible ambiguity – a slippage and a confusion between real historical time and mythical time – and it is this elision that is so crucial to Campion's use of history in the film.

How these distinct temporal registers are implicated in the construction of femininity has been explored in a now famous essay by psychoanalytic theorist Julia Kristeva. 'Women's Time' argued that female subjectivity is associated with three temporal registers: *cyclical* time or repetition; *monumental* time which encompasses mythic prehistories; and *linear* time, the time of history, of 'departure, progression and arrival'. Linear time is also the time of speech and writing: 'that of language considered as the enunciation of sentences'. These distinctive temporal categories, encode different forms of representation as well as different ideas of change, and Kristeva associates them with psychic states and psychopathology, notably hysteria. The hysteric's dysfunctional relationship to the past leads Kristeva to suggest that the 'hysteric (either male or female) who suffers from reminiscences would, rather, recognize his or her self in the anterior temporal modalities: cyclical or monumental'.[22]

As Kristeva puts it, this temporal preference is one that the hysteric actively chooses, whether or not this 'choice' is a sign of illness. Ada is a case in point; she tells us that she chooses not to speak, even if her 'will' is a somewhat alienated and independent actor: her father fears that the day she 'decides to stop breathing' will be the day of her death.[23] Locked in the 'anterior' time that is the rebus of her own history, and the paradox in which her muteness is an active not passive response to trauma, only

132   *Victoriana – Histories, Fictions, Criticism*

the intervention of the plot can release her. One of the objectives of the narrative is the rescue of Ada from this regressive, speechless stasis, powerful but pathological, and the enabling of her re-entry into the historical time of modernity and of language. For while Stewart initially associates Ada through her dumbness with the simplicity and harmless-ness of the animal world, the film uses her muteness to confer on her the mystery, menace and supernatural powers of a sibylline and mythic femininity – an identity which is in tension with her desire for more modern forms of agency, sexual and artistic. Ada's movement across these temporalities is indicative of the film's own narrative and aesthetic ambitions to deliver a stylish historical pastiche, as appealing and some-what fresher than popular adaptations of classic authors, in the shape of a magical pre-history of twentieth-century modernity.

In *The Piano*'s opening sequence this double imperative, and the prob-lems it produces, is hinted at through the dislocation of voice, that leading trope of the melodramatic imagination. For Brooks, the gesture or mime that the text cannot translate (often a woman's gesture) is, like muteness, characteristic of the genre. Drawing on Diderot and Rousseau, Brooks argues that gesture was seen by enlightenment thinkers as the origin of language – a view which complicates the genealogy and author-ity of those characters who prefer sign to voice.[24] But *The Piano* never represents Ada as entirely silent even if her voice never has a punctual origin. The film itself does not trust its audience to find Ada fully human unless we can 'hear' her conventionally. Ada's first words in the opening sequence tells us that the voice-over that we are hearing – a film con-vention that viewers might ordinarily take for granted as stream-of-consciousness – 'is not my speaking voice, but my mind's voice' and that 'today' her father 'married me to a man I've not yet met', a man who naively imagines her as without mind, as a 'dumb creature'.[25] The unknown cause of Ada's dumbness, the supernatural evocation of her mindspeaking, and the deliberate obscurity of her father's motivation in so disposing of her, are all conveyed in a poetic prose that rhetorically evokes both fairy tale and myth, registers which work in a kind of dynamic apposition to the historical realism of the film's visual and aural effects. Yet every gesture that the film makes towards verisimilitude high-lights the mythical/magical and realism as dissonant, even rivalrous, tem-poralities. In line with the film's narrative logic that tells us that Ada has not spoken since she was six years old, the Scottish-accented voice that we hear is not in fact the actor Holly Hunter's voice, but that of her daughter in the film, the actor Anna Paquin. This aural prosthesis yokes a child's voice to a woman's mind and body, highlighting the way in which Ada may be seen as psychologically stuck in early childhood, and

echoing with a difference the more prosaic fact that Flora acts throughout the film as the daily interpreter of Ada's sign language, thus supple-
menting, perhaps even competing with, the piano's function as Ada's
voice. Yet there is nothing childish or naïve about what this voice says:
for example Ada's sophisticated and contemptuous evaluation of
Stewart's regressive association of her dumbness with that of animals, or
her sibylline warning at the beginning of the film that 'silence affects
everyone in the end'.[26] Depicted in the film as a composite nineteenth-
century figure drawn from fiction, social history and fantasy, Ada combines the attributes and powers of early and late romantic heroines of
Victorian novels, figures which mutate towards the end of the century
into those of the hysteric, the dark lady of sensation fiction and the
telepath – identities which the film and its heroine both embrace and
reject, as is made clear in the double ending, in which Ada forgoes – but
with regrets that the film graphically visualises in its very last sequence –
the timeless world of death and silence underwater for the quotidian
delights of true love and family life in a colonial town. While the narrative, as I have argued, propels its characters towards this more mundane
domestic conclusion – romantic with a small 'r' only – one of *The Piano*'s
chief pleasures is the way in which it dwells in, and on, the warp between
the monumental time of myth and the linear time of historical change.

Melodrama, Morality, Femininity and Nineteenth-Century Fiction

We can best see this effect in the film's clever handling of its nineteenth-
century intertexts, which serve at once to give it the illusion of historical
specificity and depth and to signal its claim to be telling a universal story
about human nature. In one sense Campion uses these references in much
the same way as nineteenth-century authors deployed classical and biblical allusion, both overt and subliminal, to confer cultural prestige on
their tales of bourgeois life. Shakespeare and the nineteenth-century
novel is probably as close as we can get today to pre-twentieth-century
common cultural capital, and there is a strong case to be made that these
stories – for example, *Jane Eyre, Moby Dick, David Copperfield, or The
Scarlet Letter* – have displaced Greek and Roman classics or biblical
narrative in providing the mythic structure of the early staging of our
own modernity. But while any of these cited sources can act as a guarantor of the modern text's ethical, aesthetic and narrative credentials,
they do not remain inert or static within it – often acting, on the contrary,
as a catalyst for its revisionist aims.

Much of the Victoriana I have been discussing – and *The Piano* for all its innovation is no exception – is fuelled by the desire either to express the sexuality that they understand the Victorians to have repressed in their writing and their lives, or to uncover the 'real' history of Victorian sexuality presumed to have gone on pretty well everywhere, despite the denials made by genteel fictions. Whether the modern writer is into post-hoc liberation – a kind of fictional reparation of a past supposedly denied its libidinal birthright – or is more taken with the muckraking glee of the historian cracking the thin façade of a prior age's respectability, the outcome is much the same – a text whose full frontal nudity exposes and censors the modesty or hypocrisy of past times. In *The Piano* Campion draws from both these hypotheses about Victorian sexuality but leans more heavily on the former: most strikingly in her portrait of the virginal and repressed Stewart, the character who she says most interests her.

The film's theme and story, adultery in a repressive colonial society, has as its most obvious canonical source Nathaniel Hawthorne's 1850 'romance', *The Scarlet Letter*, itself an historical novel about the effects of repression, set in seventeenth-century Puritan America. *The Scarlet Letter* functions at several levels as a kind of ur-text for *The Piano*. Indeed the film makes most sense when considered generically as a remake of the hybrid form of nineteenth-century romance in which extreme psychological states are explored through narratives replete with gothic trappings, and often, but not always, set in the past. In Hawthorne's hands the romance is weighed down with symbolism and moral seriousness – melodramatic in every respect, including a heroine who bears the visual stigmata of her sin, a large scarlet A. The tale's ethical absolutes are Hawthorne's weapons in what is intended as a scathing critique of the punitive mores of his colonial ancestors. And if generically *The Piano* greatly resembles *The Scarlet Letter*, ideologically too both narratives have almost too much in common, notably their covert conservatism in relation to the sexual politics of their own day, a timidity masked by the way in which they seem to speak on behalf of their sexy historical heroines. Hawthorne is unsparing in his portrait of the unforgiving regime of state and church which first imprisons the beautiful Hester Prynne for adultery, then exposes her on the town pillory as a spectacle of shame for the coarse, censorious crowd, and finally turns her forever into an exemplary 'symbol . . . of woman's frailty'.[27] Hawthorne may have hated the bad faith of early American Calvinism, its double standard which punished women's sexual pecca-dilloes but not men's, and there are hints throughout *The Scarlet Letter* that it was meant to be read as exemplary also of the narrowness of mid-nineteenth century mores, mores not so very different in sentiment, if less draconian in practice, from that of the author's Puritan forefathers. In fact, the moral trajectory he imagines for Hester, who refuses to betray her lover, the young and charismatic local minister, is very similar to that which Elizabeth Gaskell invents for her unmarried mother, a farmer's daughter seduced and abandoned by a middle-class cad, in a contemporary English novel, *Ruth* (1853). Hester ends her days as a kind of nurse confessor to the women of the community, redeemed in their eyes by socialising her experience instead of simply suffering its effects. *Ruth's* reputation in her northern English town (and with Gaskell's intended readers) is only restored when she dies nursing her community through a cholera epidemic, among them her seducer who is now standing for parliament. The cost of sexual transgression in the nineteenth century – whether it is the past or the present that was its imagined location – was still very high. Hawthorne's pro-woman stance is skin deep also, especially towards the beautiful exotic femme fatales of his literary imagination about whom he is deeply ambivalent. Misogyny is rarely more than a clause away in Hawthorne's novels and stories, which punish the 'impulsive and passionate' women his fictions invent.[28] His mixed feelings about women as a sex, as opposed to their exceptional representatives, is expressed powerfully in his sketch of the 'hard-featured', 'ugly', 'man-like', morally 'coarse-fibred' women who form the chorus of informal 'judges' who witness Hester's humiliation with relish.[29] Unexpectedly, there is more than a little of this generic distaste for women in *The Piano*, masked here as it is in *The Scarlet Letter*. It is striking how well the foolish female representatives of Campion's settler community – Stewart's Aunt Nessie and her simple-minded daughter, for whom Ada is an unsolved puzzle – fit into this coarse-grained, narrow version of white femininity, Ada being the exception rather than the rule. And if Campion's difference from Hawthorne is to reward Ada in this life by legitimising her earthly pleasures, Ada's perverse nostalgia for the oceanic, monumental world of unfulfilled desire and death indicates that bourgeois pleasures are bought, at the very least, at the price of the poetic imagination.

But the female figure in *The Piano* most fully reminiscent of *The Scarlet Letter* is Flora, and it is through the story of possessed and possessive little girls that the sexual conservatism of both stories – conservative for their respective times of course – is conveyed. Pearl and Flora are both the illegitimate children of impulsive and passionate women. The namesake of another female child overexposed to the unregulated sexuality of adult carers and trapped in its malign field, Flora in Henry James's *The Turn of the Screw* – a text itself in debt to *The Scarlet Letter*, especially in its depiction of children who become the bearers of the sins of others – Campion's Flora owes more to Hawthorne's initial invention. Pearl and Flora are children whose uneasy dyadic relationship with their transgressive mothers – relationships represented as both natural and too close for comfort – negatively affect their own psychic well-being. Engendered and bound by secrets not of their own making – as all children necessarily must be – they are by turns clingy, stubborn and aggressive – baby fantasists prone to magical thinking. Hester's refusal to name and shame her child's father is somehow responsible for her daughter Pearl's peculiar behaviour, so out of sync with the sober Puritan children. An 'elfish', 'freakish', 'wild' child, she can be released from the pathological field of silence that surrounds her origins and implicates her in its 'sin' only when Arthur Dimmesdale acknowledges her and her mother in public.[30] Pearl is an agent not simply a victim. Jealous at Dimmesdale's encroachment of her exclusive relation with Hester, she challenges the good faith of his affectionate overtures in the forest's safe seclusion. Pearl thus becomes aligned, however innocently, with the social law that requires confession and punishment. Dimmesdale's admission of his paternity is quickly followed by his death, which releases Pearl from the cruel enchantment of sin and secrecy, allowing her to mature more normally and be decanted at the novel's end into legitimate marriage, motherhood and wealth in faraway Europe, thus following the normalising, modernising endgame of melodramatic narrative.

Flora is depicted also as a wilful, wild child both hostile to and in search of her missing father. Her declared plan to reject Stewart – 'I'm not going to call him Papa. I'm not going to call HIM anything. I'm not even going to look at HIM.' – becomes revised when Flora sees how indifferent Ada is to her husband, and how little he affects the established intimacy of mother and daughter.[31] Reversing her position, Flora not only accepts Stewart but embraces uncritically the empty form of patriarchal family life he offers. Her jealousy is only aroused by her exclusion from the piano lessons, the scene of Ada's growing closeness with George, from which Flora is literally and figuratively shut out, her disturbance expressed initially by her own eroticisation of nature in a comic scene where she and the Maori children mime sex by masturbating against the trees. Spying on her mother's lovemaking with George, she reveals their secret to Stewart, but her revenge doesn't stop there. She further betrays her mother when Ada tries to contact George by writing her love on a key torn from the piano, and sends a reluctant and rebellious Flora to deliver it. This betrayal in turn is the catalyst for Stewart's violence to Ada – he chops off the top half of her finger – a denouement so shocking to all parties that it precipitates the resolution of the film.

With the aid of a little extempore mindspeaking in which Ada tells Stewart to let her go, Stewart's violence brings everyone to their senses, eventually resulting in the reunion of Ada and George, and their recomposition, with Flora, into a real – i.e. sexual and loving – family unit. The next to last scene of the film which shows them all in Nelson, with Ada under George's tutelage learning to speak, and Flora turning innocent, exuberant cartwheels in the garden, suggests that, freed from the task of ventriloquising the psychic disturbances caused by Ada's loss of speech, or acting as the go-between for her unregulated desires, the little girl has been liberated into ordinary asexual childhood.

In the relationship between Ada and Flora, Campion reprises one of the most enduring themes of the melodramatic imagination, the problem of maternal femininity. In classic Hollywood film the sacrifice of the mother's extra-maternal femininity – her sexuality, her agency – is often required so that the daughter can survive. King Vidor's Hollywood film, *Stella Dallas* (1937), is usually seen as the exemplary twentieth-century text for this particular narrative, one in which the lower-class mother deliberately alienates her daughter, seeming to abandon her so that she may take her rightful place in genteel society – a story that is itself reminiscent of *The Scarlet Letter*, if more punitive. At first it might seem that Campion is reversing this sacrificial fate by allowing Ada to keep her lower-class lover and her bastard daughter. But in twentieth-century texts there is more room for invention; there are sacrifices short of ultimate sacrifice, sacrifices that to the modern sensibility have the conservative and sentimental resonance of the Victorian happy ending, while still seeming to evade its forms, a paradox that Campion seems to recognise in making death and silence an alternative fate that attracts Ada even as she relinquishes it. If we juxtapose *The Scarlet Letter* and *The Piano*, we can see how daughters of passionate, impulsive women (and no visible fathers) pay them back by rescinding their dangerously won liberty, turning them into reasonable simulacra of conventional motherhood, and shying away themselves from the freedoms and difficulties of their example. The moralising function of daughters in the nineteenth-century text allows Hawthorne and his readers to enjoy Hester's sexuality and her silent defiance of propriety within the safe boundaries of narrative and social convention. The orphaned Pearl will keep Hester on the straight and narrow – she must die a virtuous mother in order to be redeemed as a virtuous woman – a lesson entirely in accord with mid-nineteenth-century maternalism, and, it seems, an ideological message that has not yet been superseded – at least not by any filmmaker with mainstream ambitions – for the familial logic of Hollywood cinema in every genre is, if anything, stronger than ever.

If Campion reproduces something of Hawthorne's moralism without the forms of female sacrifice it entailed in nineteenth-century fiction, the influence of Henry James can be seen in the quest for sexual knowledge in *The Piano*, a quest in which adults and children are engaged. In James's fiction epistemological and generic issues are conflated; his literary realism is grounded in his characters' search for knowledge, often sexual knowledge – knowledge which, although frequently a burden and sometimes a tragedy, offers them at least the freedom to know, if not to change their social and personal circumstances. On the tragic side, the theme of children forced to come to terms too early with adult sexuality is one that James explored several times in the late 1890s in *What Maisie Knew* (1897) and *The Awkward Age* (1899) as well as in *The Turn of the Screw* (1898). *The Piano*'s wayward child takes her name from the little girl in James's *The Turn of the Screw*, a novella in which a neurotic young governess must protect her young charges, Miles and Flora, a brother and sister, from the corrupting legacy of her dead predecessors Miss Jessell and her lover Peter Quint. Campion's film memorialises both children, and, I would argue, the dead fornicators also, who are reworked not as malign but as virtuous transgressors in Ada and George. James's Flora, although spooked and fascinated by the sexual antics of her last governess and her lover, the evil Quint, avoids the fate of her brother Miles, who, the story hints, is driven to reproduce, albeit in some childish form which James prudishly and prudently conceals from his readers, the deviant sexuality of his mentor. Miles dies – his 'little heart, dispossessed' gives out – either from the conflict such precocious knowledge induces or from something more sinister, a traumatic crisis about what happened in the past that is largely generated by the persecutory attentions of his governess.[32] *The Piano*'s Flora, by comparison, reacts more healthily: true, she indulges in sexual play with the other children and is punished for it like Miles, but she also acts out her anger both at her exclusion from and her co-optation into the scene of Ada's illicit sexuality. To know in James is to suffer, sometimes in silence; to know in Campion is to give vent to the mixed emotions such knowledge evokes.

But the genius of James's story, and its difference from his other fiction about children, is its radical ambiguity, so that while the reader is compellingly moved to discover the horrid 'truth' of the past, truth itself becomes a more and more elusive and problematic idea. In *The Melodramatic Imagination* Brooks argues that James cleverly turns melodrama into a mental activity, and in *The Turn of the Screw* this is expressed in at least two ways.[33] First, the corruption of the children may be one largely constructed by the guilty projection of their lonely and repressed governess, a corruption imagined by adults as a screen for their own fascination with the illicit. Second, the mental drama of the governess is not a solipsism that can disturb only herself, but, in favoured critical readings of the story, has fatal consequences for at least one of her charges. But James's scepticism about modern marriage, his unsentimental notion of mothers or maternal instinct in general, his view of sexual desire as both powerful and amoral, fuelling unlimited selfishness and greed, is such that he resolutely avoids turning these bleak and scary stories of hapless children into little homilies for happy families, although this often makes them even more punishing for the women within them. *The Piano* reflects one aspect of James's realism, which is about the drive of characters to 'know' their situations at whatever cost to themselves. In James's world renunciation and death are common results of their curiosity, so that we might, if we think of the film in its Jamesian register, view the alternate ending in which Ada drowns with her piano as drawing both from 'romance', but also, in another key, 'realism'. The alignment of melodrama and realism, sometimes thought to be opposed, is complete in James, and adumbrated in Brooks's very Jamesian take on the positive power of melodramatic thinking. This convergence also holds true in Campion's film.

Campion, as filmmaker, richly rewards our scopophilia, and that of her characters, with explicit sexual scenes. Her next film after *The Piano* was an adaptation of *The Portrait of a Lady* in which, with calamitous effect, she could not resist incorporating such scenes – the heroine's supposed sexual fantasies – which are absent in the novel. Yet in spite of this urge to show and tell, she is in many ways more comfortable with the late romanticism that infuses the mid-Victorian sensibility – one where women and men's anarchic desires are almost always tamed – and not tragically – into the domestic and the familial. If Ada and little Flora in their different styles start out like Charlotte Brontë's recalcitrant Jane – as resistant children whose stubborn silence or wilful unregulated speech critiques the hypocrisies of grown-ups – they end up in a version of family life, however heterodox and unusual that configuration may be. In *Jane Eyre* the fire-damaged and otherwise compromised adulterer, Edward Fairfax Rochester, regains his lost sight but retains his mutilated hand, signifying the reduction of his phallic power. In Nelson, Ada sports a metal finger crafted by clever George, exchanging the power of her muteness – the phallic femininity that belongs to the mythic, monumental time that precedes and is outside of the social – for the minor discomfort of a missing digit, a physical reminder of the way in which that power has been literally as well as figuratively checked by patriarchal imperatives. In losing her finger and her fetishised piano, and learning to speak, Ada becomes, in one sense, a woman like any other, a woman

within the realm of the social and the economy of exchange. In safe
Nelson her metal finger seems in one way merely the memento of the
gothic nightmare from which she and her 'family' have escaped only a
little less than intact. Yet it remains the visible sign of her difference – not
only from men, but also from ordinary women. Less bulky than her
piano, less an impediment to social life than wilful or hysterical dumbness, it reassuringly reasserts her status as a 'freak' – and this, she says in
her final voiceover, 'satisfies'.[34] Ada's vestigial freakishness may be all
that is left of the film's feminist agenda, a reminder of *its* claims for difference and distance from the normative familial logic of Hollywood
melodrama. But while, obliquely at least, it thumbs its nose at those
Victorian domestic fictions – Dickens's *Bleak House* or Dinah Mulock
Craik's *Olive* – in which scarred or crippled heroines are magically
restored to almost unblemished femininity at the end of the story, *The
Piano*, by making Ada ironically treasure her little souvenir of the marriage from hell – a bad trip that has turned into her salvation – also reproduces what it mocks.

Campion's borrowings from nineteenth-century fictions about women
and children are poised somewhere between nostalgia and critique,
between a return to their more conservative motifs and messages and a
more radical rewriting of them. And this in turn affects the ideological
time of the film so that the viewer is suspended between these positions,
like an international traveller in a plane in transit between then and now
and there and here who knows that not only is the time on her watch
rarely the time she is in, but is at odds with her body clock. In *The Piano*,
because its imagination inhabits so many modalities of the melodramatic, the viewer, like the reader of a literary text which has chosen free
indirect discourse as its narrative mode, is never quite sure who, in fact,
is speaking or from just when and where in historical or interpretative
time. Indeed we might say that the only consistent 'modern' register of
the film is the medium itself, and its production values, the eerie cinematography and Michael Nyman's pastiche score.

Disability, Femininity and Colonialism

Yet the film's refusal to lock the viewer into a simple version of ideological time does not mean that it can somehow avoid any fixed ethical and
political assumptions. *The Piano* selects, edits and interprets its historical sources in order to provide a framework in which it can safely play
with temporality, genre and narrative. Nowhere is this more apparent
than in its treatment of Ada's muteness and its related take on the vexed

history of colonialism and race, and it is to these questions that I now want to turn.

Muteness is, as Brooks suggests, the symbolic disturbance of sense most closely associated with melodrama (as blindness is with tragedy and deafness with comedy); it had a fascination for the Victorians that exceeded its figurative uses in drama or fiction. The deaf-mute, like the indigene, represented for Victorians the problem of human hierarchy, the unresolved question of nature and nurture. Campion's extrapolation of nineteenth-century historical representations of female muteness is a case in point. In the nineteenth century, muteness was primarily associated with deafness of which the inability to speak was mostly a by-product; both in the nineteenth and twentieth century the training of the deaf and of the deaf and blind became a matter of extended controversy – especially about the use of sign language – but also of great public interest. Successful teachers and their pupils became celebrated, although the public display of their achievements often crossed the line and became hard to differentiate from those exhibitions and entertainments of freaks and indigenous peoples so perennially popular with nineteenth-century audiences. Such spectacles reassured Victorians as to their own normative humanity and superior ethnic attributes – they helped to frame questions, and provide answers, about the limits of both the human and the civilised. The capacity of blind, deaf and dumb persons to communicate and to become reasoning, social beings, both literate and Christian, came under this same set of enquiries, which were as much about the responses of the so-called 'normal' as about the deportment of the afflicted. The long debate, extending from the eighteenth century through the present, about sign language versus orality as the medium of communication for the deaf has become one of the key instances of how modern societies try to deal with human difference. Both those who worked with the blind and deaf, and the ordinary public, were concerned that their behaviour was not seen as disturbing or – the most common term – 'disgusting'; it was crucial to campaigners that these institutionalised men, women and children commanded sympathy and invoked as little as possible the atavistic fear of radical disability. The difference between the sexes was an important testing ground in these demonstrations; the ability to conform to western ideas of femininity in particular was a sign of successful acculturation for those robbed of their senses. Deaf, dumb and blind women were peculiarly fascinating for their mentors and trainers and the lay public; in their deprived condition and successful socialisation lay a tangle of contradictory perceptions and fears about women – their potential for wildness, inferior rationality, innate docility and imitativeness.[35] While visiting Boston's Perkins Institute and

Massachusetts Asylum for the Blind in the early 1840's, Charles Dickens was particularly taken with Laura Bridgman, perhaps the most celebrated such woman until Helen Keller. Bridgman was of especial interest because of her high intelligence combined, in Dickens's perception of her, with the kind of femininity he most admired – she was, he exclaimed, a 'gentle, tender, guileless, grateful-hearted being'.[36] Towards the end of his enthusiastic account of Bridgman's accomplishments – she could write as well as read and sign – Dickens notes, as others had, the occasional involuntary 'uncouth' noise that was 'painful' to hear which escaped her lips when she was pleased or excited and which her teachers had to remind her to suppress, lest she offend the hearing and sighted.[37]

The Piano seems, in its opening moments, as if it might be about to explore in some depth the relationship between the settlers' assumptions about Ada's muteness – her likeness to dumb animals, her possible lack of or excess of feeling – yet it ends, disappointingly, by miming the mores of the nineteenth-century dominant culture, suppressing what might give offence. It does so even while writing Ada's femininity in tune with more modern expectations of an intelligent woman – nothing 'gentle, tender, guileless' or 'grateful-hearted' in Ada. In making Ada dumb but not deaf, Campion edits out of Ada's disability anything that might evoke distaste or aversion in modern viewers, still a common response to many forms of physical or sensory impairment. In this way the film and the modern viewer can take their distance from the clumsy and patronising treatment she receives from Stewart and Nessie, aligning themselves unproblematically with the disdain that Ada expresses in her opening voiceover to those who would see her dumbness as 'animal' not human. The settlers' attitude towards Ada is equated in the film with the class condescension shown to the illiterate George Baines, a condescension that is made explicit in the Christmas pageant scene where George is teased by other men in the community. The overt contempt that George receives, and the mixed attraction and repulsion that Ada evokes, draws them together as victims of the supposedly normal. Nothing painful or disgusting in Ada's dumbness interrupts our erotic identification with Ada and George's love affair. Instead Campion cleverly grafts the nineteenth-century narrative about female disability on to the more seductive one of those women who became celebrated for their paranormal talents as mediums or telepaths – figures prominent in sensation fiction, realist novels such as Henry James's *The Bostonians* (1886), and the horror genres of the *fin de siècle*. These women in life and fiction were meant to be alluring and even sinister, though they were frequently revealed as pathetic and victimised as well. They were often mixed up with con men, or were charlatans themselves, exploiting their supposed gifts for publicity and gain.

And while it is true that Ada's murky sexual past remains a matter for conjecture and fantasy – that she and Flora, like Hester and Pearl before them, shatter the thin veneer of settler respectability – Ada's telepathic talents are used only *in extremis* and for self-preservation – good witch-craft, rather like the supernatural communication that Jane Eyre hears from Rochester when she is being bullied into marriage by the appalling St John Rivers. Pushed, like Jane, to her limit, Ada mindspeaks Stewart, persuading him to let her go.

Campion has compressed an extraordinarily rich composite of nineteenth-century narratives and fictions into her heroine, and one can only admire her skill, whether one agrees or not with the social politics that guide the way she edits and incorporates her sources. Yet Ada's muteness, perhaps the film's most original touch, is most persuasive, and most poignant, as a Freudian symptom – hysteria with muscle – a wilful, willed pathology that outlives its usefulness. Twentieth-century viewers connect positively with hints about childhood trauma – even if its etiol-ogy remains unknown – in a tried and tested way from Hitchcock's *Marnie* (1964) forward. Yet even here *The Piano* is concerned that we must always identify with Ada, offering an anodyne, highly-edited version of nineteenth-century representations of disabled and/or extrasensory femininity, or female madness, one that excludes its most troubling aspects, a version aimed to sever, rather than to connect in uncomfortable ways, the sensibilities of the past with those of the present. Ada never tests the boundaries of our modern sympathy for dis-ability or pathology; indeed in its scrupulous avoidance of what its audi-ence might find anaphrodisiac in female physical and psychic defects, *The Piano* is at its least adventurous, carefully sidestepping a whole set of questions about both disability and 'normal' femininity, extending from the nineteenth century to the twenty-first, that are still unresolved.

Human defect, gender and racial difference were conceptually so closely linked in the Victorian period that it was often hard to tell where one set of assumptions left off and the other began, and this overlap presents an opportunity but also a problem for the film's representation of women, the European settlers as a whole and the indigenous popula-tion of New Zealand. *The Piano*'s approach to racial difference runs into related difficulties, as it attempts not only to negotiate the ideological fields of the past – including its fictional referents – but also those of the present in a way that is both progressive and inoffensive. Temporality is a key term here also. Acting as the ideological ground of imperial expansion and policy within the empire, theories of racial hierarchy and difference before and after Darwin used the metaphor of human devel-opment from infant to adult to discriminate between racial types and also between the stages of civilisation that native peoples were assumed to have reached. Non-Europeans (and sometimes women) were often thought to be fixed in a perpetual childhood – monumental in the sense that it remained undeveloped. Even when non-European cultures or non-white peoples were thought to be able to achieve 'civilised' status through education and acculturation, they were imagined as developing within a different, and slower, temporality, their 'catching up' with Europeans often measured vaguely in centuries rather than decades or generations. The ideas that racial types were fixed, but also capable of improvement, were therefore formally in conflict, and fiercely debated by ethnologists and social and political thinkers. Popular opinion often entertained the two ideas at once. Like women, white working-class sub-jects of both sexes in the nineteenth century were racialised, associated with lesser white races such as the Celts, or with non-white races, and assigned a place within a vertical hierarchy of human types, their move-ment upwards impeded by a glass ceiling of racial thinking.

In Campion's film, George Baines is the link between the Maori and the European settlers, an illiterate working-class male, possibly an ex-whaler, who nevertheless becomes a property owner in the new world. For George, Campion has once more drawn on canonical nineteenth-century American authors, this time borrowing from both James Fenimore Cooper and Herman Melville, whose critiques of imperialism and whose imperial prejudices filter through in the film's general take on empire and its effects. In George, however, we can easily recognise aspects of the white scout, Natty Bumppo or Chingachgook (his 'Indian' name), from Cooper's *Leatherstocking Tales*, and – more subtly – the protagonists in Melville's fiction, both his South Sea novels, *Typee* and *Omoo*, but also *White-Jacket* and *Moby Dick*.[38] Like Natty, George is a man 'without a cross', i.e. of 'pure' European stock without the supposed stain of miscegenation in his 'blood' or on his character, yet someone who appreciates the qualities of the indigenous population, and treats them with a respect that is reciprocated. Despised by the more middle-class colonists, George prefers the community of the Maori who befriend him. He wears their tribal markings on his face, speaks their language and hangs out with them in his leisure time, although a crucial scene early in the film makes it fairly clear – through the sexual joking that passes between them and is relayed to us in subtitles – that he has resisted cohabiting with Maori women – or men.

Natty is a less tormented figure than George Baines, but his is a life of constant contradiction and considerable irony; one of his many roles in Cooper's novels is to interpret the indigenous civilisation to the Europeans, but his employment is with the latter, and as a guide he leads the American settlers ever deeper into Indian territory, inevitably aiding the rolling tide of settlement and the concomitant despoilment of natural resources, which he regrets and even deplores. The absence of 'a cross' regulates his sympathies in the long run; he may run with the red men but his bottom-line loyalties are with white skin. Natty/Chingachgook is never allowed to marry or reproduce. In spite of his racial purity, his partial identification with the Indians makes him too racially unstable a character to form part of the future tense of white America. George may be similarly placed in relation both to the white and to the indigenous population of New Zealand but his narrative takes a different turn. Ada, George and the Maori are all linked to each other through their subaltern status as this is perceived by the settler community. George's class, his past and his temperament, the film implies, all contribute to his greater sympathy for the Maori as well as his attraction to Ada. But Ada, who develops even less kinship with the Maori women or men than with those of the settler community, serves to detach George from them. Just as he rescues her from her marriage and her hysteria, moving her into linear time, so she rescues him from his partial retreat from the white community – pulls him back from the cyclical and monumental time supposedly inhabited by 'tribal' societies, into European time, the time of modernity where they become reasonable imitations of its crucial unit, the bourgeois family. Within the political parameters of the film this move is made possible because George has avoided entangling himself romantically or sexually with the Maori community. In spite of the seductions of their derepressed life (as the film represents it), so much more attractive than the costive Victorian prudery of the settlers he too has remained a man without a cross. Campion's appropriation of the lower class go-between rewrites Cooper's racial conservatism albeit in a liberal guise. The evolving figure of Natty in Cooper's five *Leatherstocking Tales*, whose compromised position vis-à-vis colonist and Indian cannot be simply resolved, is, within its own terms and in its own period, more radically imagined than Campion's.

The novel-of-the-film, written by Jane Campion and Kate Pullinger, makes explicit George's previous career as a whaleman, something only hinted at in the movie itself.[39] Nevertheless the film invokes Melville's sea stories, especially the half-fictionalised South Sea travel books *Typee* and *Omoo* through his magnum opus *Moby Dick*.[40] Rather than acting as explicit correspondences, except in one instance that I will come to presently, Melville's oeuvre resonates within *The Piano*, striking a familiar note from time to time, but more often, through its difference, illuminating the difficulties Campion had with the whole question of cultural imperialism – her own and that of her white *pakeha* forbears.

Melville's whalemen, all more or less intellectuals manqué, the voice, at least in part of his political and philosophical meditations, have little in common with the inarticulate and illiterate George, whose relationship with the Maori does not have the ethnographic self-consciousness – the reserve of Western judgement – that Melville's protagonists have. That role is reserved for the camera, supplemented by the promotional literature surrounding the film, the publicity rather heavy-handedly emphasising the cordial relations established between the Maori who took part in the film and the western members of the company.[41] Yet in some respects the film itself and the extra-diegetic material imitates the fictionalised travel genres of the mid-nineteenth century. The published film script of *The Piano*, for example, comes with a Maori glossary of terms and fulsome testimonials by the western actors on the life-enhancing effects of cross-cultural interaction. And Melville's own dilemma – his desire to criticise Western interventions in the cultures of the South Seas, especially the interference of missionaries, without abandoning western values for a dangerously unexamined relativism – is, in fact, Campion's issue also. Beneath the idyllic innocence of the Marquesans that the protogonist Tommo encounters in *Typee*, for example, Melville finds the rituals of cannibalism for which Tommo has an 'unqualified repugnance' and what is almost worse, as Mitchell Breitweiser points out, their utter unfamiliarity with personal identity and desire as it is conceived of in the west and the 'unified and internally teleological life' that follows from it.[42] For Melville/Tommo this absence of self and ambition are coupled with what he sees as their inability to understand abstraction – without these desires and capacities the Typee have no history; in their world time stands still and Tommo is 'appalled and sickened by the thought that the Typees are indifferent to meaningful time'.[43] Even the innocence or egalitarianism that Melville at first seems to approve in the Typee is, Breitweiser argues, merely comparative, a way of setting in relief the tyranny or false modesties of the west; when confronted as an alternative way of life it no longer appeals. Tommo must finally escape from a culture which threatens in more ways than the physical his sense of identity and futurity

Much of this sort of sensibility, shorn of a direct critique of non-western culture, survives in Campion's text. As she herself says, her story is about her own European ancestors, not the Maori.[44] From the opening scenes, when they appear with Stewart and Baines to escort Ada and Flora to their new home, their place in the film is to add context and colour, and to provide cheap humour and easy verisimilitude to the unfolding colonial melodrama, which they may observe and comment on irreverently but not directly affect. The Maori men's coarseness – the scatological and sexual humour of their subtitled commentary on the colonists – highlights the prudery, ignorance and sheer social awkwardness of Stewart and his Aunt Nessie, faced with Ada's mute strangeness and Flora's eccentric boldness. Visually, as critics have pointed out, the Maori are present so that whiteness may be constructed as a self-conscious value, their presence in the *mise-en-scène* make Ada and Flora's paleness, accentuated by Ada's severe black clothing, especially noticeable and desirable.[45] And they confer value too on what at first the film seems to critique, the sexual conventions of the settlers. The white settlers are in time – the cultural time of Victorian repression and prejudice which determines the conditions for desire within the film – while the Maori are somehow outside it. In the film's sexual economy their permissiveness is definitively anti-erotic, a contrast expressed in the playful idyllic scene by the water referred to earlier in which Baines jokingly fends off their offers of sexual contact and marriage, revealing he has a wife in 'New Jersey'. In contrast, Baines's obsession with the over-wrapped Ada emphasises the necessity of the hidden and the forbidden in western sexuality. (In *Typee*, Tommo dresses the beautiful Fayaway in an approximation of western dress, at least from the waist down, so that he can reinstate desire as he knows it by admiring her 'bewitching ankles' as they appear below her skirt.)[46] In the film, interestingly, the Maori taboos are represented as to do with death – the ground where ancestors are buried – not sex. A second and more casual order of repugnance on their part relates to racial mixing, a passing slur on a half-caste, and Hira's aesthetic disapproval of Baines's badly incised and unfinished half-face tattoo. Yet the infiltration and destruction of Maori culture is indicated through their partial adoption of western dress to ludicrous effect – cultural hybridity as degradation. Indeed the waterside tableau, so painterly – even Gauginesque – in its composition of a colonial scene, is one of the few episodes in which the camera focuses fully upon them. This scene, in which the Maori attempt a lazy seduction of Baines, and in which he, unshocked, resists, positions him as a virtuous 'modern' man – classless, sexually knowing, but unwilling to compromise himself and others – adumbrating his renunciation of his unfair bargain with Ada which, he will say, is 'making her a whore and him wretched'.[47] But if on the surface the scene shows him at ease with his Maori friends, able to speak their language as it were, it really emphasises not his adoption of Maori customs but the line he and his European viewers must draw between them if he is to emerge as the ethical hero of the film.

However hard Herman Melville wrestled with issues of race and imperialism, and Toni Morrison credits him with being the white writer who took on those issues at their deepest philosophical level in his epic novel *Moby Dick*, making whiteness visible as a constructed rather than as a natural attribute, he could never quite sustain an even-handed cultural relativism.[48] The black harpooners of *Moby Dick* are noble figures, but the mulatto Babbo, the mutineer of Melville's 1856 novella, *Benito Cereno*, is vengeance personified. Yet although cultural others might be demonic as well as noble, animal rather than human, Melville was not so eager to grasp the ethnological cliché which infantilised non-white races as other contemporary writers. The monumental time, the pathless paths of Typee that lead nowhere, and certainly not to market, the failure to think abstractly, all these represent not the time and geography of perpetual childhood so much as some other, stranger, cultural universe – more, we might now think, like the time and place of the unconscious where ego does not reign. Campion, however, is eager to take on and resolve the childhood/culture paradigm; her solution is to make all the persons that we see – Ada and Flora, Stewart, Baines, the settler community, the Maori – intermittently childlike, often in their relation to each other, and always to the viewers, for whom their lack of development is one aspect of the way in which they belong irrevocably to the past. At the same time, as I have argued, the viewer cannot escape being aligned with children and the childlike. The film makes children of us all. Flora, the 'real' child in the story, behaves like one, demanding, sulky and jealous, her shifting loyalties from mother to stepfather precipitating the film's denouement, but childish incapacities and capricious behaviour marks almost all of the leading characters. Ada's silence, possibly triggered by trauma, but at the same time determined by a six-year-old's mutinous act of wilfulness that she can no longer reverse, undermines her adult authority, a point visually made by her smallness. Baines's illiteracy – humiliatingly he must ask children to read to him Ada's declaration of love written on the piano key – is the mark of his failure to progress. And Campion, reflecting on her film, singles out Stewart as the character who interests her most precisely in terms of his virginity, the ignorance and inexperience that she argues would be more typically found in a middle-class, middle-aged Victorian man than a modern one.[49] Childhood innocence in adults and children cannot, for Campion, be equated with harmlessness, for they seem to be accompanied by an undeveloped psychology and morality. Stewart swings dangerously from almost infantile passivity to near-murderous violence. Like Flora, who is too young to contemplate the violent consequences of betraying her mother, Stewart cannot really understand the meaning of his act. The settlers as a group are represented as comically lacking in subjective complexity; apart from Aunt Nessie and her subnormal companion we see them mostly in the scenes to do with the Christmas pageant, excited as the children by the performances they have devised. And the Maori too, at least when negotiating angrily in buttons, blankets and guns for their land and labour, or as servants to the white women or men – are infantilised by their contact with the Europeans, whose forms of exchange are exploitative and whose ideas of representation are alien to them.

In *Typee*, Tommo is disturbed by the islanders' incapacity for abstract thought, a deficiency linked, as I have suggested, less to imputed childishness, than to Melville's imaginative evocation of the non-progressive nature of their culture. Campion, similarly, depicts the young Maori men who watch the Christmas shadow play of Bluebeard as unable to distinguish between performance and reality: nobly but ludicrously they rush on stage to rescue the endangered woman. The mimed performance of Bluebeard, and the failure of the Maori to comprehend it, are, as well, a shadow text of Ada's muteness, and the settler community's inability to understand her highly performative subjectivity. But this vignette is also perhaps a timely reminder to the cinema viewer of his own credulity, a lesson in the power of melodrama – the film's medium as well as that of the pantomime – over us, as much as the Maori.

Conclusion

At the beginning of this essay I suggested that the density of references in *The Piano* actually discouraged rather than encouraged viewers and critics to pursue particular citations or associations. The very richness of citation is distracting, demanding a short attention span, which in turn obscures the strategies of selectivity that the film uses. It is as if the viewer's gaze is so pleasurably crowded with half-familiar objects that she keeps moving from one thing to another without dwelling too long on their provenance or on how they are positioned within the archive. Viewing the film, for those having even a passing acquaintance with Victorian culture, resembles a trip to the Great Exhibition of 1851, where visitors were reported to be overwhelmed by the variety and number of artefacts. The film's pleasures depend, to a great extent, on just this difficulty of disentangling its referents, the near impossibility of rearranging them in an orderly manner so that their constellated relationship to its story and its meaning is clarified, an effect which is strikingly at odds with Campion's much simpler account of her own interests and intentions. But this does not consign the film to that category of pastiche, 'blank parody', in which historical depth is disavowed, a category invented by Fredric Jameson as a despicable, apolitical characteristic of the postmodern 'loss' of affect and diachrony.[50] On the contrary, as I hope I have shown, it raises rather than suppresses the question of history and temporality with great sophistication. And through the very strategies of overload and distraction that seem at first to inhibit a conversation with the past, it creates a dialogue, generically, thematically, and politically, with its nineteenth-century British and American literary and cultural referents and its twentieth-century theoretical influences, a dialogue that is not less interesting for being so deliberately fragmentary, an overlapping of cut-off, unfinished conversations. Nor is *The Piano*, for all its clever cosmopolitanism and its compromised post-imperial politics, expressive only of a cynical commercialised globalism: like its referents – *The Scarlet Letter, The Turn of the Screw, Wuthering Heights, Jane Eyre, The Last of the Mohicans, White-Jacket* and *Typee* – it is freighted with the unresolved psychic and social violence that was a structural element of the colonial and imperial project. Its use of melodrama too, while meeting many of the criteria set out in Peter Brooks's *The Melodramatic Imagination*, stops just short of the helpful clarification of ethics and choices he ascribes to the genre. We might read *The Piano* as marking out the limits of modern melodrama's ability to offer us Manichaean choices.

Campion's attraction to early Romantic excess – as fantasy if not reality – was the starting point of her interest in the story, and it is the last image in *The Piano*. The drowned piano with Ada floating above it, and her prosthetic child's voice reading Thomas Hood's weird lullaby – 'There is a silence where has been no sound/There is a silence where no sound may be/In the cold grave, under the deep deep sea' – resonates retrospectively through a film which describes the imperial impulse and the colonial experience, not least among the colonists themselves, as a near fatal encounter with desire and death.[51] The film is, as most of its admirers and detractors have admitted, more than the critique of its parts. Viewers need not, after all, make a decision between its ironising or its sentimental trajectories or the supposed choice between endings, that of the bourgeois novel with its relentlessly social and familial logic or its morbid romantic longings, both products, of course, of the same moment of western modernity. Unlike Ada we can 'have' both, and together they make the film an instructive and creative paradox. Its exuberant use of nineteenth-century subtexts, its witty juxtaposition of temporalities and geographies, give it an extra dimension, and one that most Victoriana lacks. As a representative of the genre it achieves what its mute but rebellious heroine (and perhaps her piano too) longs for – a life of its own.

Notes

1. Mort Gerberg, *The New Yorker*, 24 January 1994.
2. *The Piano* has generated wide critical debate, especially but not exclusively about its colonial and postcolonial narrative and treatment. For a sense of its contours, see Harriet Margolis (ed.), *Jane Campion's 'The Piano'* (Cambridge: Cambridge University Press, 2000) and 'Special debate: *The Piano*' , *Screen*, 36:3, Autumn 1995.
3. Peter Brooks, *The Melodramatic Imagination: Balzac, Henry James, melodrama, and the mode of excess* (New York: Columbia University Press, 1985) preface, pp. ix–xvi.
4. Jane Campion, *The Piano* (New York: Miramax Books, 1993) p. 9.
5. Peter Brooks, *The Melodramatic Imagination*, p. 56.
6. Peter Brooks, *The Melodramatic Imagination*, p. 22.
7. Geoffrey Nowell-Smith, 'Minnelli and melodrama' in Christine Gledhill (ed.), *Home is Where the Heart is: studies in melodrama and the woman's film* (London: British Film Institute, 1987) p. 73.
8. Peter Brooks, 'Melodrama, Body, Revolution' in Jacky Bratton, Jim Cook and Christine Gledhill (eds), *Melodrama: stage, picture, screen* (London: British Film Institute, 1994) pp. 11–24.
9. *The Melodramatic Imagination*, chapter 3, 'The Text of Muteness', pp. 56–80, *passim*.
10. Peter Brooks, *The Melodramatic Imagination*, p. 206.
11. Peter Brooks, *The Melodramatic Imagination*, p. 206.
12. Cooper's *Leatherstocking Tales* include *The Pioneers* (1823); *The Last of the Mohicans* (1826); *The Prairie* (1827) and *The Pathfinder* (1840). Herman Melville's relevant fiction includes *Typee: A Peep at Polynesian Life* (1846); *Omoo: A Narrative of Adventures in the South Seas* (1847); *White-Jacket: or The World in a Man-of-War* (1850); *Moby Dick* (1851).
13. See especially Ann Hardy, 'The Last Patriarch' in Harriet Margolis (ed.), *Jane Campion's 'The Piano'* (Cambridge: Cambridge University Press, 2000) p. 62.
14. Jane Campion, *The Piano*, p. 140.
15. Jane Campion, *The Piano*, pp. 121–43.
16. For a discussion of the response to *The Piano*, see Barbara Johnson, 'Muteness Envy' in Diana Fuss (ed.), *Human, All Too Human* (New York: Routledge, 1996) pp. 141–7.
17. Max Weber, 'The History of the Piano', in W. G. Runciman (ed.), trans. Eric Matthews, *Weber: selections in translation* (Cambridge: Cambridge University Press, 1978) p. 379.
18. Max Weber, 'The History of the Piano', pp. 381–2.
19. Claude Lévi-Strauss, *Structural Anthropology* (Harmondsworth: Penguin, 1963) p. 61.
20. Claude Lévi-Strauss, *Structural Anthropology*, pp. 61–2.
21. This crucial insight I owe to anthropologist Professor Ann Whitehead of Sussex University, with whom I discussed this section of the essay.
22. Julia Kristeva, 'Women's Time' in Toril Moi (ed.), *The Kristeva Reader* (Oxford: Basil Blackwell, 1986) pp. 187–213.
23. Jane Campion, *The Piano*, p. 9.

24. Peter Brooks, *The Melodramatic Imagination*, pp. 65–8.
25. Jane Campion, *The Piano*, p. 9.
26. Jane Campion, *The Piano*, p. 9.
27. Nathaniel Hawthorne, *The Scarlet Letter and Selected Tales*, Thomas E. Connolly (ed.) (London: Penguin, 1986) p. 104.
28. See, in addition to Hester Prynne, the exotic Zenobia, based on the writer Margaret Fuller, in *The Blithedale Romance*, but also the doomed women in his stories, 'The Birthmark' and 'Rappaccini's Daughter'.
29. Nathaniel Hawthorne, *The Scarlet Letter*, pp. 78–9.
30. Nathaniel Hawthorne, *The Scarlet Letter*, pp. 266–8.
31. Jane Campion, *The Piano*, p. 17.
32. Henry James, *The Turn of the Screw*, in Anthony Curtis (ed.), *The Aspern Papers and The Turn of the Screw* (London: Penguin, 1986) p. 262.
33. See chapter 6, 'Henry James and the Melodrama of Consciousness', in *The Melodramatic Imagination*, pp. 153–97.
34. Jane Campion, *The Piano*, p. 122.
35. On the history of deafness and sign language see Harlan Lane, *When the Mind Hears: a history of the deaf* (New York: Random House, 1976) and Douglas C. Baynton, *Forbidden Signs: American culture and the campaign against sign language* (Chicago: University of Chicago Press, 1996). Two very different but equally important analyses of deafness and sign language are Oliver Sachs, *Seeing Voices: a journey into the world of the deaf* (Basingstoke: Picador, 1991) and Lennard J. Davis, *Enforcing Normalcy: disability, deafness, and the body* (London: Verso, 1993).
36. Charles Dickens, *American Notes For General Circulation* (Harmondsworth: Penguin, 1972) p. 82.
37. Charles Dickens, *American Notes*, p. 91.
38. *White-Jacket* is also evoked in the first ending of *The Piano*. Near the end, in chapter 42, its sailor protagonist falls from his ship, the *Neversink*, into the sea; he is wearing the white jacket that has become his protective covering, a second self like Ada's piano. Heavy with water, it threatens to become his shroud. Only by taking it off is he allowed to surface and survive. Herman Melville, *White-Jacket: or The World in a Man-of-War* (Oxford: Oxford University Press, 1996) pp. 395–9.
39. Jane Campion and Kate Pullinger, *The Piano: a novel* (London: Bloomsbury, 1994).
40. There are several scenes in *Moby Dick* of death or near-death by drowning, but most notable is the accident that befalls the black child Pip, who, like Ada, is first saved after being caught in the line and pulled overboard, and later, when he falls a second time, almost abandoned. He goes mad, Melville suggests, from seeing the indifference of God. Herman Melville, *Moby Dick* Harrison Hayford and Hershel Parker (eds) (New York: Norton, 1967) chapter 93, pp. 344–7.
41. Jane Campion, *The Piano*, pp. 142–6.
42. Mitchell Breitweiser, 'False Sympathy in Melville's *Typee*' in Myra Jehlen (ed.), *Herman Melville: A Collection of Critical Essays* (Englewood Cliff, NJ: Prentice Hall, 1994) pp. 15–26.
43. Mitchell Breitweiser, 'False Sympathy in Melville's *Typee*', p. 22.
44. Jane Campion, *The Piano*, p. 142.

45. See especially Stella Bruzzi, 'Tempestuous petticoats: costume and desire in *The Piano*', *Screen*, 36:3, Autumn 1995, pp. 257–66; and Linda Dyson, 'The return of the repressed? Whiteness, femininity and colonialism in *The Piano*', *Screen*, 36:3, pp. 267–76.

46. Herman Melville, *Typee: A Peep at Polynesian Life* (London: J. M. Dent, 1993) pp. 138–9.

47. Jane Campion, *The Piano*, p. 76.

48. See Toni Morrison, *Playing in the Dark: whiteness and the literary imagination* (New York: Vintage Books, 1992) and 'Unspeakable Things Unspoken: The Afro-American Presence in American Literature', *Michigan Quarterly Review*, 28, Winter 1989. Samuel Otter argues that 'Melville offers neither a transcendent critique nor a symptomatic recapitulation of racial beliefs [. . .] Melville both inhabits and manipulates contemporary racial discourse, giving a material sense of its structures and functions'. See ' "Race" in *Typee* and *White-Jacket*' in Robert S. Levine (ed.), *The Cambridge Companion to Herman Melville* (Cambridge: Cambridge University Press, 1998) pp. 12–36.

49. Jane Campion, *The Piano*, pp. 135, 138.

50. See Fredric Jameson, 'Postmodernism, or The Cultural Logic of Late Capitalism', *New Left Review*, I: 146, July–August 1984, pp. 53–92.

51. Thomas Hood, 'Silence' in Walter Jerrold (ed.), *The Complete Poetical Works of Thomas Hood* (London: Henry Frowde, 1906) p. 196. The poem was first collected in *The Plea of the Midsummer Fairies, Hero and Leander, Lycus the Centaur, and Other Poems* (1827). The final lines of the sonnet, suggesting that 'true silence' 'self-conscious and alone' is to be found not under water or in deserts but 'in green ruins, in the desolate walls of antique palaces, where Man hath been', speak to the way in which human history and story is both remembered and repressed in *The Piano*.

Afterword – The Empire at Home

In *Wide Sargasso Sea* (1966), Jean Rhys's bravura prequel to *Jane Eyre*, Edward Fairfax Rochester's self-pitying tale of his catastrophic marriage to a crazed colonial heiress is rewritten from the point of view of Bertha Mason, his white Jamaican wife.[1] *Jane Eyre* is the inspiration and point of departure for Rhys's late, great novel, but *Wide Sargasso Sea*, set in Rhys's native Caribbean in the first half of the nineteenth century, imitates neither the style nor the narrative structures of its 1847 original. A vanguard piece of Victoriana, spawning imitations of its own, it is strictly modernist in form, echoing – and further extending – the elliptical mode of storytelling that characterised Rhys's brilliant quartet of novels published between the world wars: pitiless, quasi-autobiographical accounts of the predicament of modern women at once liberated and lost in post-Victorian Britain and France.[2] As well as expanding *Jane Eyre*'s backstory, *Wide Sargasso Sea* also sketches in an imaginary prehistory for Rhys's twentieth-century fictions about sexually adventurous but loving women from Britain's colonies, at risk from predatory metropolitan men. Written two decades before postcolonial scholars had turned their attention to the politics of race and empire in Brontë's canonical novel, *Wide Sargasso Sea* provocatively introduced those questions about sexuality and empire which have become a central theme in the rewriting and reinterpretation of the Victorian.

Banishing the Victorian happy ending is one effective narrative strategy for dispersing the long shadow that the imperial imagination cast on colonisers and colonised. In Rhys's return to Brontë, the monstrous Bertha, rechristened Antoinette, is transformed into a tragic heroine, and Rochester unmasked as her betrayer not her dupe. Rhys's emphatic rejection of the Victorian mores which linger on in later Victoriana from *The French Lieutenant's Woman* through *The Crimson Petal and the White*, combines, in *Wide Sargasso Sea*, with her appetite for sexual melodrama that ends badly for women who love too much. Rochester's xenophobia, brutality and sexism, his attraction to and fear of sexual woman, fit Rhys's animus against that aspect of Brontë's English metropolitan sensibility which projected degeneracy and unspeakable desires onto the Empire's white colonial subjects. But anti-imperialist Victoriana could also write another narrative with a happy ending that better suits late modernity's aesthetic and political tastes, one in which domestic happiness is achieved through defying laws and social convention. Australian Peter Carey's haunting *Jack Maggs* (1997) does just that in his 'twentieth-century post-colonial Dickens novel'.[3] *Jack Maggs* reinvents a parallel life for *Great Expectations*'s tormented convict, Magwitch. In a predictable postmodern turn, widely deployed in Victoriana, Carey includes the original fiction's author as a character – here an ambitious, sinister young Dickens figure, Tobias Oates, who finds out and exploits the social and psychological secrets of the vulnerable.[4] Magwitch, Pip's rough benefactor in *Great Expectations*, solicits sympathy only on his deathbed, but his alter-ego, Jack Maggs, marries happily, has six kids and dies a respectable, even honoured, man in his adopted Australia. New Zealander Jane Campion makes a similar narrative choice, as we have seen, in *The Piano*, allowing Ada, Flora and George Baines to settle in Nelson as a family, creating a simulacra of the domestic structure of Victorian Britain while breaking its moral codes. Like Rhys before them, Campion and Carey use Victorian reference as an international idiom for exploring the uneven development of subjective and social modernity in Britain and its Empire, but these twentieth-century remakes and riffs on the Victorian are not without their contradictions and blind spots. As postcolonial critics have pointed out, Rhys and Campion, as much as Brontë, privilege the story of European settlers over that of the non-white or indigenous population of the colonies.[5] Anti-imperial Victoriana of this kind retroactively counters some Victorian prejudices, but leaves others, if only by default, in place.

These retold stories of empire have also tended to prioritise one gender over another. True, Rhys makes Rochester into a fascinating figure, and Campion, in her notes on *The Piano*, highlights her interest in Stewart, Ada's virginal, violent husband, but while these fictional men embody both the bullying and emotionally clueless elements of the imperial and the patriarchal, it is the women who are the affective and symbolic centre of both the narratives, the figures with whose fate the reader or viewer is strongly engaged.[6] *Jack Maggs*, on the other hand, is a man's story, like its Victorian referent. Although not without its fully imagined women characters, it shares with the biofictional treatments of Henry James, and even Ackroyd's *Dickens*, a fascination with the masculinity of that suspect figure the nineteenth-century author, explored by Carey through both Oates and Maggs. For contemporary novelists the legacy of nineteenth-century writing, however admired and cheerfully plundered, presses hard on the living. In Victoriana by the postcolonial descendants of white Europeans this anxiety of influence is figured as an aspect of imperialism, and women writers as well as men find clever ways of fielding it in their fiction. Carey, we might say, is doubly engaged with Dickens, recreating him within the novel as the intrusive, manipulative Oates, as well as through his own pastiche of Dickensian narrative.[7] Maggs is Carey's surrogate, as Bertha/Antoinette is Rhys's; as sacrifice or survivor these reborn characters offer a critique of English character and ethics, part of their author's mission to expose the skeletons closeted in the metropole's house of culture.

Rhys, Carey and Campion chip away at Britain's class system and imperial complacencies, exploring the violence that kept such systems going – but even in *Wide Sargasso Sea*, set in the decade after Emancipation, with Black characters as a strong presence, the themes of slavery and racism are kept at arm's length. Historical novels set in the eighteenth century have been keener to tackle racial issues within as well as outside Britain; Victoriana does so much less often, as if the abolition of colonial slavery just before Victoria took the throne made race a redundant issue. On the contrary, anxieties about racial contamination in the British Isles were a persistent trope in Victorian writing after abolition.[8] Reflecting the expansion of racial thinking in post-emancipation Britain, this fear is subliminally present in the racialisation of Bertha in *Jane Eyre*, terrifyingly transformed after her passage from Jamaica to Thornfield from a beautiful white woman into a masculinised grotesque with 'blackened', inflated 'lineaments'. In a more realist, less gothic register, it is made fully visible in Dinah Craik's *Olive* (1850) and 'The Half-Caste' (1849), stories in which mixed-race women from the Empire, the illegitimate and legitimate children of its colonisers, upset the peaceful homogeneity of the English polity.[9] These fictions echo and elaborate a much wider public debate about the meaning of Englishness and Britishness that developed, with heightening urgency, throughout Victoria's reign, ending in the first modern piece of immigration legislation, the 1905 Aliens Act.[10] In the century following, the control of immigration, the end of empire and decolonisation, the porous borders of the European Union, and the rise of terrorist threats from the East and from 'home grown' disaffected Muslims have produced the controversy in new and constantly mutating forms. In multi-ethnic Britain today, it remains a bitterly divisive issue, exploited endlessly by the media and at the top of poll-driven political agendas.

Racism and Englishness within Britain – the Empire at home – is the subject of Julian Barnes's restrained and moving novel, *Arthur &*

George. Bridging the Victorian and Edwardian periods, *Arthur & George* is based on a true story – Sir Arthur Conan Doyle's successful campaign to free a young solicitor, son of the local vicar, a Parsee, who had been convicted of the bizarre crime of maiming livestock – cows and horses – in his home village of Great Wyrley, Staffordshire. The maimings followed years of mysterious local persecution of the Edalji family through poison-pen letters and other cruel practical jokes, which the local police and Chief Constable also laid at the victims' door. Barnes has compared this disturbing episode to Zola's championship of the Dreyfus case in France in the same time period. Accounting for its obscurity in British popular history compared to the continuing visibility and symbolic resonance of Dreyfus, Barnes argues that the British, unlike the French, like to forget the history of such scandalous – and emblematic – miscarriages of justice, once they seem to be resolved.

Told in the third person, but from the alternate positions of Doyle and Edalji, the novel charts the men's parallel histories as 'unofficial Englishmen' – a status that the Scottish-born Conan Doyle suggests to the mixed-race George Edalji that they have in common. The startled George, whose mother is also Scottish, finds this a strange concept. He 'regards Sir Arthur as a very official Englishman indeed' and wonders, supposedly for the first time, in what way he himself is

> less than full Englishman? He is one by birth, citizenship, by education, by religion, by profession. Does Sir Arthur mean that when they took away his freedom and struck him off the Rolls, they also struck him off the roll of Englishmen?[11]

These naïve, essentially defensive self-perceptions of identity are the central irony that shapes the novel. Arthur's acute sense of his aspirant and eccentric Englishness and George's box-ticking satisfaction that he has fulfilled its legal and cultural criteria are harmless, if instructive, illusions. More dangerous, Barnes points out, in an understated but beautifully realised scene in which Conan Doyle meets with the blimpish Chief Constable, Captain Anson, there is another and more powerful version of Englishness constructed through what it excludes, fuelled by the unshakeable, insidious prejudice, the systemic xenophobia and racism of the persons and the society that are responsible for George's false imprisonment. The scene illustrates both the extent and the limit of Conan Doyle's own liberal sympathies when he responds to Anson's tirade against mixed marriages and Indians with the tight-lipped and ironic observation that 'the introduction of a coloured clergyman into such a rude and unrefined parish was bound to cause a regrettable situation. It is certainly an experiment that should not be repeated'.[12]

The tone of the book is low-key, measured, almost stiff at times, as if it suffered from a literary variety of the sexual inhibitions ascribed to the two men. George, though allowed to be wistful about marriage, is made out to be virtually asexual, and the twice-married Arthur is an affectionate caricature of repressed, respectable Victorian masculinity, both too uptight and too honourable to commit adultery with the woman he loves. The novel's linguistic restraint mimes this lowered libidinal and affective threshold, noting its downside but also its unfashionable virtues. 'There is a tradition of English emotional reticence which can easily fall away into emotional inexpressiveness and frigidity', Barnes has said but he prefers that tradition to the 'banal' 'Oprahfication of the emotions'.[13] His contrast has its own unpleasant racial and sexual overtones; it cannot be an entirely unconscious choice that his shorthand for the unwelcome hegemony of American confessional society is represented by an ambitious, successful and vocal black woman. His preference for reticence is, however, also a key to the novel's successful minimalist style. The spare but telling use of pastiche, always filtered through the ironic third person, keeps the period at once in focus and at a necessary remove, amassing detail in short episodic chapters for its effects, rather than heightening the prose to exaggerate what is naturally dramatic and sensational in the story. Both victimhood and heroism are discursively played down. Readers are made to do the work of imagining George's suffering and that of his family; any flare-up of satisfaction deriving from Arthur's success in getting George off the main charge is quickly dampened by both men's dismay that George is never exonerated from the accusation that he wrote the offending letters, or given compensation for his three years of imprisonment.

Not all critics have found Barnes's self-denying writing strategies in *Arthur & George* appealing. Natasha Walter, in her *Guardian* review, compared the novel unfavourably with Barnes's earlier and more flamboyant *Flaubert's Parrot*, and Terry Eagleton thought that *Arthur & George* had not quite translated its history into a viable fiction.[14] These seem to me rather lazy readings of a book whose terse, monochrome prose is itself a reproof to the showier styles of Byatt, Fowles or Faber, and which suits the novel's form as a slow-building piece of crime fiction, a genre Barnes had tried out with some success in three modern detective stories written pseudonymously.[15] Nor does Barnes give in to the temptation of making Conan Doyle into his celebrated sleuth; he has, he said, 'deliberately' avoided the strategy of 'bouncing off' the Sherlock Holmes stories, a relief since they have been already stripped bare to furnish material for third-rate faux Victorian thrillers and detective fiction.[16] In *Arthur & George*, Conan Doyle does his own detective work well

enough, helped by his medical background as an eye-doctor, but the negative case that he puts together to get Edalji's free pardon by proving that
he could not have seen well enough to commit the crimes against
animals, is much sounder than the more speculative one he constructs to
find the 'true' culprit. George, his dignified, rational, unimaginative
client, the rule-governed author of *Railway Law*, definitely thought
Conan Doyle took his speculations too far, and his last 'true' comment
on the case in 1934, as cited in the novel, does not, Barnes notes, mention
either racial prejudice or Conan Doyle's shaky theories.[17] Together these
'unofficial', self-made Englishmen, one with a creative gift and a believer
in spiritualism, the other solidly empiricist, a lover of rules and a
guardian of the nation's law, make up the two halves of what Barnes, a
'quintessential' Englishman himself, admires in Englishness at its best,
whatever the class, national or ethnic origin of those who acquire it.
From Barnes's definitively postmodern but ultimately quite conservative
point of view it does not matter that the 'traditional' national trait is
cultural, invented; cut loose from biology it has even greater ethical
resonance.

　　Neither Arthur or George are depicted as particularly introspective or
self-knowing, yet both are survivors. Barnes has Arthur, the campaign-
ing liberal in this incident at least, pronouncing in high dudgeon on the
Englishman's tendency to produce 'no fault' as a response to official
wrongdoing. George, on the other hand, as the bewildering humiliation
of his prison ordeal fades a little, is made to think pragmatically about
small changes to the system, structural reforms to the conduct of cases
that would reduce the chance of such prejudicial prosecutions being successful.[18] 'Truth' in *Arthur & George* is elusive; in common with much
Victoriana, and the fictions they imitate, the novel is bulging with undis-
closed secrets, emotional and sexual, not all of them meant to be
unpacked. These repressive tendencies, their Victorian and Edwardian
sources, and the ways in which they shape the men's lives and their relationships are registered with great subtlety, but they are not the object of
Barnes's critique – quite the reverse. The novel shares with so much of
the narrative Victoriana I have been discussing, respect verging on nostalgia for a long gone chastity, a supposed national as well as masculine
innocence that may be class-bound and only historically relative, but is
notwithstanding an object of regret and desire. This version of innocence
and loss is immanent in Fowles, Lodge, Byatt and perhaps even Tóibín:
they find a kind of apotheosis in the figure of Henry James, another unofficial, self-made 'Englishman'. At the same time as it brings to light the
ugly, pervasive racism of late Victorian and Edwardian Britain, whose
respectable face is Anson and the country gentry, *Arthur & George* also

constructs a fantasy scenario of cultural separation and false equivalence in which the lives of different orders of 'Englishmen', each with a belief, however frustrated, that the laws and society could, rightly used, deliver race-free justice, touch briefly and amicably, and diverge. Modesty and dignity – the dignity of the put-upon Edaljis, the relative modesty and disinterest of Conan Doyle's action – these are qualities of English masculinity, whether home-grown or acquired through imitation and emulation, that *Arthur & George,* and Barnes himself, values. The problem is that in his expressed liking for 'the idea that countries are different', his 'regret' for the fact that England, 'an artificial notion in the first place' is nevertheless 'endangered, commercialised, Americanised and Europeanised', leads him, and by default the reader, to a broadly assimilationist model of national identity and virtue in which cultural differences are problematic and must be made to adhere to a national norm.[19]

Beautifully crafted and subtle as it is, it is never clear quite what we are meant to intuit about the past from *Arthur & George,* or what insights its readers in today's Britain might draw from it. Barnes does not see himself as a writer with a political message, but his 'true' tale is a political parable nevertheless, as much as his earlier *England, England* (1998) which takes place in a 'not-too-distant future' in which a British entrepreneur turns the Isle of Wight into a surreal tourist theme park of everything English, an in-your-face postmodern novel with narrative and philosophical affinities to Brian Moore's earlier *The Great Victorian Collection.* The neo-Arnoldian spirit of Barnes's desire for a lost national homogeneity, based on culture rather than nature, makes it especially difficult to place *Arthur & George,* a story of everyday racism, innocence and liberal good will at the turn of the twentieth century, in apposition to the reality of Britain in 2006, a nation in which outsiders, especially but not only those with dark skins, are still commonly perceived by government and media to be potentially violent as well as culturally other – as much, if not more so than in the late 1840s or at the turn of the twentieth century. Under the pretext provided by the threat of terrorism, British residents are witnessing an unprecedented contraction of their civil rights, which has become, in New Labour discourse, a derided concept, like liberalism itself. The government has made increasingly strong moves to ensure that immigrants seeking citizenship or even just residency, be forced by law rather than pragmatism or inclination to assimilate, or at least perform assimilation by learning basic English and British geography and promising to respect Britain's 'rules' and way of life. Unofficial Englishness is becoming less a chosen than a coerced identity – the government's reference to a 'way of life' supposed to reflect a tolerant and just society more hollow by the day, and accordingly a less attractive one for the constituency it is targeting. It is from within this uneasy national context that Barnes's enigmatic quasi-fictional exploration of England's 'Dreyfus case' has been written, and in part, read.

Barnes's contrast between Dreyfus and Edalji suggests – rather dubiously perhaps – that modern France learns and profits from its less than glorious historical moments through a greater attachment to popular memory, while houseproud but slatternly Britain deliberately sweeps hers under the carpet, leaving the task of retrieving these key moments in its hidden history of Empire to its novelists. This public, historical reticence presumably represents the pathological end of Barnes's model of national character – the point where the affect that should attach itself to such moments, so that they may inform the present, gets 'frozen'. Everything, it seems, depends on moderation. Barnes's idealisation of modest English 'manliness' has a direct correspondence with his view that writers are *not* generally activists, but live, to a great extent, a 'life deferred'. This way of positioning authorship as knowledgable but also passive, keenly responsive to political and intellectual currents of its time but at another level only their medium, has had a distinct resonance in recent criticism, biography and biofiction focused on figures like Charlotte Brontë, Charles Dickens and Henry James. These innovative social novelists have endured because their representation of the everyday was particularly powerful, but the mix of political conservatism and radicalism in their lives and work, analysed from a present in which these categories are themselves in ideological flux, seems ever harder to pin down. Paradoxically this has made their lives more, not less, interesting to us, their contradictions more familiar, even homely. What they have foregone to write fiction or poetry has become as fascinating, and humanising as any account of their libidinal satisfactions. Moreover this view of writers and writing implies that it is books, rather than their authors, that have historical agency, if, to paraphrase Marx, not necessarily the agency they imagine or intend. Narrative and biographical Victoriana, from *The French Lieutenant's Woman* through *Arthur & George*, seem to gather around this value-laden idea, which, while retaining a version of humanism and even an idea of 'truth', ascribes the major work of agency to fictions rather than to historical persons. The 'new' literary humanism – to give it a name – represented and elaborated in Victoriana, has not shown much respect for the authorial intentions of even its most admired and eminent referents. In its most irreverent instances – as in Rhys, Carey, Campion – it honours Victorian reticence and repression by outing it – a move with its own sexual and political ambiguities. It is likely that the inversions of *Wide Sargasso Sea* would not have struck Charlotte Brontë as a compliment; Dickens would no doubt be horrified to find himself so fully remembered in Sarah Water's lesbian Victoriana or Carey's pastiche, and Henry James might well have found *The Line of Beauty* something less than a literary tribute.

In *Repression and Victorian Fiction*, critic John Kucich advances an interesting theory about the effects of what he terms 'the nineteenth-century cultural decision to value silenced or negated feeling over affirmed feeling, and the corresponding cultural prohibitions placed on display, disclosure, confession, assertion'.[20] In Kucich's psychoanalytic reading, which he applies to the way characters act in Victorian fiction, repression is deliberate – evoked by those very familiar Victorian terms 'renunciation' and 'self denial' – 'repression heightens and vitalises emotional autonomy' becoming 'libidinal acts, forms of luxuriously self-disruptive and autoerotic experience'.[21] It is something like this dynamic, or rather its traces, together with an ambiguous sense of its loss, and a desire to recreate it in another form, that one finds in so much Victoriana. Even as we take pleasure in its inventiveness and energy, it is well to remember that as a popular genre with undiminished vitality, it has no choice about its participation in a much wider, transnational as well as national, debate, reaching beyond the boundaries of Britain's former empire: a debate about historical memory and the direction of the political future in which we, as readers and citizens, do have a voice and a role to play.

Notes

1. Jean Rhys, *Wide Sargasso Sea* (London: Penguin Books, 1997).
2. Jean Rhys: *Postures* (later known as *Quartet*), (London: Chatto & Windus, 1928); *After Leaving Mr. Mackenzie* (London: Jonathan Cape, 1930); *Voyage in the Dark* (London: Constable, 1934); *Good Morning, Midnight* (London: Constable, 1939). All these novels were reprinted by Andre Deutsch in London and W. W. Norton in New York in the late 1960s and early 1970s, following the success of *Wide Sargasso Sea*.
3. Peter Carey, *Jack Maggs* (London: Faber, 1997). Hermione Lee, *The Observer*, 28 September 1997.
4. See for example D. M. Thomas, *Charlotte* (London: Duckworth, 2000) with its modern Charlotte Brontë figure, and Lynne Truss, *Tennyson's Gift* (London: Profile Books, 2004).
5. See Gayatri Chakravorty Spivak, 'Three Women's Texts and a Critique of Imperialism' in Henry Louis Gates, Jr (ed.), *'Race', Writing and Difference* (Chicago: University of Chicago Press, 1986) pp. 271–3; Leonie Pihama, 'Ebony and Ivory: Constructions of the Maori in *The Piano*', in Harriet Margolis (ed.), *Jane Campion's 'The Piano'* (Cambridge: Cambridge University Press, 2000) pp. 114–34; Lynda Dyson, 'The Return of the Repressed? Whiteness, femininity and colonialism in *The Piano*', *Screen*, Summer 1995, pp. 267–76.

6. Jane Campion, *The Piano* (New York: Miramax, 1993) pp. 138–9.
7. He uses this strategy again to great effect in two recent novels, *My Life as a Fake* (2003) and *Theft: A Love Story* (2006), both of which are concerned with Australia's sense of its subaltern status in class and cultural terms and, like *Jack Maggs*, challenge the discourse of authenticity and integrity for art and artists.
8. See for example David Dabydeen, *The Harlot's Progress* (London: Jonathan Cape, 1999); Barry Unsworth, *Sacred Hunger* (London: Hamish Hamilton, 1992).
9. See Dinah Mulock Craik, *Olive: The Half Caste*, Cora Kaplan (ed.), (Oxford: Oxford University Press, 1999). Craik capitalises on the success of *Jane Eyre* (1847) by reworking the themes of race and empire in this novel and related short story.
10. Some of this sources in this debate can be sampled in Antoinette Burton (ed.), *Politics and Empire in Victorian Britain: a reader* (New York: Palgrave, 2001). For a multi-faceted view of the Empire at home, see Catherine Hall and Sonya Rose (eds), *At Home With the Empire: metropolitan culture and the imperial world* (Cambridge: Cambridge University Press, 2007).
11. Julian Barnes, *Arthur & George* (London: Jonathan Cape, 2005) p. 217.
12. Julian Barnes, *Arthur & George*, p. 266.
13. Barnes quoted in Stuart Jeffries, 'It's for self-protection', *The Guardian*, Wednesday, 6 July 2005.
14. Natasha Walter, 'Our mutual friends', *The Guardian*, Saturday, 2 July 2005; Terry Eagleton, 'The Facts', *The Nation*, 20 February 2006.
15. Under the pseudonym Dan Kavanagh, Barnes wrote *Duffy* (1980), *Fiddle City* (1981), *Putting the Boot In* (1985), and *Going to the Dogs* (1987), evocative London thrillers with Duffy, a bisexual private detective, as their protagonist.
16. Barnes quoted in Stuart Jeffries, 'It's for self-protection', *The Guardian*, Wednesday, 6 July 2005.
17. Julian Barnes, *Arthur & George*, p. 359.
18. Julian Barnes, *Arthur & George*, p. 316.
19. Barnes quoted in 'It's for self-protection', *The Guardian*, Wednesday, 6 July 2005. As I have suggested in 'Historical Fictions', David Lodge expresses the anxiety about cultural and racial difference as unassimilable and dangerous in *Nice Work*.
20. John Kucich, *Repression in Victorian Fiction: Charlotte Brontë, George Eliot, and Charles Dickens* (Berkeley: University of California Press, 1987) p. 3.
21. John Kucich, *Repression in Victorian Fiction*, p. 3.

Index

market forces, uselessness of
  resistance to, 101–2
political conservatism, 105–6
Thatcher's Britain, 101, 102–3
work ethic, Victorian, 100–1
Nowell-Smith, Geoffrey, 122
Nyman, Michael, 140

Orange Prize, 111
Otter, Samuel
  '"Race" in *Typee* and *White-
    Jacket*', 153n48

Piano, The (Campion) (film)
  asexual childhood, liberation of
    child into, 136–7
  cinema, and representations of the
    past, 126–7
  colonial past, take on, 9, 125
  critical debate generated by, 151n2
  as 'dark' postcolonial romance,
    9–10
  difference, visible signs of, 139–40
  as gothic romance, 121
  happy endings, 155
  language, origin of in the exchange
    of women, 129–30
  New Yorker cartoon, 119
  nineteenth-century referentiality,
    use of, 123–4, 133–40, 149–50
  piano, metaphorical possibilities of,
    119, 127–9
  Romantic excess, 150
  scopophilia, and explicit sex
    scenes, 139
  sexual knowledge, influence of
    James in quest for, 138–9
  sexual narrative, reaction to, 125–6
  temporality, levels of and female
    subjectivity, 131–2
  see also melodrama; muteness;
    racial difference, and indigenous
    population; *The Scarlet Letter*
Pihama, Leonie
  'Ebony and Ivory: Constructions of
    the Maori in *The Piano*', 162n5
pleasuring the reader
  Barthes on, 107, 108–9, 115
  Byatt and, 106–7

politics, and 'postcolonial
  melancholia', 77
Pope-Hennessy, John, 39
popular fiction genres, escape
  literature, 43
Possession (Byatt), 2, 4, 8–9, 91,
  92–3, 114
  academic characters, 94–5
  Fowles, engagement with,
    99–100
  homophobia, 109, 110
  literary and philosophical
    influences, 116n14
  poetry and prose, invented, 94–5,
    116n15
  political stance in, 105, 106
  reading, pleasure of, 106–7
  reading expectations, disordering
    of, 107–8
  reward and punishment, balance
    between, 110
  as romance, 87, 98–9, 102
postmodernism
  and biography, 38
  and historical fiction, 88
poststructuralism, 4, 44, 51
  and biography, 37–8
print culture, reinvestment in, 87
psychoanalysis, 4, 9, 45
  and biography, 79–80
  and melodrama, 122, 123

Quarterly Review, The, 17
queer fiction, 69

racial difference, and indigenous
  population
  childhood/culture paradigm, and
    underdevelopment, 148–9
  clothing, and cultural hybridity,
    147
  developmental theories, 143–4
  imperialism, critiques of, 144
  Melville's sea stories, and cultural
    imperialism, 144–9
  Natty Bumppo, 144–5
  racial hierarchy, theories of, 143–4
  settlers, sexual conventions of,
    147